# The Year of Reading Dangerously

### How Fifty Great Books
### (and Two Not-So-Great Ones) Saved My Life

## Andy Miller

FOURTH ESTATE • *London*

First published in Great Britain by Fourth Estate in 2014

A catalogue record for this book
is available from the British Library

ISBN 978-0-00-725575-7

Typeset by Palimpsest Book Production Ltd, Falkirk, Stirlingshire

Printed and bound in Great Britain by
Clays Ltd, St Ives plc

No surrender to the LRB.

For Alex, love Dad

# WARNING!

THIS BOOK CONTAINS SPOILERS.

'I long to reach my home and see the day of my return. It is my never-failing wish.'

Homer, *The Odyssey*

'What's the point of going out? We're just going to wind up back here anyway.'

Homer Simpson

# A Word of Explanation

Let me begin on the back foot and linger there awhile.

This book is entitled *The Year of Reading Dangerously*. It is the true story of the year I spent reading some of the greatest and most famous books in the world, and two by Dan Brown. I am proud of what I achieved in that year and how the experience changed my life – really altered its course – which is why I am about to spend several hundred pages telling you about it. However, the book you are holding has not always been called *The Year of Reading Dangerously*. I started out with that title but then had second thoughts. For a while *The Miller's Tales* seemed like it might work. After that, I briefly considered *Up! From Sloth*, then *The Body in the Library*. Other possibilities included *Hunting Paper Tigers*, *Real Men Don't Read Books*, *Memoirs of a Born-again Pessimist*, *Croydon Till I Die* and *Bast Unbound*. For about five minutes, it was called *Outliars*. Then there was *Against Nature II: Resurrection*, which was followed by *What Are You Staring At?*, which in turn gave way to *We Don't Need to Talk About We Need to Talk About Kevin (To Have a Good Time)*. After one particularly difficult morning, I amended the title page to *F\*\*k the World, I Want to Get Off*. Finally, however, that first thought prevailed and I turned back to *The Year of*

*Reading Dangerously*, or, to give it its full title, *The Year of Reading Dangerously and Five Years of Living with the Consequences*.

Because there are a lot of Andy Millers in the world, several of whom are writers, I also contemplated a change of pen name. For the record then, this book was not written by Andrew Miller, the bestselling novelist, or Andy Miller, winner of the Yeovil Literary Prize for poetry, or Andy Miller, the television scriptwriter, or A.D. Miller, whose thriller *Snowdrops* was shortlisted for the 2011 Man Booker prize and whose Christian name turns out to be Andrew. Nor was it written by Andrew Miller, pitcher for the Boston Red Sox, Andy Miller, guitarist in the Britpop band Dodgy, Andrew Miller, the Labour MP for Ellesmere Port and Neston, Andrea Miller, founder of Brooklyn's Gallim Dance company, nor any of the hundreds of Andy Millers on Facebook, especially the one who counts 'Women bringing me sandwiches' amongst his activities and interests. Each of these Andy Millers has some-thing to recommend him – or her – but none of them is me. So for this book, I have decided to stick with Andy Miller because that is the name of the man who wrote it; I make my own sandwiches (see page 20). Further activities and interests will be made abundantly clear in due course.

It may come as a relief to learn that the book's subtitle has remained immoveable throughout and that, by and large, it is factually accurate: *How Fifty Great Books (and Two Not-So-Great Ones) Saved My Life*.

The backbone of *The Year of Reading Dangerously* is a list of fifty books; I started out with just a dozen or so but then found I couldn't stop. In an age of communications overload, we seem to find lists like this irresistible. As we are called upon to consume ever more information and broadcast quick and decisive opinions, so we are drawn to this basic method of data-handling: directories of best and worst, top hundred countdowns, another 1001 things to do before you die. The reader is at liberty to flip to Appendix One: The List of Betterment (see page 297) whenever he or she likes, that's why we have included it. However, my list differs from others in one crucial regard: it is neither a prescription nor a set of numbered instructions. Rather, it is the inadvertent by-product of the process described in these pages. It is the cast left by the bookworm.

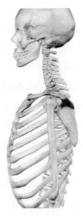

*Fig. 1: Profound misconception of the work in the mind of uncomprehending reader.*

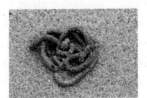

*Fig. 2: The reality.*

*The Year of Reading Dangerously* emerged from an honest attempt to read a number of books which, for reasons which will be divulged later, I had succeeded in dodging during an otherwise fairly literate thirty-seven years on Earth. If you glance through the titles and are surprised at the omission of certain novels or authors, or certain types of novel or author, it is because either I had already read them or I did not want to. Likewise, if you are unconvinced by a particular non-canonical choice, it was not an attempt to be unorthodox or provocative but simply intuitive – intuitive and honest. At a certain point, if I felt like reading *The Silver Surfer*, say, or *The Epic of Gilgamesh*, or something by Henry James, Julian Cope or Toni Morrison, I did so. There were no quotas. This selection of books, therefore, does not constitute a deliberate or alternative canon. If you scan Appendix One: The List of Betterment, and think to yourself, hang about, where is Updike, Woolf or Trollope? Martina Cole or Jules Verne? That's not the novel by Cervantes I'd have chosen . . . What about *Ulysses*? *The Catcher in the Rye*? *Girl With a Pearl Earring*? How can this list be taken seriously when it finds no place for *my* favourite authors or at least those writers *I* consider indispensable?, then I respectfully suggest you write your own book – unless your name is Andy Miller, in which case you have probably already done so.

Above all, wherever possible I tried to avoid bad faith. First I lived this book. Then I thought about it for ages. Then I wrote it down.

So the List of Betterment represents a diary rather than a manifesto; a ledger, not an agenda. I am not urging you to read all the books in this book – there is no need, because somewhere in the back of your mind you will already have a tentative list of your own, the contents of which are drawn from your curiosity or enthusiasm or guilty conscience, rather than mine.

What kind of a book is *The Year of Reading Dangerously*? To the extent that we are governed by the laws of copyright and 'fair use', it is a work of literary criticism. It is also a memoir and a confession. I have not tried to explain these books solely in terms of their relationship to other books; instead, what follows is the story of an attempt to integrate books – to reintegrate them – into an ordinary day-to-day existence, a life which was becoming progressively less engaging to the individual living it. In this book you will find footnotes, emails, personal reminiscences, blog extracts, recipes, potted biographies, strong opinions and jokes. You could conceivably use it as a reading group crib, though I don't advise it; you might receive some strange looks across the nibbles. This book also contains strong language and a tweet, for which I apologise in advance (the tweet, not the cursing).

In 1945, the author Malcolm Lowry was asked by his publisher to account for the idiosyncrasies of a novel he had just submitted called *Under the Volcano* (Book 35). In the persuasive forty-page letter he wrote in reply, Lowry described his book as follows:

'It can be read simply as a story which you can skip if you want. It can be read as a story you will get more out of if you don't skip. It can be regarded as a kind of symphony, or in another way as a kind of opera – or even a horse opera. It is hot music, a poem, a song, a tragedy, a comedy, a farce, and so forth. It is superficial, profound, entertaining and boring, according to taste. It is a prophecy, a political warning, a cryptogram, a preposterous movie, and a writing on the wall. It can even be regarded as a sort of machine: it works too, believe me, as I have found out.'

A sort of machine: I like that. Every book is a sort of machine and this one is no exception. You have to read it to find out how it works.

What makes a great book? That depends both on the book and the operator. I think of *Under the Volcano* as a 'great book' because a) I like it and b) the body of expert critical opinion supports me in this view. But we must acknowledge that greatness recalibrates itself from person to person and book to book. To one reader, 'great' may denote unbridled cultural excellence, e.g. the greatness of Tolstoy or Flaubert; to another, it is an exclamation of pleasure, e.g. '*One Day* by David Nicholls: what a great book!' It may be that when we speak of 'a great book' we are referring to a pillar of the Western canon: a classic, in other words.[1] 'Great books' of this kind may be important but they are not always straightforward or entertaining. Some, such as *Under the Volcano* or *Ulysses*, may require other great books to help make sense of them. Difficulty in a book constitutes a sort of unappealing literary masochism to some; to others it is a measure of artistic genius. Either way, a great book does not have to be a good read to be a great book. Some books become great because the public embraces them en masse; others are judged great by the critical establishment despite public apathy – or even because of it. All these sorts of book feature in *The Year of Reading Dangerously*, which could yet be called *Fifty Shades of Great*. Every single book herein may be considered great in one way or another, either because it was born great, achieved greatness, had greatness thrust upon it, was declared great by Oprah, or came thirty-first in a poll conducted by *Take a Break* magazine or the *Literary Review* to find the greatest books of all time. And this even applies to the two not-so-great ones. I hope that's clear.

1 'Definition of a classic: a book everyone is assumed to have read and often thinks they have.' Alan Bennett, *Independent on Sunday*, January 1991.

Recently, BBC TV broadcast the first series of *My Life in Books*, in which well-known personalities are interviewed about five special books which have shaped their lives. The day after the first episode, I was poking around a second-hand bookshop – nothing remarkable about that, as you'll see – when I chanced on a volume with the mirror-image title, *The Books in My Life*. This was no more than a coincidence. *The Books in My Life* was published fifty years ago; I had never heard of it and I doubt the producers of *My Life in Books* had either. However, on closer inspection, *The Books in My Life* was similar to *The Year of Reading Dangerously* in a number of significant ways. Just as in this book, the author of *The Books in My Life* discourses at length on the stories he read as a child, the influence of fiction on his imagination,

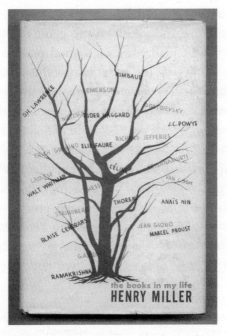

*Fig. 3: 'Indubitably the vast majority of books overlap one another.'*

the conundrum of personal taste, the problem of 'great books'. He incorporates letters and diary excerpts into the text. There are appendices which catalogue the author's favourite titles; there is even a satirical, though not unserious, chapter entitled 'Reading in the Toilet'. And, with a certain inevitability, the writer's name is Miller. Somewhat spooked, I bought the book. On the up side, at least he wasn't called Andy.

*The Books in My Life* is the work of Henry Miller, author of *Tropic of Cancer* and other racy *romans à clef*. In the opening chapter, he offers a simple phrase to sum up the authors or books that had remained with him over the years: '*They were alive and they spoke to me!*' I cannot think of a more eloquent definition of greatness than that and I borrow it from my predecessor and semi-namesake with gratitude. It encapsulates the type of book I was hunting for during my year of dangerous reading, books that were alive and that spoke to me while I tried to deal with the trials of everyday existence: commuting, working in an office, being a new dad, getting older. *The Year of Reading Dangerously*, then, is a book about great books – reading them, writing them – and how life can get in the way. Whether it is great in itself will depend on whether, as you turn the pages, the machine begins to hum; on whether it comes alive and speaks to you.

The first decade of the twenty-first century was, superficially, a good time to be a book lover. You heard about a new book from a friend or on a television book club. Maybe a customer review caught your eye. You purchased the book from a superstore or supermarket, or you bought the audio edition to listen to in the car or at the gym. Over a glass of wine, you talked about it with your friends or reading group. How did it make you feel? Were you broadly in agreement? Later, perhaps you saw the author discuss the same book at a sold-out event or literary festival. You raised your hand and asked a question; you got involved. And if you had the technical know-how, it became possible to achieve all of the above *virtually*. You read off the screen of an ereader or a tablet computer and shared your thoughts on the Internet. You tweeted and blogged, on the train or up the top of a mountain. The humble book was transformed from a clumpy bundle of paper and glue into a pass-key that unlocked a variety of interactive book-based experiences, most of which involved the chatty participation of other users. In comparison, the more traditional method of reading – i.e. sitting alone, looking at lines of words until the pages ran out – seemed distinctly starchy and pre-millennial.

In short, this was a period in which the phrase 'you're never alone with a good book' started to sound less like a promise and more like a threat.

However, it wasn't all stimulating debate, dry white wine and a healthy queue in the signing tent. At the same time these innovations were captivating a certain class of reader, libraries and bookshops were struggling to survive. Ever since the advent of the big chain bookstores in the 1980s, with their armchairs and coffee shops, local independent booksellers have found it hard to compete. Now the chains' market dominance was threatened in turn by the twin forces of the supermarkets – who offered deep discounts on the most popular titles, depriving booksellers of a vital source of income – and the Internet which, either in the guise of an online bookseller or as a provider of downloadable ebooks, can pulverise a bricks and mortar store in terms of stock. An average bookshop might hold a few thousand titles; the Internet provides instant access to these, plus millions more no bookshop could possibly contain, however super the store, comfy the chair or aromatic the coffee. Independent or otherwise, the dedicated bookseller started to vanish from the high street.

Meanwhile, public libraries continued to lose funding and the support of the local authorities who ran them. Budgets for books dwindled away. For a while, it seemed as though these institutions might survive as 'community hubs' – Internet terminals were installed and government ministers made speeches where they referred to the library of the future as 'Facebook-3D'. [2] However, in the wake of the credit crunch and the austerity cuts that followed, many libraries were deemed a luxury the community could no longer afford. Librarians were told their expertise was dispensable and that their roles could be performed by unpaid volunteers. Library closures gathered pace. Accusations of 'cultural vandalism' abounded; legal actions were launched. Some were successful and some were not. School libraries suffered a similar fate. In bankrupt California, Governor Arnold Schwarzenegger proposed to scrap new school textbooks in favour of ebook and Internet access as the state's main portal to knowledge: 'It's nonsensical and expensive to look to traditional hard-bound books when information today is so readily available in electronic form.'[3]

Not very long ago, my family and I were staying at a cottage in the country. In the mornings, I worked on the second draft of this book – which was overdue – but in the afternoons we would explore the surrounding countryside or drive to the nearest town to pick up supplies from the local shop. The cottage was an authentic retreat and had

2 Andy Burnham, former Culture Secretary, from a speech to the Public Libraries Association, 9 October 2008.
3 *San Jose Mercury News*, 7 June 2009.

no telephone or Internet access. One morning, I needed to double-check something I had written about *Moby-Dick* in Chapter VI. However, my copy of *Moby-Dick* was at home on the Shelf of Betterment. Never mind, I thought, if we go into town this afternoon, I'll find a copy and look up what I need.

But *Moby-Dick* was nowhere to be found. The town's bookshop had closed down the previous year and the library did not hold it in stock. I asked the volunteer behind the desk if I could use one of their Internet terminals but she told me their server was down and they weren't expecting it to be restored for several days. Finally, in a supermarket on the ring-road, I located Melville's great novel. It was one of a hundred classic books in the *Nintendo 100 Classic Book Collection*, a cartridge for the Nintendo DS handheld games console. I don't know if you have ever tried to read *Moby-Dick* on a DS in a Tesco car park – I doubt you have – but I cannot recommend it. The two miniature screens, so in harmony with the escapades of Super Mario and Lego Batman, do not lend themselves to the study of this arcane, eldritch text; and nor does the constant clamour of a small boy in the back seat asking when he can have his DS back.

I accept that this story illustrates that it is technically possible to buy a copy of *Moby-Dick* on what passes for the high street. It might also be advanced as further evidence of the adaptability of the book. But to me it demonstrates how marginal good books might become in the future. Surely *Moby-Dick* deserves to be something more than just a sliver of content on a screen? I feel much the same when I see books piled up on pallets in supermarkets, like crates of beer or charcoal briquettes, and I am shocked to be reminded that there is nothing intrinsically special about books unless we invest them with values other than 'value' and we create spaces in which to do it.

Reading is a broad church. But it is still a church.

So it has been my mixed fortune to be occupied with this book about books in a period of frenetic cultural upheaval, with further trouble ahead. Several competing forces threaten to alter the way we think about reading, what we read and how we read it – the Internet, bookstores, libraries, our governments. Meanwhile, the last decade has given us blogs, book groups, festivals, all the chatter of the social network, developments which, while they may indeed be progress, are not the thing itself. They are not reading.

Having begun on the back foot, let me finish on the front. I have wasted enough ink telling you what this book is not. Over the course of a year or so, the slow process of reading these fifty great books, and the other two, gave me back my life. The actions I describe here, inspired by a particular volume or a passage of writing, were often the direct result of chatting with no one except myself. I was my own 3D Facebook; number of friends: one. And therefore, as you read this book, please consider it a passionate defence of those two elements I consider most at risk from our neophiliac desire to read fashionably, publicly, ever more excitedly: patience and solitude.

Because, when you stop and think about it, the rest is time off.

Andy Miller
The Garden of England
Summer 2013

I

'Writing brings scant relief. It retraces, it delimits. It lends a touch of coherence, the idea of a kind of realism. One stumbles around in a cruel fog, but there is the odd pointer. Chaos is no more than a few feet away. A meagre victory, in truth.

What a contrast with the absolute, miraculous power of reading! An entire life spent reading would have fulfilled my every desire; I already knew that at the age of seven. The texture of the world is painful, inadequate; unalterable, or so it seems to me. Really, I believe that an entire life spent reading would have suited me best.

Such a life has not been granted me.'

Michel Houellebecq,
*Whatever* (*Extension du domaine de la lutte*)


'I may, if I am lucky, tap the deep pathos that pertains to all authentic art because of the breach between its eternal values and the sufferings of a muddled world – this world, indeed, can hardly be blamed for regarding literature as a luxury or a toy unless it can be used as an up-to-date guidebook.'

Vladimir Nabokov, *Lectures on Russian Literature*

# Book One

*The Master and Margarita* by Mikhail Bulgakov

My life is nothing special. It is every bit as dreary as yours.

This is the drill. Every weekday morning, the alarm wakes us at 5.45am, unless our son wakes us earlier, which he sometimes – usually – does. He is three. When we moved into this house a year ago, we bought a Goodman programmable radio and CD player for the bedroom. The CD player, being cheap, is temperamental about what it will and will not play. When it works, which it sometimes – usually – doesn't, the day begins with 'I Start Counting', the first track on *Fuzzy-Felt Folk*, an arch selection of children's folk tunes on Trunk Records. (For a few weeks after we got the CD player, we experimented with alternative wake-up calls, from Sinatra, to the Stooges, to Father Abraham and The Smurfs, but the fun of choosing a different disc every night quickly turned into another chore, one more obstacle between us and our hearts' desire – falling asleep.) 'I Start Counting' is a lilting and gentle song, a scenic shuttle-bus ride back to Morningtown, and the capricious CD player seems to like it. So we have settled for 'I Start Counting'. *'This year, next year, sometime, never . . .'*

But on those mornings when the CD won't take, the radio kicks in instead. These are the days that begin at

5.45am not with a soft dawn chorus of 'I Start Counting', but with the brutal twin reveille of *Farming Today* at ear-splitting volume and the impatient yelling of our only son, who has invariably been awake for some time. 'Is it morning yet?' he enquires, over and over again at the top of his lungs. We lie there, shattered. Someone somewhere is milking a cow.

I stumble downstairs and make a cup of tea. In the time it takes for the kettle to boil, I put some brioche in a bowl for my son – his favourite – and swallow a couple of vitamin supplements, cod liver oil for dry skin, and high-strength calcium (plus vitamin D) for bones. The calcium tablets are a hangover from a low-fat diet I put myself on four years ago, wanting to get in shape before Alex was born, one of the side effects of which, other than dramatic weight loss, was to make my shins ache from a real or phantom calcium deficiency. The pains soon went but the tablets have become another habit. At that time, my job was making me miserable. For too long I compensated by eating and drinking too much, wine at lunchtime and beer in the pub after work, with the result that for the first time, in my early thirties, I had become a fat man with a big, fat face. I shed three stone and have successfully kept the weight off, so that now, combined with the effects of sustained sleep deprivation, my face is undeniably gaunt. Acquaintances who haven't seen me for a while look concerned and wonder whether I'm ok. 'Have you been ill?' they ask. I love it when they do this.

The kettle boils. I pour the hot water onto the Twinings organic teabag nestled in the blue cat mug which came from Camden market in the early 1990s, soon after my wife, Tina, and I first started going out, and which for reasons both of sentimentality and size remains her preference for the first cup of tea of the day.[1] Sometimes I put out the mug and bag in readiness the night before, sometimes I don't. I stir the teabag, pressing it against the side of the mug and squashing it on the bottom. Then I throw it in the bin, pour in the organic semi-skimmed milk, give the tea another stir and put the spoon to one side so I can use it again in an hour's time to eat half a grapefruit – another surviving component of the low-fat diet. Actually, to all intents and purposes, I am still on the low-fat diet. I don't drink beer any more and I rarely eat cakes, chocolate, biscuits, etc.

If reading about this is sapping your spirit, you should try living it.

I take my wife her tea in bed. On a good morning, she will be waiting to take the hot cat mug from me, but sometimes, when I arrive in the bedroom, hot tea in hand, she has gone back to sleep and so I have to wake her up and cajole her into a sitting position. This does irritate me. I have been performing this small, uxorious duty for the last thirteen years; surely I am entitled to a measure of disgruntlement that she, luxuriating in precious minutes of sweet sleep I have already forgone on her behalf, cannot even be bothered to sit up? By now, three-year-old Alex has climbed into bed, though, so all slumber soon ceases. We lie in bed together, our whole family, complete. The best minutes of the day.

At this point, a fork appears in the road, depending on which of us has to go to London today. Tina and I both have jobs that permit us to work selected days from home. I look after Alex on a Thursday and his mother spends the day with him on Monday. On Tuesday, Wednesday and Friday, he is in nursery from 7.30am until 5.30pm. My mother-in-law helps with the pick-ups and drop-offs, as well as the

1 While the mug is blue, the cat itself is ginger.

washing and ironing. We pay her a small monthly retainer for these chores, which discreetly bumps up her pension and helps keep her grandson in chocolate buttons. However, by placing this arrangement on a financial footing, my mother-in-law is understandably reluctant to perform any grand-motherly tasks which fall outside her remit. We rarely arrive home after a long day at the office to discover, to our surprise and delight, someone has baked a cake or hidden a thimble.

So one of us goes to work in London, sometimes two of us. If it's me I make sure I have enough time to eat break-fast, which is the same breakfast I eat every day except Sunday – half a grapefruit, a glass of orange juice from a carton, a slice of wholemeal toast and Marmite, and a mug of strong black coffee, brewed in a one-person cafétière. On Sundays I have black coffee, warm croissants and good strawberry jam. After six days of abstinence, the sudden Sunday combination of sugar, caffeine and pleasure propels me to a state of near-euphoria. This is usually the most alive I feel all week. For about half an hour, things seem possible.[2]

The philosopher Ludwig Wittgenstein is said to have remarked that he didn't mind what he ate, as long as it was always the same thing, although I imagine Wittgenstein rarely, if ever, bagged up his own packed lunch. If I am working in London, I always take the following with me: a ham sandwich, a tomato, a bag of baked crisps and an

2 In the interests of full, Patrick Bateman-like disclosure, here are the brands which make up this breakfast. Grapefruit: Jaffa, pink, organic. Orange juice: Grove Fresh Pure, organic. Bread: Kingsmill, wholemeal, medium-sliced. Low-fat spread: Flora Light. Marmite: n/a. Coffee: Percol Americano filter coffee, fairtrade, organic, strength: 4. Sundays – All-butter croissants: Sainsbury's, 'Taste the Difference'. Jam: Bonne Maman Conserve, strawberry. I drink the orange juice from a type of Ikea glass called Svepa which, through a process of trial and error, I have determined is the perfect size for consuming a carton of orange juice in equal meas-ures over four successive mornings. Then I go out and disembowel a dog.

apple, which I eat at my desk.[3] If I am having lunch in a restaurant with a colleague or a client, I still make and pack this exact combination of items and eat it twelve hours later on the train on the way home, where it tastes absolutely desperate. Why do I always do this? Because I don't have the energy to be bothered to think about doing something different, even though the thing I am doing will, I know, stick in the throat.

(FYI Mrs Miller skips breakfast – tut – and makes her own sandwiches only infrequently – tsk – although she does put a banana in her handbag and keeps a box of Oat So Simple instant porridge in her desk drawer.)

One or both of us leaves home at about 6.30am, certainly no later than 6.35am. We both prefer the 6.44am train, run by Southeastern Trains. There is very little chat on the 6.44; many of the other passengers are asleep. (The 7.03 lands you at Victoria at the height of the rush-hour crush, while the 7.22 usually fills up by Chatham, and its human traffic, having had an extra hour in which to wake up, make-up and caffeinate, is significantly rowdier.) But the 6.44am train has its drawbacks, too. We both travel in fear of sitting next to the woman who boards the train at Sittingbourne and without fail performs the same daily manicure: fingernails with emery board till Rainham, application of hand cream at Gillingham, greasy massage to Rochester. Once treatment is complete, the hands' owner takes a power nap, mouth agape, to Bromley South, where she leaves the train. We refer to the woman as 'Mrs Atrixo'. If she sits down next to one of us, we text the other: 'Eek! Atrixo!'

3 'I sometimes feel like Nietzsche in *Ecce Homo*, feeling it appropriate to give an account of his dietary habits, like his taste for "thick oil-free cocoa", convinced that nothing that concerns him could be entirely without interest.' Michel Houellebecq, *Public Enemies*.

Our train arrives in town. Then follows the bus or Tube ride. Then work. Work lasts all day, sometimes longer.

Meanwhile, at his nursery, my son enjoys a day of structured and unstructured activity in the company of a mixture of children and young women – few of whom are older than eighteen and none of whom are older than twenty-five. He might play with the Duplo™. He might pretend to be Doctor Who for a while. He might tell one of the girls what he got up to on his last 'Mummy day'. We don't know for sure because we're not there. He usually has his breakfast and his lunch and his tea sitting at a little table with some of his friends. Of course, they are only his friends by virtue of being the children with whom he is obliged to pass much of his time (three days in every seven). They are more like colleagues than friends. At the end of the day, they all sit around the television, children and helpers, and watch a video until someone, a parent or grandparent, comes to collect them.

Sandwich, bath, a little more television, bed, stories, sleep. Also a telephone call from the parent – or parents – who may or may not get home in time to say goodnight.

The parental evening routine follows a very similar pattern, with half a bottle of wine and maybe some cooked food, sometimes even cooked from scratch. Sleep follows swiftly at 10pm, unless some detail of the day sticks in mind, some professional slight, some office skirmish to come.

That's how the week goes. Weekends and family days are less restricted but still have their structures and patterns and duties – paperwork, haircuts, the weekly shop, visits from friends with children, long car journeys to close family. There is some fun but there is little in the way of spontaneity. We do not have the time. Then Monday comes around and we start counting all over again. *'This year, next year, sometime, never . . .'*

I assume we are happy. Certainly we love each other.

We have been working parents for three years. In that time I have, for pleasure, read precisely one book – *The Da Vinci Code* by Dan Brown.

It is Thursday, and Thursday is a Daddy day. So we have packed the Wet Wipes and a change of trouser and after lunch the boy and I set off for Broadstairs.

Broadstairs is half an hour up the coast from where we live. For a part-time child-minding parent, it has several attractions to recommend it. The bay encloses a sandy beach with swings and trampolines. There is a small, old-fashioned cinema. Along the promenade, overlooking the bay, lies Morelli's famous ice-cream parlour. And the long walk downhill from the station to the seafront almost guarantees an afternoon nap for members of the party travelling by pushchair.

However, this is a Thursday in late November. The cinema is closed. The swings and trampolines are shrouded in winter tarpaulins and the sea is too boisterous and cold for paddling. The rain that greets us at the station thickens as we trudge into town, facing the wind, and we have to shelter in the doorway of a charity shop to unpack the PVC rain cover, which flaps about uncontrollably until skewered to the metal frame of the buggy by ruddy red hands – mine. No one feels much like a snooze.

In Morelli's, we are the only people eating ice creams. We also appear to be the only customers younger than sixty. Around us, pensioners eke out their frothy coffees and try not to make eye-contact with me. It has been my experience over the last few years that people are generally more at ease with the dad and toddler combo on TV than in reality, where it seems to disconcert them. Is the mother dead? Are

23

we witnessing an abduction? In spring and summer, this place is full of life, with holidaying families and little children boogieing in front of the jukebox. But today the view across Viking Bay has vanished behind fogged-up windows.

We leave Morelli's and walk up the promenade to the Charles Dickens museum. Hmm, some other time. But around the corner on Albion Street is the Albion Bookshop. I yank the pushchair up the steps, holding open the heavy door with one foot, and once inside try to find a corner where we shan't be in anyone's way, even though the shop is empty. Down the street a little way is another Albion Bookshop, a huge, endearingly dingy secondhand place – fun for Dad, who could easily lose hours in there, but less so for three-year-old boys. So while Alex decides which Mr Men book he would like, I browse this shop's smaller selection of titles. There is a cookery section, a local interest section – *Broadstairs In Old Photographs,* etc. – and a Dan Brown section, with his four novels to date: *The Da Vinci Code, Angels and Demons* and the other two, and a plenteous range of spin-offs and tie-ins: *Cracking the Da Vinci Code, Rosslyn and the Grail, The Holy Blood and the Holy Grail.*[4] On the fiction shelves, between Maeve Binchy and *The Pilgrim's Progress,* I am surprised to find Mikhail Bulgakov's *The Master and Margarita.* I pick it up – small format, £3.99, good value. The grinning cat on the front cover[5] makes Alex laugh, so I take it to the till along with his choice, *Mr Small.*

It is time for us to go home. On the long climb back up the hill to Broadstairs station, the combination of sea air and ice cream finally catches up with Alex and he nods off. We find the space on the train next to the disabled toilet

4 I am aware *The Holy Blood and the Holy Grail* was published long before *The Da Vinci Code.* The Albion Bookshop has since closed down.
5 The book is orange, the cat is black.

and, with my son still asleep and nothing to do for half an hour, I start to read.

'Mr Small was very small. Probably the smallest person you've ever seen in your whole life.'

No, better wait till Alex wakes up. I turn my attention to the other book.

'At the sunset hour of one warm spring day two men were to be seen at Patriarch's Ponds . . .'

Later that evening, after reading *Mr Small* three times in a row, after Alex is tucked up and sleeping, I hazard a few more pages of *The Master and Margarita*. The two gentlemen at Patriarch's Ponds in Moscow are Mikhail Alexandrovich Berlioz, editor of a highbrow literary magazine, and the poet Ivan Nikolayich Poniryov, 'who wrote under the pseudonym of Bezdomny'. Before they have had a chance even to exchange pleasantries, a third character materialises:

'Just then the sultry air coagulated and wove itself into the shape of a man – a transparent man of the strangest appearance. On his small head was a jockey-cap and he wore a short check bum-freezer made of air. The man was seven feet tall but narrow in the shoulders, incredibly thin and with a face made for derision.'

It seems this character, '*swaying from left to right . . . without touching the ground*', is the Devil. But no sooner has He manifested himself, than the Devil vanishes. Shortly thereafter, Berlioz and Bezdomny are joined by a 'professor', a foreigner, country of origin unclear. The three of them have a rambling, opaque conversation. At the end of the first chapter, the action suddenly shifts to Rome at the time of Christ, and the palace of Pontius Pilate. What?

I cannot really fathom it. But the sheer novelty of reading a book of this sort after such a long lay-off is reward in itself. I am doing something difficult – good for me.

'*Your head will be cut off*!' the foreigner informs Berlioz in the course of their baffling chat, '*by a Russian woman, a member of the Komsomol.*' (I have no idea what the Komsomol is.) After the mysterious detour to Rome in Chapter 2, back at Patriarch's Ponds the editor and poet decide this 'professor' is certifiably crazy – '*his green left eye was completely mad, his right eye, black, expressionless and dead*'. Leaving Bezdomny to watch over this lunatic, Berlioz runs to telephone the authorities. ('*The professor, cupping his hands into a trumpet, shouted: "Wouldn't you like me to send a telegram to your uncle in Kiev?" Another shock – how did this madman know that he had an uncle in Kiev?*')

Then this happens:

'Berlioz ran to the turnstile and pushed it. Having passed through he was just about to step off the pavement and cross the tramlines when a white and red light flashed in his face and the pedestrian signal lit up with the words "Stop! Tramway!" A tram rolled into view, rocking slightly along the newly-laid track that ran down Yermolayevsky Street and into Bronnaya. As it turned to join the main line it suddenly switched its inside lights on, hooted and accelerated.

Although he was standing in safety, the cautious Berlioz decided to retreat behind the railings. He put his hand on the turnstile and took a step backwards. He missed his grip and his foot slipped on the cobbles as inexorably as though on ice. As it slid towards the tramlines his other leg gave way and Berlioz was thrown across the track. Grabbing wildly, Berlioz fell prone. He struck his head violently on the cobblestones and the gilded moon flashed hazily across his vision. He just had time to turn on his back, drawing his legs up to his stomach with a frenzied movement and as he turned over he saw the woman tram-driver's face, white with horror above her red necktie, as she bore down on him with irresistible force and speed. Berlioz made no sound, but all around him the streets rang with the desperate shrieks of women's voices. The driver grabbed the electric brake, the car pitched forward, jumped the rails and with a tinkling crash the glass broke in all its windows. At this moment Berlioz heard a despairing voice: "Oh, no . . .!" Once more and for the last time the moon flashed before his eyes but it split into fragments and then went black.

Berlioz vanished from sight under the tramcar and a round, dark object rolled across the cobbles, over the kerbstone and bounced along the pavement.

It was a severed head.'

Google tells me the Komsomol was the popular name for the youth wing of the Communist party of the Soviet Union and not the Moscow municipal tram network. But it's academic: I'm in.

Right here is where my life changes direction. This is the moment I resolve to finish this book – a severed head bouncing across the cobblestones. Life must be held at bay, just for a few days, if for no reason other than to prove it can be done. I need to know what happens next.

Mikhail Bulgakov was born in Kiev in 1891 and died in

Moscow in 1940 and at no point in-between, as far as I can establish, did he ever visit Broadstairs – never toured the Dickens Museum on a drizzly afternoon, never ordered a milkshake at Morelli's. But let's pretend he did. Imagine he manifested himself in the Albion Bookshop on Albion Street and discovered, as I had done, a copy of something called *The Master and Margarita*, with his name on the spine and cover. For a number of reasons, he would be astonished.

Мастер и Маргарита, usually translated as *The Master and Margarita*, was unpublished at the time of Bulgakov's death – unpublished and, in one sense, unpublishable. For many years, it was available only as *samizdat* (written down and circulated in secret); to be found in possession of a copy was to risk imprisonment. Even its first official appearance in the journal *Moskva* in 1966 was censored; the first complete version was not published until 1973. Yet here it is in Broadstairs, available to purchase and in English to boot. 'Боже мой!'[6]

Another reason Bulgakov might be astounded to find his novel, in English, in a small Kent bookshop, might stagger out onto the pavement to catch his breath and, with a trembling hand, light a cigarette – 'Я нуждаюсь в дыме!'[7] – is that back when he died, the book remained unfinished. The first draft was tossed into a stove in 1930, after Bulgakov learned that his play, *Cabal of Sanctimonious Hypocrites*, had been banned by the Soviet authorities (who, unsurprisingly, did not care for the title). After five years' work, he abandoned a second draft in 1936. He commenced a third draft the same year and chiselled away at it, making corrections and additions, until April 1940, when illness forced him to

6 'Good Heavens!'
7 'I need a smoke!'

abandon his labours. A few weeks later, Bulgakov expired, exasperated. Мастер и Маргарита was completed by his widow, Elena Sergeevna; and it was she who spent the next twenty-five years trying to get it published. ('Елена, моя любовь, есть кое-что, что мы должны обсудить . . .'[8])

Have you read *The Master and Margarita*? It cannot be denied that the early part of the book is often inscrutable, a barrage of in-jokes savaging institutions and individuals of the early Soviet era which only an antique Muscovite or an authority on early twentieth-century Russian history would recognise or find amusing. And then there is the business with Rome and Pontius Pilate. Essentially, it is a book one has to stick with and trust.

Here are the bare bones of the plot. The Devil lands in Moscow, disguised as a magician. With Him is an infernal entourage: a witch, a valet, a violent henchman with a single protruding fang, and an enormous talking cat called Behemoth, a tabby as big as a tiger. The diabolic gang leave a trail of panic and destruction across the literary and governmental Moscow landscape. Sometimes this is grotesquely amusing, at others terrifying; frequently it is both. In a lunatic asylum we are introduced to the master, a disillusioned author whose novel about Christ and Pontius Pilate (ah, I see!) has been rejected for seemingly petty reasons. His response has been to burn the manuscript and shut out the world, even turning away his lover, Margarita, who ardently believes in his work.

Of course, I only appreciated the autobiographical significance of this in retrospect and the communistic targets of the satire remained obscure to me. In terms of the story itself, the promise of the severed head was slow to be realised. Had

8 'Elena, my love, there is something we need to discuss . . .'

it not been for the half-forgotten kick of reading a book at all, I probably would not have carried on; for the first couple of days, I was compelled to do so by little more than my own stubbornness. This is only a book; I like reading books; this one will not get the better of me. But the more I read, the more I understood – or rather, understood that I did not need to understand. If I let it, the book would carry me instead.

*The Master and Margarita* begins as a waking nightmare. It has the relentlessness of a nightmare, the same persistent illogic one finds in *Alice's Adventures in Wonderland*, but nastier, crueller – dead eyes, derision, severed heads, a cat whose mischievous grin betokens only black magic. Once in train, it is pitiless. But for the nightmare to take hold, the reader must fall asleep and wake up somewhere else.

Back in reality, though, I had to stay awake. I read in fifteen- or twenty-minute bursts, in lunch breaks or during *Tikkabilla*. It wasn't a good way to go about it. To engage with this book when there were tasks to be performed, emails to be sent, ham sandwiches to be packed, or a purple dragon singing a song about being friends, was hard. It required sacrifices. Wine, TV and conversation were all postponed. It also required selfishness and cunning. 'Just off to the Post Office,' I would announce at the busiest hour of the day, 'I won't be long.' And in the gloriously slow-moving queue, I would turn a few more pages.

At the beginning of the second half of the novel, Margarita is transformed into a witch at the Devil's command. She accepts an invitation to His great Spring Ball. This is when both Margarita – and *The Master and Margarita* – take flight. She soars naked across Mother Russia – across the cities and mountains and rivers – transformed, ecstatic and free. And as she does, borne aloft on Bulgakov's impassioned words, I felt the dizzying force of books again, lifting me off the 6.44, out of myself, away from Mrs Atrixo and her hands. How had I lived without this?

*The Master and Margarita* is a novel about many things, some obscure, others less so. To me, at this point in my life, it seems to be a book about books; and I love books. But I seem to have lost the knack of reading them.

After the ball, Margarita is granted a wish by the Devil. She asks only that the master be restored to her from the asylum. And then: *'Please send us back to his basement in that street near the Arbat, light the lamp again and make everything as it was before.'*

'An hour later Margarita was sitting, softly weeping from shock and happiness, in the basement of the little house in one of the sidestreets off the Arbat. In the master's study all was as it had been before that terrible autumn night of the year before. On the table, covered with a velvet cloth, stood a vase of lily-of-the-valley and a shaded lamp. The charred manuscript-book lay in front of her, beside it a pile of undamaged copies. The house was silent. Next door on a divan, covered by his hospital dressing-gown, the master lay in a deep sleep, his regular breathing inaudible from the next room . . . She smoothed the manuscript tenderly as one does a favourite cat and turning it over in her hands she inspected it from every angle, stopping now on the title page, now on the end.'

But of course an arrangement with the Devil has its price. Life cannot stay the same. For the master and Margarita to live forever, their old selves must die. She will stay at the Devil's side, he will be free to roam the cosmos:

'"But the novel, the novel!" she shouted at the master, "take the novel with you, wherever you may be going!"

"No need," replied the master. "I can remember it all by heart."

"But you . . . you won't forget a word?" asked Margarita, embracing her lover and wiping the blood from his bruised forehead.

"Don't worry. I shall never forget anything again," he answered.'

It took me a little over five days to finish *The Master and Margarita*, but its enchantment lasted far longer. In death, the master and his book become as one. The book is no longer a passive object, a bundle of charred paper, but the thing which lives within his heart, which he personifies, which allows him to travel wherever and whenever he likes. The deal Margarita makes with the Devil gives him eternity. And this is how *The Master and Margarita* had made its journey down a century, from reader to reader, to a Broadstairs bookshop. Some part of that book, of Bulgakov himself, now lived on in me. The secret of *The Master and Margarita*, which seems to speak to countless people who know nothing about the bureaucratic machinations of the early Stalinist dictatorship or the agony of the novel's gestation: words are our transport, our flight and our homecoming in one.

Which you don't get from Dan Brown.

So began a year of reading dangerously. *The Master and Margarita* had brought me back to life. Now, if I could discover the gaps in the daily grind – or make the gaps – I knew I could stay there. Could I keep that spark alive in the real world, I wondered? Yes! Because to do so would truly be to never forget anything again. All I needed was another book; that was the deal. This was not reading for pleasure, it was reading for dear life. But, looking back, perhaps I should have stopped to think. With whom, exactly, had the deal been struck?

'The master, intoxicated in advance by the thought of the ride to come, threw a book from the bookcase on to the table, thrust its leaves into the burning table-cloth and the book burst merrily into flame.'

# Book Two

*Middlemarch* by George Eliot

'He had two selves within him apparently, and they must learn to accommodate each other and bear reciprocal impediments. Strange, that some of us, with quick alternate vision see beyond our infatuations, and even while we rave on the heights behold the wide plain where our persistent self pauses and awaits us.'

*Middlemarch*, Book 2, 'Old and Young'

There is a classic episode of the television comedy *Hancock*[1] called 'The Bedsitter', in which Tony Hancock, in a characteristically vain attempt at self-improvement, decides to 'have a go' at Bertrand Russell's *Human Knowledge: Its Limits and Scope*.[2] Every few sentences – few words even – he has to put the book down and consult the large dictionary on his bedside table (*'Well, if that's what they mean, why don't they say so?'*). Soon, frustration gets the better of him:

1 Formerly *Hancock's Half Hour*. The title changed in 1961 after the departure of Sid James.
2 A knowing transposition? The correct title of Russell's book is *Human Knowledge: Its Scope and Limits*.

'No, it's him. It's him that's at fault, he's a rotten writer. A good writer should be able to put down his thoughts clearly in the simplest terms understandable to everybody. It's him. He's a bad writer. Not going to waste my time reading him.' (*Drops* Human Knowledge: Its Limits and Scope *on the floor and picks up another book*.) 'Ah, that's more like it – *Lady Don't Fall Backwards*.'

Fifty years later, a similar scene was being played out in our house. I lay on the bed with a nice new copy of George Eliot's *Middlemarch*, and tried to silence my inner Hancock.

**Eliot** (from the 'Prelude'): 'Who cares much to know the history of man, and how the mysterious mixture behaves under the varying experiments of Time . . .

**Hancock** (from 'The Bedsitter'): No, no, I should know. It's in English, I should know what he's talking about.[3]

**Eliot**: Some have felt that these blundering lives are due to the inconvenient indefiniteness with which the Supreme Power has fashioned the natures of women . . .

**Hancock**: He's a human being the same as me, using words, English words, available to us all. Now, concentrate.

3 George Eliot was a woman, real name Mary Ann Evans. For minor comic effect, however, I have left Hancock's words unaltered, thus giving you, the reader, the impression that he, Hancock, thinks George Eliot is a man. Ha ha! Sorry for these nit-picking footnotes, by the way, I know they disrupt the flow, but fans of George Eliot, Tony Hancock, Bertrand Russell *et al.* are an unforgiving lot and it is necessary to reassure them that what they are reading is unimpeachably correct, to the extent that I have compromised, even ruined, the opening of this chapter in order to secure their trust, solely to prevent the wholesale dismissal of a book it has taken me almost five years to write, simply because they, the so-called experts, might mistakenly assume that I don't realise George Eliot was a woman. Of course George Eliot was a woman! But where experts are concerned, it goes without saying that nothing goes without saying.

I succeeded in reading the 'Prelude' in its entirety. (*'Yes, it's hard graft for we intellectuals these days.'*) Then I read it again. It was only three paragraphs long, so I took a quick turn round the room, and then read it a third time. No, it was no good. I could hardly understand a word. But, unlike Hancock, I had no *Lady Don't Fall Backwards* to fall back on. *Middlemarch* and I were going to have to get along.

Of course, the problem was not *Middlemarch*. Despite my surprise conquest of *The Master and Margarita*, and the blast of confidence it gave me, I quickly knew I had overreached myself. *The Master and Margarita* had been an obstacle course; *Middlemarch*, on the other hand, gave every indication of being a 688-page punishment beating. Once upon a time, I had been in the habit of reading this kind of elaborate, circumlocutory prose. But that was when I was a student, full of piss and vinegar and blithe ignorance. Two decades on, I was gravely out of condition, short of breath, barely limping along. It was too much, too soon, too old.

In those days, as an English literature undergraduate at a self-consciously progressive university, it was possible to read a couple of classics every week – unlikely, almost unheard of, but possible. In contrast, an audit of my current week's reading would look something like this:

200 emails (approx.)
Discarded copies of *Metro*
The *NME* and monthly music magazines
Excel spreadsheets
The review pages of Sunday newspapers
Business proposals
Bills, bank statements, junk mail, etc.

CD liner notes

Crosswords, Sudoku puzzles, etc.

Ready-meal heating guidelines

The occasional postcard

And a lot of piddling about on the Internet

Of these, the Sudoku was the most inexplicable to me. What a waste of time! I loathed it. Yet I could pass a whole train journey wrestling with one small grid, a long hour that brought me little or no pleasure, even on the rare occasions it ended in success. The shelves of WHSmith at Victoria station were packed with competing Oriental number tortures: Sudoku, Sun Doku, Code Doku, Killer Sudoku . . . As a former student acquaintance had written in the concluding sentence of a 10,000-word dissertation on mechanical engineering: '*It doesn't matter anyway, because it's all a load of shit.*'[4]

So, accepting I was in no fit state even to complete an *Evening Standard* 'brainteaser' – Grade: Beginner – why had I felt compelled to attempt *Middlemarch*, one of the high peaks of the English novel?

As I approached my mid-thirties, before our son was born, while he was still a Nice Idea In The Not Too Distant Future, I started getting the first pangs of a feeling which soon grew acute. The feeling was this: one day soon, I am going to die. Previously, I had enjoyed brooding on my own mortality, because I was young and death was never going to happen to me. Now, however, like many people on the threshold of middle-age, out there in the jungle somewhere I could discern a disconcerting drumbeat; and

4 Our university may have considered itself progressive but these eleven words earned him an F (for TELLING THE TRUTH).

I realised that at some point in the aforementioned Not Too Distant Future, closer now, the drumming would cease, leaving a terrible silence in its wake. And that would be it for me.

Immediately, we produced a child. But if anything, this only made things worse.

I had heard that other people dealt with this sort of problem by having ill-advised affairs with schoolgirls, or dyeing their hair a 'fun' colour, or plunging into a gruelling round of charity marathon running, 'to put something back'. But I did not want to do any of that; I just wanted to be left alone. My sadness for things undone was smaller and duller, yet maybe more undignified. It seemed to fix itself on minor letdowns, everyday stuff I had been meaning to do but somehow, in half a lifetime, had not got round to. I was still unable to play the guitar. I had never been to New York. I did not know how to drive a car or roast a chicken. Roasting a chicken – the impossible dream! Even my mid-life crisis was a disappointment.

I told myself I had a lot to be thankful for. I had a loving family, lived by the sea in a house which in thirty years I might own, had written a couple of books, knew Paris via its *arrondissements*, could ride a bike, play the piano and bake a potato on demand. Yet I was not satisfied.

One of the certainties I found myself questioning was my belief in art. For as long as I could remember, from childhood on, I never doubted that 'great' books or 'fantastic' singles or 'brilliant' films were the prerequisites of a balanced and full existence. Their presence in my life as an adolescent and a young adult was constant and their absence unimaginable. If I needed to go without food so I could buy an important record or novel, I went without food – the hungry consumer. But lately I had begun to ask myself whether this loyalty had amounted to anything more than a shed-load of stuff; two shed-loads in fact, one at the bottom of the garden in a bona fide shed and the other in a storage unit up the road.

However meagre my spiritual beliefs, however much I toed the modern secular line, my faith in art had never faltered. Culture could come in many forms, high, low or somewhere in-between: Mozart, *The Muppet Show*, Ian McEwan.[5] Very little of it was truly great and much of it would always be bad, but all of it was necessary to live, to be fully alive, to frame the endless, numbered days and make sense of them.[6]

Lately, though, I had been feeling like a sucker. As I contemplated the stacks of CDs and VHS tapes, old theatre programmes and superhero comics, wearing a fading t-shirt for some group that had probably split up, they seemed to represent the opposite of the enlightenment they had originally promised. Like me, they were nudging obsolescence. I saw I had got it wrong. I had confused 'art' with 'shopping'.

Books, for instance. I had a lot of those. There they all were, on the shelves and on the floor, piled up by the bed and falling out of boxes. *Moby-Dick*, *Possession*, *Remembrance of Things Past*, the poetry of Emily Dickinson, *Psychotic Reactions and Carburettor Dung*, a few Pevsners, that Jim Thompson omnibus, *The Child in Time*, six more Ian McEwan novels or novellas, two volumes of his short stories . . . These books

5 If one were to plot a graph where the 'x' axis is 'high culture' and the 'y' axis is 'low culture', with Mozart at the top of the former and *The Muppet Show* at the far end of the latter, Ian McEwan's corpus would perfectly bisect the two – the Bonne Maman Conserve in a Wonderloaf baguette.

6 In a neat QED, I have stolen the phrase 'endless, numbered days' from the title of the best Iron & Wine album *Our Endless Numbered Days*.

did furnish the room, but they also got in the way. And there were too many I was aware I had not actually read. As Schopenhauer noted a hundred and fifty years ago, *'It would be a good thing to buy books if one could also buy the time to read them; but one usually confuses the purchase of books with the acquisition of their contents.'*[7]

These books became the focus of a need to *do something*. They were a reproach – wasted money, squandered time, muddled priorities. I shall make a list, I thought. It will name the books I am most ashamed not to have read – difficult ones, classics, a few outstanding entries in the deceitful Miller library – and then I shall read them. I was thirty-five years old. Ten books maybe, ten books before my fortieth birthday. Yes, ten books in five years; one book every six months; that seemed like an easily achievable goal and vaguely decadent when you held down a full-time job and were still unable to drive to the supermarket to buy a chicken you didn't know how to cook, because you'd learned to do neither, because you'd been too busy shopping. Excellent! Books first, driving lessons later.

For the next couple of years I did nothing with this plan except congratulate myself on it. I thought about the list a little and talked about it a lot. In the pub, at parties, over lunch, I would sketch out the idea and coquettishly disclose a title or two: *The Master and Margarita, Pride and Prejudice, Middlemarch*. And each time somebody responded with a disbelieving: 'You've never read *The Master and Margarita / Pride and Prejudice / Middlemarch*?!', I would chortle at the effect my words had created, and thus pull a little further

7 From 'On Reading and Books'. Though it was written a hundred and fifty years ago, this essay by Schopenhauer still has much to tell us. Also, for nineteenth-century German philosophy, it is significantly funnier than you might expect.

away from ever beginning the books in question. Better to speak volumes than to read them.

And so two and a half years passed. Our son arrived. I was halfway to forty and I had read precisely none of the books I could have read in that time, now lost. I hadn't even drawn up the list. There was no list. It existed only in my head, occasionally summoned into being for an easy laugh, the contents of which could be reshuffled as circumstance or listener demanded. It didn't matter anyway, because it was all a load of shit.

Then two things happened.

I was talking about the list yet again with an old friend from university, in that manner of ironic bluff and counter-bluff reserved for all men who were students in the 1980s, and in their hearts are students still.

'Two and a half years gone,' I said. 'I've only got two and a half years left. I'll never do it! I'll never read *Middlemarch*!'

'No,' said my friend. 'You won't.'

He meant it. He was neither bluffing, nor calling my bluff. He knew I would not do it, was certain of it, based on his familiarity with my character, his understanding of my family and work commitments, and his appreciation of how tired we all seemed to be these days.

And I knew he was right.

(I should also add that, when we had first discussed this idea, my friend went out and bought *Middlemarch*, bought and read it and, for the record, enjoyed it. He may possibly have done this because I told him – falsely – that I had already bought, read and enjoyed it myself.)

The second thing that made me stir myself was the afore-mentioned Sudoku.

Somewhere near Gillingham on a dank November

evening, stuck between stations, scratching digits into a box like a tin monkey, after a day at work doing much the same thing in Excel, I experienced an epiphany: Why was I wasting my life like this? Words were my passion, not numbers. And there suddenly rose before me, as if to holler, STOP!, the ghosts of all the printed matter I had consumed in the preceding weeks and months: culture supplements, heritage rock magazines, photocopies and blurbs, *Private Eye* and the *Radio Times*, prescriptions and descriptions, print-outs and spreadsheets and Sudoku, Sudoku, killer Sudoku.

Something had to change and I had to change it.

So when Alex and I went to Broadstairs the following day, the appearance of *The Master and Margarita* there on the shelf of the Albion Bookshop seemed providential. Here was my chance to make good. It was a wild and inspiring and faith-renewing ride and when it was over I wanted to try another one. Plus now I was someone who had read *The Master and Margarita*. I felt like I had put something back.

*Middlemarch*, then, was the book I chose to tackle next. But *Middlemarch* was a much bigger dipper than *The Master and Margarita*. If that had been a fairground ride, this was like a trip on Space Mountain™ – a formidable test of nerve, and one I wanted to get off way before the end.[8]

If *War and Peace* is the most distinguished unread novel in Russian literature, and *Remembrance of Things Past* its even lengthier French counterpart, then *Middlemarch* has a modest claim to being the equivalent in English. ('Middlemarch, twinned with Combray and Bald Hills. Number of visitors:

8 Not the sort of comparison F.R. Leavis would make, eh readers? Actually, Frank much preferred Nemesis™ at Alton Towers, which he described in a letter to friends as both *'physically and conceptually rigorous in the Greek classical tradition'* and *'wicked – I totally spilt my drink and crisps'*.

Uncertain.') It may not be as forbidding as *Finnegans Wake* or as epic as *Clarissa*, but it seems to occupy a special status as a book that sorts the heavyweights from the halfwits. For this reason alone, it had always been a fixture of the phantom list; and I suppose it was vaguely reprehensible that a graduate of English Literature should not have read what Virginia Woolf called '*one of the few English novels written for grown-up people*'. I recall as a teenager watching Salman Rushdie on a BBC2 literary panel game – *The Book Quiz*, was it? – where Rushdie was able to identify some lines from a Bob Dylan song, but not from *Middlemarch*, which he confessed he had never read – cue much amusement amongst his fellow panel members. Was this, it suddenly occurs to me, where I first picked up the awful habit?[9]

After a week and a hundred or so hard-won pages, I knew I was in trouble. I found there were plenty of other jobs I suddenly wanted to do – cleaning the oven, a spot of long overdue filing – anything other than pick up this torturous book. There seemed to be a problem. Who were all these various doctors and ladies and landlords and parsons and what on earth were they saying to one another? The whole experience did nothing but compound the sense of my own wretched floccinaucinihilipilification. Not only was I not enjoying *Middlemarch*, it left me feeling dejected. I was not up to a task others performed with apparent ease. Perhaps I had done little more than swap number puzzles for intellectual fakery – pseudoku. When it came down to it, perhaps I was a halfwit.

Fortunately, at this point Tina staged an intervention.

9 'I made the mistake of going on a TV quiz show and admitting that I'd never read *Middlemarch* . . . and I don't think I'll ever live it down. When I saw I was in trouble I went out and bought it, and I'm planning to read it. I hear it's good.' Salman Rushdie to John Haffenden, 1983.

Much as she wished the oven to be clean and the phone bills to be in tidy, chronological order – wished it with all her heart – she also recognised that what I was doing really mattered to me. She had watched as I struggled with *The Master and Margarita*, and so she reminded me that I needed to let the book do the work. So what if not every line made sense? The drift would do for now.

'Have you actually read *Middlemarch*?' I asked her. 'There is no drift, there is only confusion. Or as the author would say, in the instance of this poor history, it would not be unfair to envisage a state of superlative driftlessness, and where driftlessness lies about us, there too – alas! – confusion may abide. Etc.'

'Oh, stop being so melodramatic,' she said. 'Just do what I did. Read fifty pages a day and leave it at that.'

Do you perceive my wife's brilliance? Is it plain to you, simple reader? It lay not in the essential nobility of her heart, or that she herself already stood atop *Middlemarch* and was gently beckoning her husband to join her. No. It was that *she had a system*. Fifty pages every day. It wasn't exciting, in itself it did not elevate the spirit, but it worked. It allowed time for books and time for life to go on. It was the key both to all mythologies and a clean oven.

And so I accepted that the first few days of *Middlemarch* would be a chore. I started over, counting down each fifty-page segment like it was my homework. Gradually, however, the mists dissolved and the sun began to shine on a fictional corner of the West Midlands. The model for Middlemarch had been Coventry, so in the short term, some amusement was had from reading the highfalutin dialogue aloud with a regional twang (*'I am fastidious in voices, and I cannot endure listening to an imperfect reader'*) and speculating how close Middlemarch lay to Ambridge. Just as with *The Master and*

45

*Margarita* though, there was something seductive about *Middlemarch* and I started to succumb; but whereas Bulgakov's technique is conjuring and grand gestures, Eliot works an intellectual seduction, a slow game of pace and frustration. Sentences picked up as I became accustomed to the rhythms of the prose. The *per diem* fifty pages increased; I stopped mucking about with the voices. I shan't pretend that I understood all the subtleties of issues pertaining to the Reform Bill of June 1832, around which the novel thematically revolves, but the layering of character and motive – and the moral issues the characters have to confront – seemed thrillingly ambitious and sophisticated. When the novel's perspective switches from Dorothea to Casaubon at the start of Chapter 29 – '*but why always Dorothea? Was her point of view the only possible one with regard to this marriage?*' – there follows a passage so sublime and wise and complex that the only word to describe it is: genius.

(A spoiler follows. As in the sport of football, look away now if you don't want to know what happens.)

By the time Casaubon dies in the summerhouse, resentful and alone, I was besotted with the book. I could not believe how much I was enjoying it.

On a seven-hour journey back from Edinburgh, I hardly lifted my head from my book, welcomed an enforced delay in the airport departure lounge, was grateful to miss a connection at Heathrow, sat in the bone-freezing cold at the station for half an hour in order to discover the ending for Dorothea Brooke and Will Ladislaw, before walking home, elated. I mean exactly that; I was elated. I felt the unmistakable certainty that I had been in the presence of great art, and that my heart had opened in reply.

Plus, now I was someone who had read *Middlemarch* and *The Master and Margarita*. Two down.

We live in an era where opinion is currency. The pressure is on us to say 'I like this' or 'I don't like that', to make snap decisions and stick them on our credit cards. But when faced with something we cannot comprehend at once, which was never intended to be snapped up or whizzed through, perhaps 'I don't like it' is an inadequate response. Don't like *Middlemarch*? It doesn't matter. It was here before we arrived, and it will be here long after we have gone. Instead, perhaps we should have the humility to say: I didn't get it. I need to try harder.

I learned to love *Middlemarch*. I had also been reminded of the value of perseverance. I determined to finish what I had started. So the following weekend, we finalised the selection. I wrote down the names of the books on a piece of paper and Tina witnessed and signed it. We christened it 'The List of Betterment'. And afterwards we sat down to a special Sunday lunch which Dad had prepared for the whole family.

Baked potatoes.[10]

## Postscript

This was not quite the end of *Middlemarch*. Of the novels I read during this period, *Middlemarch* is one that stayed with me over several years – haunted me, I should say. As one deadline after another expired, and still I came no closer to completing work on this book, I would remember poor old Casaubon and his unfinished *Key to all Mythologies*: '*the difficulty of making his Key to all Mythologies unimpeachable weighed like lead upon his mind . . .*' And I would also recall

10 An echo of Roger Hargreaves here. I am thinking particularly of the words with which he draws *Mr Strong* to its droll yet satisfying conclusion – '*Ice cream! Ha ha!*'

Dorothea's forlorn plea to her husband: '*All those rows of volumes – will you not now do what you used to speak of? – will you not make up your mind what part of them you will use, and begin to write . . .*'

And so I give thanks that, if you are reading these words, I have been at least partially successful and not conked out at my desk before I could finish what I started; and I also give thanks that we, unlike the Casaubons, are still married.

*Fig. 4: Propped up by a saint. Photo: Alex Miller.*

# Books Three to Five

*Post Office* by Charles Bukowski

*The Communist Manifesto* by Karl Marx and Friedrich Engels

*The Ragged Trousered Philanthropists* by Robert Tressell

'Let us now take wage labour.'

*The Communist Manifesto*

'They had given up everything that makes life good and beautiful in order to carry on a mad struggle to acquire money which they would never be sufficiently cultured to properly enjoy . . . They knew that the money they accumulated was foul with the sweat of their brother men, and wet with the tears of little children, but they were deaf and blind and callous to the consequences of their greed. Devoid of every ennobling thought or aspiration, they grovelled on the filthy ground, tearing up the flowers to get at the worms.'

*The Ragged Trousered Philanthropists*

'This is the job for me, oh yes yes yes.'

*Post Office*

I was sitting in Tiny Tim's Tearoom reading *The Communist Manifesto*, while I waited for my mother to finish her shopping.

'Can I get you anything else?' enquired the proprietor.

'Just the bill, please,' I said.

'Right you are, comrade,' she said. I paid for my bourgeois scone and went to wait outside.

The book I was holding was not the little red book but a slim, modishly-designed paperback from a series called 'Great Ideas'. Its cover blasted out the manifesto's rousing final declaration in embossed, faux-utilitarian type: '*Let the ruling classes tremble at a Communistic revolution. The proletarians have nothing to lose but their chains. They have a world to win. WORKING MEN OF ALL COUNTRIES, UNITE*!' Standing in the street, book in hand, it was hard not to appear as though you were trying to make a point. I tried to adopt an air of intrigued neutrality and not burning revolutionary zeal.

My mother arrived, and catching sight of the cover, uttered the reproach she still reserves for special moments of filial disappointment.

'Oh, Andrew,' she said. I slipped the book in my pocket.

Actually, I quite liked the idea of being perceived as a communist. I didn't even object to being called 'comrade'. The last time I had affected a similar display of left-wing solidarity was as a teenager in the 1980s. Back then, my blue fisherman's cap and enamel Lenin badge attracted more cries of 'wanker' than 'comrade'. But that was then. The old ideological schisms were dead. No one cared enough to call you a wanker any more.

Nestling in my pocket next to *The Communist Manifesto* was the List of Betterment, which I carried round with me like Dumbo and his feather.

# THE LIST OF BETTERMENT

*The Master and Margarita* – Mikhail Bulgakov ☑
*Middlemarch* – George Eliot ☑
*Post Office* – Charles Bukowski ☑
*The Communist Manifesto* – Karl Marx & Friedrich Engels ☐
*The Ragged Trousered Philanthropists* – Robert Tressell ☐
*The Sea, The Sea* – Iris Murdoch ☐
*A Confederacy of Dunces* – John Kennedy Toole ☐
*The Unnamable* – Samuel Beckett ☐
*Twenty Thousand Streets Under the Sky* – Patrick Hamilton ☐
*Moby-Dick* – Herman Melville ☐
*Anna Karenina* – Leo Tolstoy ☐
*Of Human Bondage* – W. Somerset Maugham ☐
*Pride and Prejudice* – Jane Austen ☐

In making this final cut, I had tried not to think too hard about what ought to be there and to let the heart take over. I only wanted to read books I wanted to read. Here, though, was the ink-blot, the echocardiogram. What did the reading say? What did it say about me?

Well, with one exception, these were all novels – six British, three American, two Russian, one Irish, one German.[1] Three women, eleven men. My internationalist credentials were intact but my gender bias could use some work.

1 This is a headache. I have divided the books along these lines but a similar exercise using the writers' nationalities would produce a markedly different result. *Post Office*, for example, is a distinctively American novel by an author who was, strictly speaking, German. Somerset Maugham, whose stories are synonymous with England and Englishness, was born, passed much of his life in and died in France. *The Communist Manifesto* is the work of a couple of Prussians. Murdoch, Tressell and Beckett were native Dubliners, but would one categorise *The Sea, The Sea* or *The Ragged Trousered Philanthropists* as Irish novels? I don't know. I don't know how it works. No doubt someone from the *TLS* will be in touch.

These were all books I had told people I'd read when, actually, I hadn't.

These were books by authors whose work I was unfamiliar with, with the exception of Beckett (plays – short) and Austen (*Emma* – as a student, could not recall anything about it), not that that had prevented me from giving the opposite impression, often to myself. Also, all the authors were dead.

There was nothing here that could be described as a thriller.

There were several books that I had previously started but been unable to finish. For instance, I knew for a fact that on 16 June 1992, after just a couple of pages, I had stopped reading *The Unnamable*, because a till receipt marked the ignoble spot. You must go on; I can't go on; I, er, didn't go on.

These were all books, to a greater or lesser extent, that defined the sort of person I would like to be. They conveyed the innate good taste someone like me would possess, effortlessly. If you asked me if I liked Patrick Hamilton's work, for example, I would almost certainly reply in the affirmative. Moreover, I thought of myself as 'a Patrick Hamilton fan' – *despite never having read anything by Patrick Hamilton*. It was easy to maintain these two apparently contradictory positions; one did not necessarily cancel out the other. It seemed inevitable that I would become a Patrick Hamilton fan once I found the time to read him, so why refrain from assuming that identity in advance? It need not even alter if I were to discover that, on settling down with a book by Patrick Hamilton, I didn't much care for it. There would always be another book I might read at some hazy point in the future and like more, confirming the high opinion I had of Patrick Hamilton, though to date I had read nothing which matched up to the esteem in which he was held by me. And with this certain prospect fixed on the horizon, so the likelihood of ever reading Patrick Hamilton receded still further. I was the victim of a self-confidence trick.

The same might be said of the entire list. Because I had already forged a connection, presumed a familiarity, with every title on this piece of paper, they summoned up friends or conversations or specific moments from the past; but what lay behind the titles was a blank, and memories which ought to have cheered me instead induced prickles of embarrassment and even guilt, for they evoked little more than my own insincerity. Finally coming to terms with these books would be like reclaiming these far-flung moments and restoring their fidelity, or simply acknowledging and settling a debt.

I considered myself to be well-read. Could someone honestly call themselves well-read without reading *Middlemarch*, *Moby-Dick* and *Anna Karenina*? Probably not. However, this list was a start. With *Middlemarch* and *The Master and Margarita* behind me, it seemed possible that in the next few weeks, all these books could tumble. They would become part of the texture of my life as it was now. Even the thought of it was revitalising; more than that, it was a relief. I could begin to stop pretending.

Marx and Engels, for example. When I was seventeen, our school organised a week-long visit to Berlin. This was several years before the Wall came down. About a dozen sixth-formers made the trip. We stayed at a hotel in the West and at night went out to bars and strip-clubs off the Kurfürstendamm – well, the others did, including the teachers. I was much too puritanical. I stayed in my room and read *Brighton Rock*.

On two occasions, we crossed over to East Berlin, which

I much preferred to the decadent West. Yes, it was dour and repressed – but I was too. I wish I could remember more about these excursions. I can dimly recollect long avenues of shabby apartment blocks lined with identical cars, and shops with sternly rectilinear window displays. Everything looked as though fashion and maintenance had abruptly ceased in the early 1960s, which of course they had.

If you were a tourist, the East German authorities obliged you to change twenty-five Deutsche Marks at the border. You were not permitted to carry this money back to the West at the end of your daytrip. In other words, while you were in East Berlin, you had to find something to spend twenty-five Marks on. In Alexanderplatz, my schoolmates converted their cash into beer and grainy strawberry ices. However, I was captivated by the State-run book and record shop, which had about four Melodiya Beatles and Pink Floyd cassettes for sale, and numerous hardbacks of Karl Marx translated into English. There was nothing modish or faux about these editions. They were big, no-nonsense bricks, with just the title on the dust jacket, bordered by orange stripes along the top and bottom, as though their designer still vaguely recalled a Penguin Library paperback he had seen decades earlier. I bought a copy of *Capital* and another volume called *The Holy Family* and smuggled them back home in my suitcase.

I'm sure I believed I might read these hefty Marxist tomes; I certainly did not buy them solely for the effect they might have on my mother. But the effect they did have on my mother was so electric and so immediately gratifying, that thereafter reading them never really entered the picture. There was no need. They were accessories to a half-formed left-wing conception of the world which I had no immediate urge to deepen. Besides, at a recent parents evening my mother had been informed in all seriousness by one teacher that me and my best friend Matthew Freedman were communists, so someone else was doing the work for us. (This notoriety was the result of a General Studies discussion in which we had ventured the heretical proposition that there might be some justification in the then-current Miners' Strike.)

So twenty years later, when my mother discovered her only son loitering on a city street corner with *The Communist Manifesto*, it must have seemed, despite his toiling obediently for the capitalist system since graduation, accumulating a significant amount of property, and raising a child along doggedly bourgeois lines, like further evidence of his stubborn refusal to grow up. And – oh, Andrew – who is to say she was wrong?

Of course, then as now, although I was happy to be perceived as a communist, I had no serious yen to be one. This was not from a position of political principle but because of the effort required to first grasp and then assimilate a set of rules to which I would be expected to adhere. So instead I went with a liberal, left-of-centre position and told myself the half-truth that I had been more militant in my youth and that I had mellowed with age. In this, I was scrupulously in step with my generation, the one which spent thirteen years fretting at the lack of socialism in the New Labour government, yet which had made a journey of its own from youthful idealism to battered pragmatism in the face of political reality, career advancement and the school run.

With this journey behind me, I found it much harder to read *The Communist Manifesto* at thirty-seven than I would have done at seventeen, not because its philosophy was difficult to grasp but because it was true to life. The gloomy picture of the world it proposed might have seemed romantic to me then; now it felt dismayingly like the one I actually lived in.

Prior to *The Communist Manifesto*, I had read *Post Office* by Charles Bukowski. Ah, Bukowski. When I was in my early twenties, it seemed like everyone I knew – every male, I should say – read Bukowski. These men of my acquaintance listened to the Go-Betweens, drank Guinness from a straight glass and loved Bukowski like little girls love ponies. From their descriptions of his work and what was good about it, Bukowski sounded like precisely the kind of writer there would be no point in liking if everyone else liked him. So I never bothered.

All these years later, I had soaked up *Post Office* in little more than a day. Bukowski's alter ego, Henry Chinaski, a substitute postman and a drunk, gambled and screwed and occasionally made his mail round and then it was over: tick. The style was fragmentary and brutal. I was given to understand his other novels told a similar, if not identical, tale in a similar, if not identical, register. In an inversion of the old saying, when you'd read all Bukowski's books, you'd read one of them; they were all postcards from the same place, scrawled in a defiantly shaky hand.

As a book about work, though, *Post Office* was even bleaker than *The Communist Manifesto*, which at least offered potential resolution, i.e. total destruction of the apparatus of capital. Henry Chinaski's solution to the same problem was a cocktail of booze, horses and pussy. It would be nice to think the latter was at least an achievable goal but as Chinaski noted in the first few pages: '*It began easy. I was sent to West Avon Station and it was just like Christmas except I didn't get laid. Every day I expected to get laid but I didn't.*' And, figuratively at least, this too rang true with the world I found myself living in.

Work was preying on my mind. I had a good job in a successful business yet every day when I set off for the office, somewhere in the back of my head I could hear Sonya's lamentation from the closing scene of *Uncle Vanya*.[2] And my subconscious seemed to have shuffled *Post Office* to the top of the pile along with *The Communist Manifesto* and *The Ragged Trousered Philanthropists*, suggesting my id urgently required my ego to look into books which might help make sense of this problem of not getting laid, figuratively speaking.

In the event, neither *Post Office* nor *The Communist Manifesto* offered much in the way of solace. That said, *Post Office* was a holiday brochure compared to the toil and hopelessness captured by *The Ragged Trousered Philanthropists*, the concluding instalment of this subliminal trilogy. Over the course of 600 pages, it catalogued the indignity of labour in painstaking, crushing detail.

*The Ragged Trousered Philanthropists* is essential to the history of the British Left, both for what it says and what it symbolises. On the wall of the house in Hastings where it was written, in a flat above a bike shop, there is a blue plaque that states: 'Robert Noonan, 1870–1911. Author as Robert Tressell of "The Ragged Trousered Philanthropists", The First Working-Class Novel.' It is the story of a year in the life of a group of Mugsborough (i.e. Hastings) painters

2 'Uncle Vanya, we must go on. We've no choice! All we can do is go on living . . . all through the endless days and evenings . . . we will get through them . . . whatever fate brings. We'll work for others until we're old, there'll be no rest for us till we die. And when the time comes, we'll go without complaining and we'll remember that we wept, and that we suffered, and that life was bitter, but God will take pity on us!. . .' Anton Chekhov, *Uncle Vanya*, Act 4.

I always wanted to copy out this speech in the 'Further Comments' box of my annual appraisal form.

and decorators and their families. They are the philanthropists of the title and their 'philanthropy' is ironical; they practically give away their skills and strength to a system that perpetuates their oppression – 'The Great Money Trick', as it is memorably laid out in the novel. Into their midst comes Frank Owen, a thinker and a Socialist, who tries to rouse his workmates from their unenlightened torpor. Robert Noonan was an accomplished plasterer and sign-painter, and an enthusiastic member of the Social Democratic Federation (a forerunner of the Labour Party). On Sundays, he was often to be seen preaching the word from a soapbox on the beach at St Leonard's-on-Sea.

For the Left, *The Ragged Trousered Philanthropists* is a totemic document. It dramatises the class conflict of *The Communist Manifesto* in a domestic setting that is immediately recognisable to millions of working people all over the world. Better than that, it was written by a real painter and decorator – the characters and situations feel authentic because they are authentic. (*'I have invented nothing. There are no scenes or incidents in the story that I have not either witnessed myself or had conclusive evidence of.'*) Furthermore, the author was a committed activist who intended his book to *'indicate what I believe to be the only real remedy, namely – Socialism'*. And, fifty years before *Coronation Street, Boys from the Blackstuff* or *The Royle Family*, it gave its readers a portrait of working-class life that was compassionate, salty and true. A TUC working group could not have come up with anything more effective.[3]

However, it isn't all friendly associations and taproom banter. Tressell's depiction of human fallibility, greed and

3 In fact, the TUC now owns the original handwritten manuscript of *The Ragged Trousered Philanthropists*. It can be browsed in its entirety at www. unionhistory.info/ragged/ragged.php.

treachery is unrelenting. I was particularly fascinated by the personality of the 'journeyman-prophet' Frank Owen, who seems to spend most of the novel in a state of perpetual rage and frustration, both at his masters' deviousness and his workmates' failure to comprehend 'The Money Trick', in spite of his repeated efforts to explain it to them during tea-breaks. If *Post Office* is an account of the working life of a man without principle, too dazed or apathetic or self-medicated to fundamentally change anything, *The Ragged Trousered Philanthropists* suggests how much worse it is to be a man of principle trapped in the same system, to know with dreadful clarity what is oppressing and wasting you, but to be powerless to do anything about it, except proselytise and wriggle and rant.

We started well. As I progressed through the novel, though, fifty pages a day, I soon encountered a flaw – the book was obviously far too long. I started reading on a Tuesday; by Friday, nothing had really happened in the plot that had not already happened several times before, most of it on Tuesday. This was alarming, because *The Ragged Trousered Philanthropists* is a doorstop and the print was very small. At this rate, I would not be in the clear till the weekend after next. On and on and on it goes. Just like the remorseless, infinite grind of capitalism, say its admirers; but if I wanted the remorseless, infinite grind of capitalism, I could get it at work.

'The Ragged Trousered Philanthropists *is less a bourgeois novel of characters and plot (with the dangers of falsification that plot can entail), than a novel of the continuing processes of working life, its themes and variations.*' This is what was written in the novel's introduction and perhaps it was true. But it seemed like a handy retrospective gloss to apply to a story that is noticeably repetitive and static, and at times overwrought and hectoring like its hero Frank Owen. Of course, to the true Socialist the novel itself is a suspect item, a bauble of the bourgeoisie which does no more than reflect and reinforce the corrupt values of that class (the true Socialist might, with some justification, point to my mountains of unread books as proof of this phenomenon). Plot is a necessary sacrifice in the struggle to create art that is not compromised by bourgeois sensibilities and modes of expression. Fair enough. But, however noble in intention, this does seem like a sure-fire method of producing a lot of boring novels.[4]

Noonan's original manuscript was quarter of a million words long – three times the length of the book you are reading. It was impossible to find anyone willing to publish it in unexpurgated form and Noonan died in 1911 without ever seeing his novel in print. After his death, his daughter Kathleen sold all rights in her father's work to the publisher Grant Richards for the sum of £25. In 1914, Richards produced a first edition of *The Ragged Trousered Philanthropists*, which slashed 100,000 words from the text. It was priced

---

4 In the late 1960s, the film director Jean-Luc Godard denounced the French film industry as inherently bourgeois and announced that henceforth he would only produce work which conformed to his increasingly Maoist political beliefs. This resulted in several short films that whatever one's opinion of them as cinematic art – and I think they are pretty wonderful – are unambiguously terrible propaganda. *British Sounds*, which Godard made around this time for (of all people) London Weekend Television, consists of uninterrupted footage of the deafening production line at Ford's plant in Dagenham, Essex, a naked woman wandering up and down stairs in a flat, interviews with a group of Ford employees, a generic bunch of hirsute students sitting around and chatting and, finally, a montage sequence of clenched fists punching through paper Union Jack flags. It is laughably pretentious and woefully inscrutable. Had the director been bold enough to screen this for the workers at Dagenham, they would have been more likely to rise up and seize Jean-Luc Godard than the means of production. *British Sounds* was never broadcast by LWT, but these days you can find most of it on YouTube.

at six shillings, too much for a housepainter to afford. Reviews were mostly very positive. A second edition appeared four years later, retailing at a shilling but shorn of a further 60,000 words. Noonan's novel was now little more than a third of its intended length. It was not until 1955 that, thanks to the efforts of Hastings Labour Party member Fred Ball, a restored and uncut version of *The Ragged Trousered Philanthropists* was made available to the general public via the Communist Party publisher Lawrence & Wishart.

In this version of events, the original publisher Grant Richards seems like a scoundrel. He exploits a dead man's daughter. He bowdlerises the novel, not once, but twice, despite which it becomes a bestseller. But hold on; if Richards had not recognised the book's power, describing it as 'extraordinarily real' and 'damnably subversive', the manuscript would have stayed sealed in a tin box under Kathleen Noonan's bed. Richards had been declared bankrupt in 1905 and was certainly no well-heeled Bloomsbury toff; and his cuts were intended to make the story more palatable to readers of popular working-class sagas by the likes of Somerset Maugham or Arnold Bennett, while bringing the book down to a length at which Richards could afford to publish it. The first edition cost a pricey six shillings because, in the words of the writer Travis Elborough, '*Richards understood that the novel's authenticity could enhance its cachet amongst reviewers, perhaps especially with the more affluent radicals who would, initially at least, be its main purchasers.*' And when, in 1918, Richards produced the yet-shorter second printing for a shilling, it was partly in response to the pleas of a Glasgow bookseller, whose potential customers included workers at the nearby Clydeside shipyard, an early home of trade union agitation.

In other words, from the very beginning, as a publisher Grant Richards did his utmost, within the system, to permit some version of Tressell's text to reach the widest possible readership. No one else would take the risk. He edited it not because he wished to suppress its message of working-class unity but because he sought to disseminate it – and because the book needed an edit. To reach the audience it deserved, from drawing room to factory floor, the novel was too long and repetitive; owing to the well-meaning efforts of those on the Left, arguably it remains so.

I am not saying one of these accounts is correct and the other incorrect. There is more than one way to look at history, as there is more than one way to interpret a book. As a writer and a liberal I am sentimentally inclined towards the former explanation; I respect the author's conception of his own work. But a reading of events which follows the money – philosophical rather than dogmatic Marxism – would conclude that the novel owes its national treasure status to the shrewd stewardship of Grant Richards. For forty years, the text which was passed from hand to hand, which spread by word of mouth in mills and workshops and barracks, which was subsequently circulated as agitprop by the nascent British Left, often in tandem with *The Communist Manifesto*, was Richards' dramatically shortened version. Only once its place in the hearts of the British public was thus assured could Lawrence & Wishart afford to take the liberty of introducing the much lengthier, purer rendition which is on sale in bookshops today.

*The Ragged Trousered Philanthropists* continues to be treasured, regularly making appearances in polls of best-loved British novels. But when we read the book of that title today, we are essentially reading a restored, unedited first draft; and the qualities that still endear it to us – its humour, its passion, its social(ist) conscience – remain so inimitable that they overcome the inevitable drag caused by its size and Tressell's reluctance to tell his story straightforwardly. I finished it, and admired it, but I felt it would not have made much difference had I started somewhere in the middle, or read my daily fifty pages from wherever the book happened to fall open. Perhaps one day someone might edit it properly – but then perhaps it would lose its power.

At this point, I should declare an interest. If I seem to be overly concerned with the minutiae of the publishing process it is because I am, in my own way, a scoundrel like Grant Richards. If I am taking this matter of the manuscript rather personally, then I have to confess that it is personal. You may, or may not, know me as the author of two other books, but I'm afraid this is not a case of brotherly solicitude towards a fellow scribbler. If only.

At the time I was reading *The Ragged Trousered Philanthropists*, and working my way through the List of Betterment, I had a day job, like many writers do. It was this day job which was causing me such anguish and which had thrust these books to front of mind. Was I a plasterer? I was not. A postman? No. My hands were soft and lily-white; the only bags I carried were the ones underneath my eyes. A journalist, then? No.

I was an editor of books. Several times a week, I commuted to a publishing house in London and sat amidst many piles of paper, more and more each day, and tried to work out which were good and which were bad, which deserved to be published and which consigned to oblivion, which could be saved by judicious editing and which were fit only to be sent to the recycling depot to make yet more manuscripts. I am a writer. Every day, for money, I held the destinies of other writers in my hands. It was a chronic bout of double alienation.

'The propertied class and the class of the proletariat present the same human self-estrangement. But the former class feels at ease and strengthened in this self-estrangement, it recognizes estrangement as its own power and has in it the semblance of a human existence. The class of the proletariat feels annihilated, this means that they cease to exist in estrangement; it sees in it its own powerlessness and the reality of an inhuman existence.'

Oh Fred, oh Karl. If only it were that simple.

# Book Six

*The Sea, The Sea* by Iris Murdoch

(Supplementary Book One – *Cooking with Pomiane* by Edouard de Pomiane)

'I was utterly horrified in the kitchen this morning to see what I took to be a grotesquely huge fat fleshy spider emerging from the larder. It turned out to be a most engaging toad.'

*The Sea, The Sea*

'There is no doubt that people in England are becoming much more adventurous in their eating habits, and snails appear quite tame compared with the bumble bees, grasshoppers and chocolate-covered ants which I believe are selling well at some of the big stores.'

*Cooking with Pomiane*

How do you go about becoming a writer? I had paper and pencils. I had a notebook for ideas. I had an Amstrad PCW 9512 word processor. But I did not know anyone who made a living from their writing and I did not know how you went from sitting in front of a blank screen to sipping Bellinis with Jeanette Winterson. So, for rather longer than planned, I got a job in a bookshop. I signed up for six months and stayed for five years.

To be precise, it was a chain of bookshops. During my time, I worked in three different branches, the last of which was an elegant superstore in a posh quarter of West London. After a couple of years there, I was allowed to run the fiction section on the ground floor, a responsibility I loved. It was a spectacular sight, shelf after shelf of new paperbacks; prize-winners, potboilers, whodunits, whydunits and all points in-between. The manager of the shop took the view that we were the chain's London flagship store – the managers of the Hampstead and Charing Cross Road stores told their staff the same thing – and therefore we had to offer what he called 'perfect stock'. 'Perfect stock' meant never running out of anything. Woe betide you if, on recommending Robertson Davies to a customer, he went to the shelf and discovered a space where, say, *The Lyre of Orpheus* should have been. In this atmosphere of edgy competitiveness, good retail sense often took a back seat to hawk-eyed completism. So when the previous incumbent suffered a nervous breakdown and went on semi-permanent sick leave, I had been the obvious candidate to succeed him.

Every day, I would patrol the fiction bays, roaming up and down with a publishers' stocklist, hunting out the tell-tale gaps. In the process, I inadvertently absorbed the names of many authors of whom I had never heard before. I also became familiar with the more obscure corners of the well-known writers' back catalogue. So, for instance, Muriel Spark became not just the author of *The Prime of Miss Jean Brodie*, but also *The Public Image*, *The Takeover* and *Territorial Rights*. I quickly came to know the works of Miss Read, Hubert Selby Jr and Lisa St Aubin de Téran, though only by sight, spine-out. It was here and not at university that

I learned all you really needed to appear indisputably bookish, i.e. titles and names. The shop was a finishing school for bullshitters.

In the never-ending pursuit of 'perfect stock', one looked more kindly on those authors whose work did not sell rather than those whose work did. Of these perhaps my favourite was Iris Murdoch. No one ever bought any of her books, except *The Sea, The Sea*, which had won the Booker Prize in 1978. The popularity of the likes of Virginia Andrews, Louis de Bernières, Jilly Cooper or Robertson Davies posed a persistent threat to 100 per cent coverage. But every time you arrived at the tail-end of 'M', stocklist in hand, you could be certain of finding *The Black Prince, Henry and Cato, A Severed Head, et al.*, exactly where you last left them. And this had the notable side-effect of giving you an easy fluency – a superficial depth of knowledge – in Dame Iris's entire oeuvre.

I met my future wife in that shop. I also met Morrissey, Dustin Hoffman and Princess Diana.[1] And because we were

1 Morrissey bought two copies of a book by Bruce Foxton (bass) and Rick Buckler (drums) of The Jam about what a bastard Paul Weller had been to them by splitting the group and abandoning them to fend for themselves. 'That's not supposed to be very good,' I said. 'Mm,' smiled Moz, 'but they're not for me.' Do you think they were intended for Morrissey's estranged Smiths bandmates Andy Rourke (the bass guitar) and Mike Joyce (the drums)? I do.

Princess Diana, in the period when she was separated from Prince Charles and trying to assert her independence by making tentative outings to McDonald's, Harvey Nichols, etc., chose something from the psychology section about the effects of bad fathering on children with eating disorders. The manager of the shop immediately forbade any of us from contacting a tabloid newspaper with this scoop, though I am revealing it here for posterity. Towards the end of the transaction, a paparazzo ran into the shop and tried to snap Diana and, to a far lesser extent, me. The next morning, the manager wrote to Kensington Palace to assure them that this breach of privacy had nothing to do with us and the Princess should feel confident that she could return to our on the publishers' promotional circuit, I also made the brief acquaintance of a lot of writers, amongst them Iris Murdoch. At a Booker anniversary evening, she gave a reading from *The Sea, The Sea* to an audience of about two dozen people in front of the gardening books upstairs.[2] Dame Iris was petite, with white hair and an impish smile, and she appeared to have come to the reading in her slippers.

'I love your work,' I told her, which was something one said fairly often to visiting authors but which on this occasion had the merit of being wholly misleading yet completely true.

All this came back to me as I began *The Sea, The Sea*. However, these feelings of nostalgia, guilt and remorse – or was it pride? – were soon swept away in a wash of bewilderment. Although the prose was bright and clear, and the scenery reassuringly English and domestic, this was quite the most head-scratching of all the novels I had tried so

---

portals whenever she wished, discretion was our watchword, etc., etc. It was that sort of shop.

Dustin Hoffman, though thoroughly amiable, said and did nothing worth noting nor did he buy a book. This should in no way be taken as an implicit criticism of him. One well-known actress, a local resident of the shop, pulled lots of memorable stunts which would probably amuse and enthral you but even twenty years later I am reluctant to publish them and give this individual the slightest whiff of publicity, even though she is no longer with us. It was not unknown for the entire staff to hide in the stockroom rather than deal with her petulant, ill-mannered demands. She was one of the rudest human beings it has ever been my misfortune to encounter but I am not going to reveal her identity here. Let's just say it's a pity her character doesn't get stabbed through the throat with a camera tripod specially adapted for the purpose at the climax of [NAME OF FILM REDACTED BUT IF YOU'VE GOT ANYTHING ABOUT YOU, YOU'LL KNOW WHAT IT IS] and leave it at that.

2 Though the event was held at the behest of Booker, Dame Iris may have chosen to read from her most recent novel *The Green Knight*, rather than *The Sea, The Sea*, and I am writing about the wrong book. Thank you, the then-future Mrs Miller, for the declarification.

far. Not to put too fine a point on it, this was one weird book.

The narrator is a retired theatre director called Charles Arrowby. The story begins just as he has moved from London to a town on the edge of the North Sea, taking up residence in a ramshackle house called Shruff End, where he plans to write his memoirs – the book we are reading – and *'to repent of a life of egoism . . . I shall abjure magic and become a hermit'*. To this end he catalogues, in the fruitiest tones imaginable, his every swim, thought and meal. (*'Food is a profound subject and one, incidentally, about which no writer lies.'*) These early pages of *The Sea, The Sea* were transparent enough. Relocating to the coast in search of a profound life change, making lists of food and drink in fiddle-faddling detail: the man was a buffoon.

However, the novel soon spins off into a kind of insanity, as Arrowby's self-obsession runs wild. He sees, or hallucinates, monsters from the deep. He is visited by a succession of friends and associates from London, who come and go seemingly at will. He indulges a renewed passion for his childhood sweetheart Hartley, who coincidentally lives in the nearby town with her husband. Is this really happening or not? The marriage is violent and unhappy, he tells us, but is it? She clearly wants Arrowby to leave them alone. Her adoptive son turns up, just like that. Then, using the son as bait, Arrowby kidnaps her. Meanwhile, he relays all this madness to the reader in a rococo monologue comprised of philosophical *aperçus*, finely-wrought pen-portraits of the sea, the sea, and periodic descriptions of really horrible meals.

It was the meals I found most perplexing. As noted earlier, food was not my strong point. I had some enthusiasm for the stuff – it keeps one alive, after all – but little knowledge;

I had never really learned to cook properly. So, when presented with some of Arrowby's more bumptious menus ('*I imagined that the only book I would ever publish would be a cookery book!*'), I was at a loss to know what they stood for. Was this fine dining or foul? For example, on page 27:

Spaghetti with a little butter and dried basil. ('*Basil is of course the king of herbs.*')

Spring cabbage cooked slowly with dill.

Boiled onions served with bran, herbs, soya oil and tomatoes, with one egg beaten in.

A slice or two of cold tinned corned beef. ('*Meat is really just an excuse for eating vegetables.*')

A bottle of retsina.

In the spirit of the List of Betterment, as a means of understanding the book, I felt I ought to at least try to establish whether this meal was edible or not. So I rode my bike to the supermarket and filled a basket with these items, brought them home and prepared them to the best of my limited ability. The spaghetti was ok, and the cabbage and corned beef were, well, cabbage and corned beef, but the boiled onion concoction was unspeakable. Thank goodness for the retsina.

I tried again a couple of days later with a lunch that required a little more planning:

Lentil soup

Chipolata sausages served with boiled onions and apples stewed in tea

Dried apricots and shortcake biscuits

A light Beaujolais

'Fresh apricots are best of course,' notes Arrowby, 'but the dried kind, soaked for twenty-four hours and then well drained, make a heavenly accompaniment for any sort of mildly sweet biscuit or cake. They are especially good with anything made of almonds, and thus consort happily with red wine. I am not a great friend of your peach, but I suspect the apricot is the king of fruit.'

I soaked the dried apricots overnight and stewed the apples in tea, as instructed, but the result was neither heavenly nor illuminating – the combination was simply revolting – and once again I got a hangover from downing a bottle of wine at lunchtime. It was a sort of Charles Arrowby drinking game, with additional unpleasant gastric consequences.

Of course, these experiments were a lark but they were beside the point. They brought me no nearer to divining the meaning of the meals, or for that matter, *The Sea, The Sea* itself.

That weekend, we had a visitor to stay, an old friend called Richard. He and Tina had known one another since infant school where, because of an accident of surname, they were allocated desks together. They then had to sit next to one another, day in, day out, for the next nine years. Richard is a hearty individual, whose general bonhomie covers a roving and somewhat intense spirit. Tina is very fond of him; he is tremendous company. He is also a somewhat intense bon viveur, in the sense that he likes to eat well and drink very well – quality in quantity.

What do you cook the man who eats everything? I considered boiling some onions *à la Arrowby* in his honour but decided against it. Instead, I did what we always do when Richard visits, which is buy a lot of wine and several extravagant cheeses and let him get on with it.

We were sitting at the kitchen table, and as I uncorked

another bottle, Richard leant back in his chair and pulled a cookbook off the shelves by the window.

'Is this any good?' he asked, leafing through it. And then, a minute later, 'God, you really look after your books, don't you? Ours are always covered in sticky marks. This looks like it hasn't even been opened.'

Inadvertently, Richard was onto something. Our cookbooks were in pristine condition because none of them had ever been used. Several years earlier, when Alex was born, I had decided that I would shoulder my new responsibilities by taking care of the cooking. I had bought a juicer and some superior measuring spoons and we started frequenting farmers' markets and high-class butchers; and of course, I had bought a lot of cookbooks, far more than we needed, most of which stayed permanently on the shelf and made the place look culinary. And it was true that I had learned a few basic dishes, though nothing with any finesse and certainly nothing I could rustle up for a gourmand of Richard's standing. However, it had not really occurred to me until this moment that my appetite for the trappings of gastronomy, which had felt so genuine, had been little more than another way of going shopping. *The heart of a man is hollow and full of ordure,* writes Pascal in *Pensées.* Ah well. I was shallow but at least I was consistent.

'Is this any good?' The uncomplicated, unreflecting answer to Richard's simple question would be, 'Yes.' I had every reason to suppose that it was good, bar personal experience of the book, of which I had almost none. But what could personal experience really add? I lacked the expertise in cookery to make this judgement. In my ignorance, it would be a matter of blurting out whether or not I liked the book, and that was not what was being asked. However, the new-born integrity spawned by the List of

Betterment, and the fine wine, was urging me towards a full confession: 'I don't know. It was in that list of the greatest cookbooks of all time, you know the one, the supermarket one, a few years ago. I haven't read it. I haven't even looked at it. I bought the whole lot and we never use them. I'm a charlatan.'

'Have some more cheese,' I said instead.

'Well, I thought it was shite,' said Richard, slipping the book back on the shelf. 'What are you working on at the moment?'

I told him the truth. I had done very little writing since Alex had been born. 'But,' I said, 'I'm doing this project at the moment with books, I think you'll like this.'

'Is this that list you mentioned the last time I saw you?' he said. Mmm, and several times before that.

'Yes, but now I'm actually doing it,' I said. And I told him about the books I had read so far.

Richard, ever the perfect guest, listened politely while I expounded on the virtues of this or that book, nodding occasionally to confirm whether he had read it or not. ('Yep.' 'Nope.' 'Awful.' 'Nope.' 'Never heard of it.') When I reached *The Sea, The Sea*, however, he suddenly sat bolt upright.

'Shit!' he yelled, the wine sloshing around his glass. 'I *love* that book!'

'I, er, I'm not sure I really get it,' I said.

'Have you finished it?' he demanded.

'Not yet,' I said.

'It's INCREDIBLE,' he said, with absolute conviction. And for the next fifteen minutes, he rhapsodised about this intoxicating novel which had so far done little but give me a sore head. As I sat and listened, a bit drunk, what struck me was not his coherent argument regarding the glory of

*The Sea, The Sea* – there was little coherence, he was drunk too – but the *joie de vivre* that was spilling out of him. Richard is a documentary filmmaker. He has seen some fairly awful sights and regularly encounters the worst of humanity: tyrants, lowlifes, TV executives. But reflecting in the glow of this book he was rejuvenated. You could see him catching his own enthusiasm.

'But the meals, Richard,' I said. 'What about the meals?'

He shouted with laughter. 'Oh, they're hilarious,' he said.

And, of course, they were. It wasn't that the meals in *The Sea, The Sea* were only hilarious, but being given permission to find them hilarious opened the novel for me. Until now it had not occurred to me that I was allowed to find anything in any of these books properly funny rather than 'witty' or 'amusing' or 'comic'. I had been reading literature, and literature mistrusts hilarity, reasoning that something that makes you laugh out loud must be making its appeal to a coarser sensibility. Yet *The Sea, The Sea*, especially in its first few chapters, is brilliantly, mischievously funny. I went back to the beginning and laughed a lot at Charles Arrowby. It felt good to laugh.

Another thing which made me smile was the discovery that no two commentators seemed to agree about the meals in *The Sea, The Sea*. A quick Internet search revealed that one newspaper considered them 'nauseating', while another preferred 'parodically rustic'. To one reviewer, they were 'elaborately described', to another merely 'tedious', to a third 'delightful'. One website singled out a couple of the dishes as 'refreshing and organic'; another noted that they were 'primarily out of tins'. Moreover, an obituary of Dame Iris in the *Independent* revealed that '*the disgusting menus were suggested by Murdoch's husband, John Bayley, who would shock people by pretending to find the food perfectly nice*'.

It was liberating to discover there was no right answer: one man's meat is another's excuse for eating vegetables. *The Sea, The Sea* is held together by the personality and preoccupations of its author, more than a consistent application of novelistic good form. It is hilarious. It is also spiritual and sexual, philosophical and frightening. The beautiful thing about it is how it holds more than one meaning within itself, releasing something subtly different to whoever picks it up. *'We are all such shocking poseurs,'* writes Arrowby, *'so good at inflating the importance of what we think we value.'* Murdoch had taken an ingredient from her own kitchen table, a practical joke, and mixed it in with all her other fascinations – her eccentricity, intelligence and spirit lived on in the book, just as the master lived on in his novel.

*The Sea, The Sea* was liberating in a more practical way, too. Having tried my hand at a few of Arrowby's nastier dishes, I could now see no reason not to attempt some authentic cooking of my own. Perhaps it would be nice to make dinner for my own spouse one evening. But where to start?

One of the cookbooks I had bought at the height of my *folie de cuisine* was a 1930s classic called *Cooking with Pomiane*, by the French chef and epicure Edouard de Pomiane, which was written in a grandiloquent register every bit as fruity as Charles Arrowby's – except of course that one author was fictional and the other flesh and blood. Take, for example, Arrowby's musings on *haute cuisine*:

'It may be that what really made me see through the false mythology of *haute cuisine* was not so much restaurants as dinner parties . . . *Haute cuisine* even inhibits hospitality, since those who cannot or will not practise it hesitate to invite its devotees for fear of seeming rude or a failure. Food is best eaten among friends who are unmoved by such "social considerations", or of course best of all alone. I hate the falsity of "grand" dinner parties where, amid much kissing, there is the appearance of intimacy where there is really none.'

This rings true, doesn't it? Now compare the fictional Arrowby with the historically verifiable figure of Pomiane on the same subject:

'First of all, there are three kinds of guests: 1. Those one is fond of. 2. Those with whom one is obliged to mix. 3. Those whom one detests. For these three very different occasions, one would prepare, respectively, an excellent dinner, a banal meal, or nothing at all, since in the latter case one would buy something ready cooked . . . To make a dinner for people one can't bear is to try and keep up with the Jones's, as you say in English. Whatever you do, you are bound to be criticized, so it is better to buy ready cooked food and let the supplier be criticized instead.'

Well, who could argue with either gentleman, especially when they both expressed themselves with such authority? Actually, doesn't Pomiane seem a little more fictional than Arrowby, a little more far-fetched? After all, here is a chef of some renown suggesting some guests are only fit for ready meals; Jamie Oliver, in contrast, would feel compelled to knock up a 'pukka spag bol' even for his worst enemy.

'*For a successful dinner, there should never be more than eight at table. One should prepare* only one good dish,' writes

Pomiane. *'Concentrate all your efforts on the main dish and let it be abundant. Your guests will enjoy a second helping since you will have used all your art in its preparation.'*

I flicked through *Cooking with Pomiane*, looking for a dish which fulfilled these criteria. There would only be two at table, and one of us did not eat fish, so that ruled out Codling à la Basquaise. How about Poulet Flambé à l'Estragon? Too tricky. Blanquette of Veal? Delicious, but cruel. I finally settled on a markedly Arrowbian recipe for Pork Chops and Rhubarb. Here it is.

3 pork chops
A bundle of rhubarb
1oz butter
2 lumps of sugar

*'Serve the chops surrounded by rhubarb purée. This is a very good dish,'* wrote Pomiane. We both liked pork chops, and also rhubarb, though not necessarily on the same plate at the same time. Obviously the meal needed to be prepared in abundance, as there was nothing in the recipe to indicate that anything should be served alongside these two elements – potatoes or green beans or whatnot – which was presumably why Pomiane had added that reassuring final sentence. Nothing more was needed than the rhubarb and the chops.[3]

I called Tina at work. 'I'm cooking dinner tonight,' I said. 'Something special.'

---

3 This has an unhappy resonance with the domestic arrangements of Joe Orton and Kenneth Halliwell, who would invite guests to dinner at their Islington bedsitter and treat them to a National Assistance feast of rice and sardines, with differently-cooked rice and golden syrup for pudding. 'One of the most bizarre and terrible meals I've ever eaten.' Charles Monteith, former chairman of Faber & Faber.

'Right,' said Tina, with flawless equanimity.

Later, after I had put Alex to bed and we had read *We're Going on a Bear Hunt* together ('*We can't go over it. We can't go under it. Oh no! We've got to go through it!*'), I came downstairs and began the pre-prandial routine. I laid the table. I uncorked the wine. I diced an entire sheaf of rhubarb. Then I set to work.

'Don't come in!' I called, when I heard the front door. Things were not going well.

Finally, forty minutes later than planned, a cloud of oily smoke hanging over the kitchen, extractor fan roaring at full power, the work surface strewn with dirty utensils, I was ready to dish up. Tina sat down. On her plate lay a lightly burnt pork chop and a dribbly slick of bright pink rhubarb.

'What is this?' she said.

'This is a very good dish,' I replied.

'Potatoes? Or . . .?'

'No, this is it.' The rhubarb glistened unappetisingly in the half-light. 'There's plenty more. I used all my art in its preparation.'

'I know you and Richard liked that Iris Murdoch book,' said Tina, lifting her fork. 'But I have been at work all day. Next time, would you cook something real?'

It did not seem like the right moment to correct my wife's mistake. We ate the Pomiane supper. Actually, it wasn't bad. But no one came back for a second helping.

The difference between the real and the imagined experience was one of the motifs of Iris Murdoch's writing – pork chops and rhubarb as opposed to chipolatas and boiled onions. How can we always distinguish between the two when all we have to rely on is our own unreliable perception? Which dish is 'disgusting' and which is 'parodically rustic'? Neither? Both? We are on our own. In order to puzzle it out, all we have to go on is our accumulated knowledge and our shared experience – and maybe a good book.

So that Sunday, putting aside childish things and cracking open the cookbook Richard had taken off the shelf the previous weekend, I cooked Sunday lunch, in the course of which, for the very first time, I roasted a chicken. And although it was rather dry and the gravy was only Bisto, we told one another it was superb, because it was. The book was called *Roast Chicken and Other Stories*.

Betterment was proving to be transferable.

# Books Seven to Nine

*A Confederacy of Dunces* by John Kennedy Toole
*The Unnamable* by Samuel Beckett
*Twenty Thousand Streets Under the Sky* by Patrick Hamilton

'Ignatius quickly cleared the desk by brushing the magazine articles and Big Chief tablets smartly to the floor with one sweep of his paws. He placed a new looseleaf folder before him and printed slowly on its rough cover with a red crayon THE JOURNAL OF A WORKING BOY, OR, UP FROM SLOTH.'

*A Confederacy of Dunces*

'Bob was not susceptible to the faintest glimmering of the fact that the people he was passing in the street really existed. He observed their faces, he even caught their eyes, but he had no notion of their entity other than as inexplicable objects moving about in that vast disporting-place of his own soul – London.'

*The Midnight Bell*, from *Twenty Thousand Streets Under the Sky*

'A great gulp of stinking air and off we go, we'll be back in a second. Forward! That's soon said. But where is forward?'

*The Unnamable*

Half a dozen titles into the List of Betterment and a pattern was emerging. I would start on a book; after a spell of bafflement or boredom, steady persistence would start to pay off, giving way after several days to hard-won but tangible pleasure, which in turn spread into a blush of accomplishment, at the end of which: ☑. However, book number seven bucked that trend. I blushed almost from the first page.

*A Confederacy of Dunces* is one of the great American cult novels of the last fifty years. It was published in 1980, a decade after the suicide of its author, John Kennedy Toole, known to his friends and family as Ken. '*Every reviewer has loved it. For once, everyone is right,*' wrote Greil Marcus in *Rolling Stone* magazine. It won the Pulitzer Prize for Fiction the following year.

The hero of *A Confederacy of Dunces* is the unsavoury figure of Ignatius J. Reilly, a pompous, overweight, flatulent malcontent in a green hunting cap who, at the age of thirty, is still living at home in New Orleans with his drunkard mother. He scorns popular culture; his preferred reading is Boethius's *Consolation of Philosophy*. Ignatius is a slob who has never been in paid employment; when he masturbates, he does so to childhood memories of Rex, 'the large and devoted collie that had been his pet when he was in high school'. He is devious, arrogant and self-obsessed. Essentially, he suffers from a terrible superiority complex.

In what I am sure must be a coincidence, many of the people I know who count *A Confederacy of Dunces* amongst their favourite books are writers. *A Confederacy of Dunces* is exquisitely constructed and stylistically extraordinary; it is also consumed with bitterness and a misanthropic loathing of the world and everything in it. Furthermore, its author killed himself owing to the indifference of publishers, which confirms the sustaining notion that the few publishers who aren't bastards are idiots and vice versa. Toole can also be praised uninhibitedly by other writers because he is dead and safely in the ground. As I say, a coincidence.

Ignatius's trial in the novel is to get a job – 'UP FROM SLOTH', as he writes on the front of his journal. He goes to work in a pants factory. He pushes a hot dog cart, gulping down the weenies as he goes. Ken Toole did both these jobs. He also lived at home with his mother and believed he was a genius. If Ignatius Jacques Reilly is a self-portrait by John Kennedy Toole, it is a vicious and eviscerating one. It is also stupendously funny. I have never read such an accurate description of the inner life of the writer, made mountainous flesh. What is Anthony Horowitz really like, people want to know. Nigel Slater? Lionel Shriver? Rachel Cusk? To which the answer is: really, most writers are like Ignatius J. Reilly but some are more successful than others at disguising it. I am no exception.

Of course, loudly admiring *A Confederacy of Dunces* did not make me a proper writer, just as running into a burning building does not make you a fireman. But, as one with Ignatian tendencies, I could relate to it, which was not always the case with the great cult books. In Britain, we probably read more American cult writing than that of any other country, including our own (the same is true of film but not of music); Salinger, Kerouac, Thompson and so forth, coming over here, snatching our kids, on heroin. As a teenager, I skipped a lot of these products of the US counterculture. My heroes were Graham Greene, George Orwell and Philip Larkin, none of whom were very rock'n'roll nor, it must be observed, particularly nice people. But I was English; as the singer of *C86* indie band the

Bodines said in the *NME*, he could identify more with *Billy Liar* than *Rebel Without a Cause*.[1]

My favourite book at this time was *Absolute Beginners* by Colin MacInnes. To a boy from the suburbs, its portrait of London was kaleidoscopic and exciting. It made me feel like my life was going to be an adventure. I had not read it for years. I needed to read it again.

I moved to London from Brighton in 1991 to be with a girlfriend who was to undergo major heart surgery. She came through the operation safely and promptly dumped me for a male nurse she had met on the cardiac ward. I was devastated. This unhappy experience brought to mind Graham Greene's short story about a boy whose father is killed when a pig falls on top of him, and who then spends the rest of his life trying to tell people about this tragedy without making them laugh. And a fat f\*\*king comfort it was too.

In Stephen Sondheim's *Sweeney Todd*, the young hero Anthony sings joyfully of his arrival in the metropolis – '*There's no place like London*!' The word peals off Anthony's tongue like the chime of a bell. This is how I imagined I would feel on the day I made it to the city. Instead, I lurched onto the stage of my new home like the Demon Barber himself, red-eyed and murderous, the voice inside my head clanging ominously:

> 'There's a hole in the world like a great black pit
> And the vermin of the world inhabit it,

1 Turn to Appendix One: The List of Betterment, for additional examples of American cult writing, some of which we shall return to later, e.g. 37, *On the Road*; 39, *American Psycho*; 40, *The Dice Man*. I never got round to *Naked Lunch* or *One Flew Over the Cuckoo's Nest*, both of which may be found in Appendix Three: Books I Still Intend to Read.

And its morals aren't worth what a pig could spit,
And it goes by the name of London.'

You get the idea. Unhappily for me, I looked nothing like Johnny Depp in the film. Around this time, I had grown a goatee beard, which lent me an uncanny resemblance to the actor Steve Buscemi in Quentin Tarantino's *Reservoir Dogs*, aka Mr Pink – a fine actor but no matinée idol. Nevertheless, for about a year I found it difficult to walk down the street or go to the pub without passers-by turning

*Fig. 5: Portrait of an artist's impression of someone who looked a bit like the artist as a young man.*

their heads: 'Excuse me, are you . . .?' Thank God no one had cameras on their phones in those days. Or phones.[2]

---

2 One evening, on a late shift at the shop, I was standing alone at the ground-floor till. That afternoon, I had been to a funeral. I had come straight to work and so had not had a chance to change out of the black suit, white shirt and black tie I had worn to the service. I was feeling tired and sad.

Customer: (STARTLED) Mr Pink! Er, has anyone said to you . . .?
Me: Yes, they have. Can I help you?
Customer: It's amazing! Let's go to work! Would you mind if I ran and got a couple of mates?

After this uncertain start, however, I soon came to love living in London. I was single and I knew nobody beyond work. On a day off, I could step outside my front door and not meet anyone I knew all day, which was bliss. I went to gigs in Camden and record shops in Soho. I joined the early morning queues on the South Bank for tickets to the theatre. I hung around the Tate in Pimlico and Sir John Soane's Museum in Holborn. I went to readings in the Charing Cross Road and Sunday morning film screenings in Leicester Square. I drank beer at book launches in Bloomsbury and pubs in Fitzrovia, Earls Court, Dalston, Hampstead and Clapham. I passed out on the Tube and woke up at Heathrow or Arnos Grove with no money for a cab. Occasionally, I got lucky with girls from Crouch End, Kentish Town or the King's Road who may, or may not, have seen *Reservoir Dogs*. The postcode was unimportant; it was all terrific.

For a while, London belonged to me. However, I never really belonged to London. At heart I remained an in-comer, a day-tripper from Metroland. And when, fifteen years later, we finally moved out to the coast, I realised I had been waiting to leave from day one, and my residency in the capital had been a protracted blip – a bliiiiip, if you like. I felt calmer as a visitor, a spectator, restored to my suburban self. But I missed the Rough Trade shop, museums and good pubs – and the option of the Rough Trade shop, museums and good pubs – and my new hometown by the sea could feel small and close. Soon, I was always bumping into people I knew. I missed disappearing into the crowd.

--------

Me: Actually, I have just been to a funeral today, so I'm not really . . .

Customer: Oh yeah, of course. Sorry. (PAUSE.) Can I bring them in tomorrow to have a look at you?

That night, I shaved off the beard.

The break with London was not proving to be a clean one.[3]

However, the commute was looking up. For a year, it had been dead time, a three-hour return trip to London to earn money to pay for the train fares to continue making the trips to London to earn the money, etc., etc. Something to be endured. But thanks to the List of Betterment, it had become the highlight of the day. What I was really buying with my weekly ticket, I belatedly realised, were between twelve and fifteen hours of doing whatever I wanted, circumscribed by the regulations of Southeastern Trains. And what I wanted to do, with increasing determination, was read. I looked forward to my days in town, to climbing aboard the 6.44, because I knew I would achieve something before the working day had even begun. By the time I arrived at my office, two hours and fifty or more pages further on, I was energised, fortified, fit to deal with the multiplying piles of paper.

I was now on to *The Unnamable* by Samuel Beckett. As I said earlier, Beckett was an exception on the list. I had seen or studied the plays *Waiting for Godot*, *Happy Days* and *Krapp's Last Tape*, so I knew what to expect: an existential babble, a screed of desolation, a few music hall jokes. *The Unnamable* is not a long novel but I anticipated it would be as dense and diffuse as much of Beckett's writing, so I had reduced the daily target to just ten pages – ten pages that

3 One of the groups I used to go and see at the Garage, Subterania, ULU, etc. was the Auteurs, led by the dyspeptic Luke Haines, a man whose demeanour, onstage and off, is more Ignatius J. Reilly than Iggy Pop. See his hilariously splenetic memoirs *Bad Vibes* and *Post Everything* (both Heinemann) for proof. Haines' album *21st Century Man* contains a song called 'Love Letter to London' which eloquently addresses those of us who have chosen to leave the city behind. '*They said that they loved you / But they used you as a playground / When they were young,*' he hisses.

I knew would require sustained focus and reflection. And this was where my troubles began.

Do not attempt *The Unnamable* on any form of public transport or in any kind of public space or anywhere where there is any kind of human distraction, such as the tish-tish-tish of crappy white earbuds, a wailing baby, the post-pub drone of football bores, the honking of a comedy ringtone, the repetitive strain of the slow-rolling refreshments trolley – TEAS! COFFEES! LIGHT SNACKS! – or the snoring of the occupant of the seat next to yours: the combined cretinous cacophony of a contemporary confederacy of dunces. (*'Oh, my God!' Ignatius bellowed. 'No! I told you before. I am not a fellow traveler.'*)

Furthermore, few of my fellow travellers were reading books. Those who were had been canny enough to choose ones with plots: thrillers, true crime, Aga sagas.[4] Plots keep the world out, which under the circumstances – WILL YOU PLEASE KEEP IT DOWN?! – was not merely justifiable escapism, it was a survival stratagem. If you go and see one of Beckett's plays in a theatre, you sit in a space dedicated to the performance of that piece and assume that the rest of the audience will sit still and keep quiet, which they often, though not infallibly, do. You focus collectively on the words and the manner in which they are delivered. You are in it together. Whereas on a commuter train, though

4 This is a statement of fact. On our line, people read newspapers, or work documents, or watched portable DVD players, or played on games consoles, or played with their phones, or nodded off. Books were relatively thin on the ground. In a year, I never saw one other person with their nose in what might be termed a 'classic'. In London, on the other hand, I frequently witnessed people on the bus or Tube engrossed in Hardy, Lessing, Flaubert, Einstein, the Koran and, on one occasion, Hitler. Does reading *Mein Kampf* make you a better person than the one playing Angry Birds? Certainly not! But it does make you more interesting. Don't shoot the messenger.

you are physically in it together, you are trying forcefully to pretend otherwise. It is not a crowd in which one disappears but a gang of individuals in noisy denial – tish, honk, bing-bong, WAAAAAAAAAAH.

Hell is other people, said Jean-Paul Sartre. Don't take this the wrong way, but I think he means you.

To read Beckett, it was obvious that the ideal accompaniment would be silence. But silence was not an option. Over the course of several journeys, I experimented with finding the music on my iPod that would block out extraneous noise, while also feeding into the experience of reading something as intense and cyclical as *The Unnamable*. Vocal music was out; concert orchestras, I discovered, were either too hushed or too bombastic; movie soundtracks were incongruously syrupy or jarringly overdramatic; Eno's *Ambient 1: Music for Airports*, though soothing, did nothing except provide a gentle sound-bed for other people's high-volume phone calls, unsought opinions and mastication. But cometh the hour, cometh the Famous Death Dwarf (© Lester Bangs, circa 1975).

I want you to stop reading for a moment and go and fetch your copy of Lou Reed's *Metal Machine Music*. If you don't have one, please find it on Spotify or YouTube. And when you are ready, turn up the volume, pick up the book, press play and carry on.

No, don't switch it off. I'm here with you. In our left ear or speaker we can hear a thousand bombs exploding, a horrific bombardment of guitar feedback and tape loops, the distant rumble of post-war pop culture being shredded by Messerschmitts and Telecasters. To our right, we can hear much the same, but with someone stabbing at our cochlea with a tiny dentist drill, like a needle or a fencing foil. Maybe you discern what *Rolling Stone* heard in 1975, '*the tubular groaning of a galactic refrigerator'*. After all, this is the fourth-worst album of all time according to *Q Magazine*, *'four sides of unlistenable oscillator noise'*. The journalist Lester Bangs, on the other hand, thought of it in these terms: *'As classical music it adds nothing to a genre that may well be depleted. As rock'n'roll it's interesting garage electronic rock'n'roll. As a statement it's great, as a giant FUCK YOU it shows integrity – a sick, twisted, dunced-out, malevolent, perverted, psychopathic integrity, but integrity nevertheless.'*

Ok, you can turn it off now. Whatever your verdict on *Metal Machine Music*, it seemed undeniably fit for my short-term purpose, which was the total obliteration of my immediate surroundings – a giant FUCK YOU to the rest of the train. Yes, *MMM* was a hellacious racket but it was *my* hellacious racket. Finally I could hear myself think.

For two weeks, I adhered to a bracing early morning regimen of *Metal Machine Music* via the ears and *The Unnamable* via the eyes. Putting aside whatever psychic damage I might be doing to myself by ingesting two such powerful stimulants simultaneously, the compound was a potent one. It successfully blotted out the carriage. It fed my Ignatian edginess and exasperation, incorporating them into Beckett's stream of imagery and Reed's sluice of noise. I read furiously, head down, teeth clenched, right to the end of the line. However, the treatment must be judged only a partial success. After a fortnight, I had completed the novel, but in a disjointed, belligerent state which only succeeded in blotting out the book too. By the end, I had no real sense of what I had spent two weeks reading.

Technically, I had now finished *The Unnamable* – but only technically. I knew I had entirely failed to connect with it. Usually I found Beckett's work very affecting. Either the book was beyond my capabilities or there was simply no space in my life where I could attempt a book like this. If I could not make it work on the train, where was left? And after all that effort, what was the difference between saying I had read *The Unnamable*, as formerly, and actually having read it, as now? I was better served by what I thought I thought about it beforehand, than by the disillusioning, uncomprehending reality. And what about the Beckett I studied at school or college, did that count? I was aware of having seen *Happy Days* twenty years ago but, save for a mental picture postcard of Billie Whitelaw in a pile of sand, I had forgotten nearly everything about it. My conception of it was shaped more by received academic opinion than a spontaneous reaction, and besides which, I had been nineteen; what I had to say about it would be half-baked at best. Or so I believed as I consigned *The Unnamable* to the shelf once more.

Am I going on? I'll go on.

When Patrick Hamilton was a half-baked young man loose on the streets of London, he fell insanely in love with a prostitute called Lily Connolly. This infatuation drove him to the brink of financial ruin, set him on the road to alcoholism and inspired his fourth novel, *The Midnight Bell*, which was published in 1929 when he was only twenty-four years old. Bob is a well-liked barman at the Midnight Bell, a pub off the Euston Road. He lodges in a room above the pub, along the landing from Ella, the barmaid who is secretly in love with him. But Bob becomes obsessed with Jenny, a West End streetwalker; little by little, and without any sexual intercourse, she parts him from his savings of £80, leaving him broke and almost broken. Around this unhappy trio, Hamilton wrote the novels which would subsequently be collected as *Twenty Thousand Streets Under the Sky*: *The Midnight Bell*, then *The Siege of Pleasure* (1932), in which we learn how Jenny fell into prostitution, and finally *The Plains of Cement* (1934), where barmaid Ella is wooed by one of the Midnight Bell regulars, the appalling Mister Ernest Eccles.[5]

It soon emerged that I had been correct in my long-held supposition that I would enjoy Patrick Hamilton's writing without having read a word of it. In the space of a few pages, I recognised it. It felt comfortable. The inter-war landscape of Lyons Corner Houses and Clapham omnibuses, the seedy London lowlife, the anguished, juvenile passion, the imminence of spiritual and financial damnation, the girls with bobbed hair, all brought back my own teenage literary crushes: Orwell's *Keep the Aspidistra Flying*, Greene's *It's a Battlefield*. Hamilton was another burgeoning Marxist but a better – or more bourgeois – craftsman than Robert Tressell. His politics inform the books but do not dictate them. He shows how it is money, or fear of poverty, that underpins the so-called 'moral choices' his characters have to make, without venturing to propose a political solution directly. Bob's £80 is both a safety net and a stake to which he is tethered; the feckless Jenny, once she has 'fallen', cannot resist the pull of 'easy money'; Ella contemplates marriage to Mister Eccles as a way of obtaining financial security for herself and her mother. It was beautifully done.

5 I did not realise *Twenty Thousand Streets Under the Sky* was a trilogy until I started it, otherwise I could have claimed it as three novels rather than one. Conversely, *The Unnamable* is the final part of a trilogy, also comprising *Molloy* and *Malone Dies*. I knew this in advance and chose to ignore it. Why? Probably because I guessed *Twenty Thousand Streets Under the Sky* and *The Unnamable* were better-known quantities, and sounded more impressive, than *The Plains of Cement* and *The Samuel Beckett Trilogy*. Again, don't shoot the messenger, even though, in this case, the messenger and the message are one and the same.

'We are all such shocking poseurs, so good at inflating the importance of what we think we value,' wrote Charles Arrowby. For the novelist Dan Rhodes, *The Midnight Bell* is a life-like study of boozing ('*[the book is] sodden with the wonderful, nasty stuff*') and boozers: '*My family had a pub for many years, and from an early age I came face to face with the horrors of the habitué. There are few things more soul-destroying than being locked into an early-evening conversation with a barfly who thinks they are funny or clever or, worst of all, "a character".*' I had been given my copy of *Twenty Thousand Streets Under the Sky* by an acquaintance for whom the book was a study in the compulsive madness of addiction, a subject he knew something about. For my part, I looked into these three novels, each successive volume of which I liked more than the one preceding it, and saw my distant younger selves – the boy who worshipped the writers of another era; the cautious adolescent agitator; the demented, jilted Steve Buscemi lookalike, and the reluctant working man.

What was the difference between saying I had read Patrick Hamilton and finally reading him? The answer was pleasure – both the pleasure of recognition and the irresistible pull of the story he told. And therefore I could read him, under siege on a train, without distractions of my own or anyone else's making.

What was really remarkable was how much of my London was in these books. Not just the saloon bars of Soho and Fitzrovia, but Shaftesbury Avenue, Hammersmith Broadway, the garden suburb of Bedford Park, the Great Western Road out past the Hoover Factory, all places I had lived or worked during my fifteen-year stay in the capital. I got drunk here, held down a day job, had my heart broken, fell in love again. This was where I grew up. And although Tina and I had left together, part of me remained here. I finished

*Twenty Thousand Streets* . . ., so much of which felt familiar, and thought: perhaps it is time to move on.

On a Sunday morning before Christmas, I caught a train into town and took the bus to Primrose Hill. Climbing to the top, I could see the Post Office Tower, the Snowdon Aviary and a homeless man shaking his fist at someone who was both much taller than him and invisible. It was still early. I planned to walk across the city, down the Euston Road, paying my respects at the Midnight Bell or a few pubs like it, through the West End, and along the river to Hammersmith or beyond. It was going to take me all day to say goodbye.

For company, I had Samuel Beckett. On my iPod was an audiobook of *The Unnamable*, read by an actor called Sean Barrett. The book ran just under six hours, long enough to carry me from Primrose Hill to Hammersmith. Perhaps it was cheating to listen to something the author intended to be read, but print on paper had not got me very far. I was going to try an alternative route.

As I set off past the zoo and the Roundhouse, along Camden High Street, past where all the record shops used to be, past the market and the Odeon cinema on Parkway, Beckett's words murmured in my ear. They drifted around me, catching my attention, retreating, returning, insinuating themselves into my train of thought. I came here a lot once. We saw Blur at the Electric Ballroom. Compendium, the bookshop, was over there, Burroughs and Bukowski tapes, gone now. The Oxford Arms, that was where I saw Glen Richardson perform his Todd Carty musical. Or was it an opera? On second thoughts, maybe that was the Hen and Chickens. It was all a long time ago. '*Some may complain that they cannot understand* The Unnamable,' Beckett's publisher and champion John Calder has written, '*but they should ask themselves how well they understand not only their own lives, but what they see when they look out at the world; how they interpret what they see, little of which could be understood anyway; and especially how they think themselves, what makes them think, what they think about and why; and how they separate what they know from everyday events, from what they know from dreams.'*

From Camden onwards, letting *The Unnamable* spool, I traversed not one but three places called London: the city I had lived in for so long; Patrick Hamilton's twenty thousand streets, still humming in my mind; and this unreal city, shaped by memory and daydreams and Beckett's unravelling commentary. After a couple of miles, I had to sit down, not from fatigue but because I was overwhelmed by what I was experiencing. In a pub I did not recognise, somewhere in limbo, I sat and nursed a pint and just listened . . .

'I hope this preamble will soon come to an end and the statement begin that will dispose of me. Unfortunately I am afraid, as always, of going on. For to go on means going from here, means finding me, losing me, vanishing and beginning again, a stranger first, then little by little the same as always, in another place, where I shall say I have always been, of which I shall know nothing, being incapable of seeing, moving, thinking, speaking, but of which, little by little, in spite of these handicaps, I shall begin to know something, just enough for it to turn out to be the same place as always, the same which seems made for me and does not want me, which I seem to want and do not want, take your choice, which spews me out or swallows me up, I'll never know, which is perhaps merely the inside of my distant skull where once I wandered, now am fixed, lost for tininess, or straining against the walls, with my head, my hands, my feet, my back, and ever murmuring my old stories, my old story, as if it were the first time. So there is nothing to be afraid of. And yet I am afraid, afraid of what my words will do to me, to my refuge, yet again. Is there really nothing new to try?'

# Book Ten

*Moby-Dick; or, The Whale* by Herman Melville
and introducing Book Zero, *The Da Vinci Code*
by Dan Brown


'Finally: It was stated at the outset, that this system would not be here,
and at once, perfected. You cannot but plainly see that I have kept my
word. But now I leave my cetological System standing thus unfinished,
even as the great Cathedral of Cologne was left, with the crane still
standing upon the top of the uncompleted tower. For small erections
may be finished by their first architects; grand ones, true ones, ever leave
the copestone to posterity. God keep me from ever completing anything.
This whole book is a draught – nay, but the draught of a draught. Oh,
Time, Strength, Cash, and Patience!'

*Moby-Dick*, Chapter 32, Cetology


'As someone who had spent his life exploring the hidden interconnec-
tivity of disparate emblems and ideologies, Langdon viewed the world
as a web of profoundly intertwined histories and events. *The connections
may be invisible*, he often preached to his symbology classes at Harvard,
*but they are always there, buried just beneath the surface.*'

*The Da Vinci Code*, Chapter 3

It was Friday and I was working from home. To my left lay an unread pile of paperwork. On my right was a half-started copy of *Moby-Dick*. And on the television screen in front of me was *Loose Women*. I believe it is important always to take a lunch break.

As usual on *Loose Women* – which I had seen before – it was Coleen Nolan who said what everyone was thinking. Perched in her usual berth between Carol McGiffin and the Oxo mum, the former 80s pop princess and bestselling co-author of *Upfront & Personal: The Autobiography* was taking her turn in a discussion segment entitled 'What Makes a Good Book?' Coleen, who according to previous debates sees nothing wrong with reasonable breast enhancement, does not think gay couples should be allowed to adopt, would rather her sons had sex with hookers in Amsterdam than 'behind a club in Ibiza with absolutely no safeguards', and really likes chocolate, was speaking up for many of those present.

'I can't stand all this snobbery about books! Ooh, that one was garbage, ooh it was trash! Ooh, la-di-dah! I mean, it's supposed to be good if we're reading, isn't it? I thought it was supposed to be good!'[1]

And the studio audience whistled and cheered and stamped its feet on Shakespeare's face, forever.

Which is not to say Coleen was wrong. There is an awful lot of snobbery around books. In the last ten years, much of it has been directed at one man. Has there ever been a more unpopular popular author than Dan Brown? For every satisfied customer of his sensational conspiracy thrillers, there is an offended Catholic, an exasperated academic or

1 This was the gist, at any rate. I don't watch *Loose Women* with a Dictaphone running.

an infuriated subscriber to the *New York Review of Books* raging at his success and fame. For every Coleen Nolan, there is a Michiko Kakutani. Notorious *Middlemarch*-shirker Salman Rushdie has described *The Da Vinci Code* as 'a novel so bad that it gives bad novels a bad name'. None of which has prevented Dan Brown becoming one of the most widely read authors of modern times. Only E.L. James, author of *Fifty Shades of Grey* and its sequels, comes close.

On average, everyone has read *The Da Vinci Code*. You have probably read it. Even if you have not read it, statistically you have. My encounter with the phenomenon of Brown was pretty typical. I picked up on the book about a year after Alex was born. Sleep deprivation and CBeebies had turned my brain to Tubbycustard. All I wanted was something lightweight and undemanding. *The Da Vinci Code* was both of these. However, as I compulsively turned the pages to discover what incredible nonsense might happen to Robert Langdon and Sophie Neveu next – incredible but gripping – I could not help noticing that the book was exceptionally poorly written. You go to a thriller for its thrills, not its poetry, but this was distractingly bad. My eye kept getting snagged on some clunking piece of expository dialogue or pseudo-scholarly statistic or shockingly ugly sentence. '*Da Vinci was the first to show that the human body is literally made of building blocks whose proportional ratios* always *equal PHI,*' exclaimed Robert Langdon, wretchedly. And the movie was even worse.

I am not saying that Dan Brown cannot write. But whilst reading *The Da Vinci Code*, I was certainly thinking it.

However, although *The Da Vinci Code* did a whole heap of things defectively, it did one thing stupefyingly well – the plot. It was as though Brown had jettisoned all traces of style and credibility from his novel because he had realised, in a flash of Leonardo-like scientific insight, that style and credibility were the very properties preventing his theoretical story-balloon from taking flight. So they had been tossed over the side, along with beauty, truth and five hundred years of literary progress.

To be clear, Dan Brown knows how to tell a story – but there is more to telling a story than just telling the story. Stephen King understands this, as do Lee Child and Audrey Niffenegger. I am keen to make this point because naysayers of Dan Brown tend to be dismissed as either 'ooh la-di-dah' snobs who disdain all escapist entertainment or jealous, sour rivals of a more successful author. '*All you haters can suck my chubby dick,*' types one web forum contributor calling himself Socrates. '*Hes got all the riches and the bitches! Does the envy hurt THAT bad? Boo hoo! Boo hoo hoo! Dan Brown's a really rich writer with millions of fans and I'm not! NO FAIR! Masturbate elsewhere, loserzzz. You people need to get lifes and go out and get laid.*'

Socrates, let me address your concerns. Liking bad books does not make you a bad person; equally nor does preferring good ones. Am I jealous of Dan Brown? I am not. I do not aspire to Dan's prose style nor do I wish to be a global figure of fun. Interestingly, although he is many, many times more successful than I am, until the publication of *The Da Vinci Code*, Dan and I sold similar quantities of books, after which he pulled ahead of me by a factor of approximately 40,000 to 1. Nonetheless, I wish him well – after all, we are all writers and we should stick together. (Are you listening, Salman?) As for the riches, of course I would love to earn just a fraction of Dan's wealth but that does not mean I want to do it his way. I would like Donald Trump's billions, without necessarily committing myself to his hairstyle.

Secondly, there is nothing wrong with escapism. I love escapism. As Brian Eno once observed, 'We're all perfectly happy to accept the idea of going on holiday, nobody calls that escapism.' I frequently yearned to escape from my dull routine and a great book – of any stripe – offers us a cheap getaway from reality. But there are all sorts of holiday destinations and a multitude of ways to travel. We don't always have to end up behind a club in Ibiza with absolutely no safeguards.

Finally, Socrates, I question whether your dick is particularly chubby. Your confrontational manner suggests otherwise. In reality, I imagine your dick to be rather twiggy and bent, like a bent twig or a Twiglet. Perhaps it is you who should masturbate elsewhere, if you are able. (I wonder if you will ever read this, you who posted your thoughts on the Internet, never thinking they would be noted down and reproduced in a book, a copy of which will reside in the British Library for future generations to consult and snigger at you and your thin abnormal penis. What a surprise you'll have if you do!)

Memories of *The Da Vinci Code*'s compelling plot had visited me often during my trawl through *Moby-Dick*, a book which might fairly be described as 'putdownable'. It is widely hailed as 'the great American novel' but as many a despairing high-school student will attest, it's no *Da Vinci Code*. *Moby-Dick* is long, gruelling, convoluted graft. And yet, as soon as I completed it, once I could hold it at arm's length and admire its intricacy and design, I knew *Moby-Dick* was obviously, uncannily, a masterwork. It wormed into my subconscious; I dreamed about it for nights afterwards. Whereas when I finished *The Da Vinci Code*, which had taken little less than twelve hours from cover to cover, I chucked it aside and thought: wow – I really ought to read something *good*.

*Moby-Dick* is a work of genius and some of its genius seemed dark or supernatural. It most reminded me of Coppola's *Apocalypse Now* or Sly Stone's *There's a Riot Goin' On*, both products of isolation and psychosis, and both somewhat out of the control of their ostensible creators. Or perhaps that is a definition of genius, a force that cannot help but beget itself, regardless of the toll it takes on the artist; in all three cases, these men struggled to locate such ungodly inspiration in their later work. Melville knew he had birthed, in his words, *'a wicked book'*. In a letter to a female neighbour, he wrote: *'Dont you buy it – dont you read it . . . A Polar wind blows through it, & birds of prey hover over it.'* *Moby-Dick* is a miscreated, mystical leviathan, often unfathomably deep, whose flaws and imperfections miraculously become the contours of the immaculate whole.

It also begs interpretation. The whiteness of the whale, its supernatural blankness, has been made to stand for society's preoccupations in any given era from the early twentieth century on – sexual, political, spiritual, military, cosmic, personal. ('Call me Ishmael.' 'No, call *me* Ishmael.') The hairs on the back of my neck stood on end – a cliché but physically what happened – as I read of *'the damp, drizzly November'* in Ishmael's soul, compelling him to flee the *'thousands of mortal men . . . tied to counters, nailed to benches, clinched to desks'*. Here was I, undertaking my own voyage of discovery, adrift on the sea of books: *'Who ain't a slave? Tell me that.'* I preferred not to think too hard about who or what my white whale might be. But at the same time, *Moby-Dick* is mesmerisingly, eternally interpretable, so much so that Melville reminds us early on that, whoever we are and whatever our discipline, we are always reading *'. . . that story of Narcissus, who because he could not grasp the tormenting, mild image he saw in the fountain, plunged into it and was drowned. But that same image we ourselves see in all rivers and oceans. It is the image of the ungraspable phantom of life; and this is the key to it all.'*

However, we should not overlook the fact that, for fifty years, few readers saw their reflection in *Moby-Dick* or hailed it as a 'great book'. It took a new century, a World War and the innovations of modernism before the critical establishment was willing or even able to comprehend it; readers only began to come aboard in appreciable numbers after World War II. In contrast with Melville's early seafarer yarns *Typee* and *Omoo*, which had attracted enthusiastic reviews and healthy sales, the publication of *Moby-Dick* in 1851 was, in the words of Robert McCrum, *'a horrible combination of a botch and a flop'*. Total earnings from the American edition amounted to just $556.37 from his publisher Harper & Brothers; forty years later, it had still not sold out its first edition of 3000 copies. Following the poisonous reaction to his next, even weirder, novel *Pierre: or, The Ambiguities* and the rejection of *Isle of the Cross* (now lost) in 1854, Melville wrote very little. He lectured; he tried his hand at poetry; he drifted. Eventually, his wife and her relatives used their influence to secure him a post at the New York City customs house where for the next twenty years he worked as an inspector, *'a humble but adequately paying appointment'*. There were whispers of insanity, heavy drinking and violence; one of his sons shot himself, another ran away from home and was never heard from again. When Melville died in 1891, he and his Leviathan were more or less forgotten.

In the 1990s, there used to be a website called Grudge Match™ which staged imaginary fights between characters from pop culture. These ranged from the obvious ('Obi-Wan Kenobi vs. Darth Vader') to the witty ('Red-Shirted Ensigns vs. Imperial Stormtroopers') to the cross-platform meta-brawl ('John McClane vs. The Death Star'). Some grudge matches even had nothing to do with *Star Wars* – 'a Rottweiler vs. a Rottweiler's weight in Chihuahuas', for example, or the epic 'Battle of the Seven Deadly Sins: Wrath vs. Greed vs. Lust vs. Gluttony vs. Sloth vs. Envy vs. Pride vs. Virtue'. The outcomes were hotly debated by contributors from all over the planet and, following a public vote, a winner would be declared, in the above cases Obi-Wan, Stormtroopers, John McClane, the Rottweiler and Lust respectively. But after ten years, the site's owners packed it in because 'long story short: we ain't in grad school any more'. (However, matches have been archived at www.grudge-match.com/History/index. html – kids, this and pornography are how your parents first harnessed the awesome power of the Internet.)

When contemplating the difference between *Moby-Dick* and *The Da Vinci Code*, it would be tempting to frame it in Grudge Match™ terms, thus:

*Fig. 6: Whale vs. Grail.*

It is the eternal dilemma for the artist and the hack alike: fame and wealth in the here and now or an impoverished, miserable life but a posthumous shot at immortality – 'Austerity vs. Posterity', or 'Riches 'n' Bitches vs. Nervous Twitches 'n' Diggin' Ditches'. The fact was this. More people had probably read – and enjoyed – *The Da Vinci Code* in five years than had read – and enjoyed – *Moby-Dick* in one hundred and fifty. The latter was awkward, demanding and brilliant. The former was accessible, electrifying and bollocks. In the white corner, high art. In the Brown corner, low schlock.

And yet, a Grudge Match™ between *Moby-Dick* and *The Da Vinci Code*, though amusing, would do little except confirm our prejudices and tell us next to nothing about what makes each novel so remarkable in its own sphere. So instead I suggest we look for the hidden – and not-so-hidden – resemblances between the lives and careers of Herman Melville and Dan Brown. What do they have in common? We may be astonished by what we uncover.

I call . . . a Love Match!

### TEN ASTOUNDING SIMILARITIES BETWEEN
### *THE DA VINCI CODE* BY DAN BROWN
### AND *MOBY-DICK* BY HERMAN MELVILLE

 ♥

## 1. QUESTS FOR THE HOLY GRAIL

*The Da Vinci Code* and *Moby-Dick* are both epic grail quests, over a hundred chapters in length, each with a scene-setting prologue and meditative epilogue. Both narratives focus on the personal quest of an individual, or individuals, who, by going against the received wisdom of their age and confronting terrible, unknown dangers, put their sanity, their lives and even their immortal souls in peril. In *Moby-Dick*, Ahab, Ishmael and the *Pequod* crew criss-cross the planet in bloody pursuit of a seldom-glimpsed killer albino whale whose metaphorical significance is practically infinite; in *The Da Vinci Code*, Robert Langdon, Sir Leigh Teabing, Interpol, Opus Dei and a seldom-glimpsed killer albino monk – metaphorical significance: nil – criss-cross the planet in bloody pursuit of the actual Holy Grail: a cup, or a code, or a cryptex, or a person, or a cup again at the end, I wasn't quite sure. But then I wasn't sure what was going on in *Moby-Dick* a lot of the time either.

## 2. FACTS

Melville and Brown both love statistics, historical anecdote and facts. The very first word of *The Da Vinci Code* is 'Fact', a statement of intent which is only undermined by the fact that so much of what follows is untrue.[2] Brown initially claimed that either '99 per cent' or 'absolutely all of [the book] is true', although he has subsequently retrenched, utilising phrases like 'alleged', 'rumoured', and 'seem to be' when discussing this controversial issue. Nevertheless, his novel is full of art history, theological supposition and precise measurements of height, depth and length, sometimes to the

2 The Wikipedia page devoted to inaccuracies in *The Da Vinci Code* lists dozens of specific mis-statements and errors.

nearest millimetre. *Moby-Dick*, meanwhile, creaks with ancient maritime lore, accurate scientific data (accurate for its time) and disquisitions on the function and harvesting of blubber, spermaceti, etc. As a young man, Melville had shipped with the whaler *Acushnet* and the purpose of his novel was, in part, to impart that hard-won knowledge to the reading public. '*I mean to give the truth of the thing,*' he wrote. However . . .

## 3. THE FACT FACTOR

Melville and Brown both wear their learning heavily. Brown will merrily disfigure a sentence if it means he can cram in one more gratuitous statistic, e.g. '*Murray Hill Place – the new Opus Dei World Headquarters and conference centre – is located at 243 Lexington Avenue in New York City. With a price tag of just over $47 million, the 133,000-square-foot tower is clad in red brick and Indiana limestone. Designed by May & Pinska, the building contains over one hundred bedrooms, six dining rooms –*' Enough already!

If a little learning is a dangerous thing, a lot of learning can be even worse. *Moby-Dick* repeatedly judders to a chapter-length halt so Melville/Ishmael can instruct the reader on the measurement of a whale's skeleton, or harpooning technique, or the best cuts of whale meat: tongue, hump, barbecued balls of porpoise ('*the old monks of Dunfermline were very fond of them*'). The author is also an incorrigible show-off. He throws in Milton, Byron, Shakespeare; pagan folklore, magazine clippings, Holy Scripture; Cleopatra, Cinderella, Thomas Jefferson and dozens more. He probably has something to say about pots calling kettles black too but I am not at home at present and do not have a copy of *Moby-Dick* to hand, so am unable to confirm. There is no Internet access at the cottage where I am currently staying. I'll get back to you.

## 4. DIALOGUE

Neither Brown nor Melville cares for naturalistic dialogue. As you will have noted, no one in real life speaks like either Robert *'I've got to get to a library . . . fast!'* Langdon or Captain *'lick the sky!'* Ahab. And why should they? This is not real life. Nevertheless, it represents a problem for cinema and theatre adaptations of both *The Da Vinci Code* and *Moby-Dick*, which can seem slightly, well, ludicrous. Of these, the flop musical theatre adaptation of Melville's novel – *Moby! A Whale of a Tale* – was perhaps more in sympathy with the original text than other, more serious efforts. I should know: I still have the souvenir mug.

The principles of brand extension make it inevitable that there will be a musical theatre adaptation of *The Da Vinci Code*. Potential producers should be aware that the book and lyrics of *Moby!* were penned by one *Robert Longden*. Coincidence? Professor Robert Langdon would tell us there is no such thing.

## 5. SYMBOLOGY

In their different ways, Brown and Melville are both obsessed with symbols and symbolism. Robert Langdon is a professor of symbology at Harvard. *The Da Vinci Code* is packed with cryptic riddles; *Moby-Dick* is a cryptic riddle in itself. And what is that elusive white whale if not a 'lost symbol'? Dan Brown particularly loves anagrams and his characters are always obliged to untangle not-very-fiendish word puzzles to reveal hidden meanings and clues. This is the sort of lexicographical riddling one associates with writers like Vladimir Nabokov, Italo Calvino and Georges Perec, only not as good.

Let us adopt a symbologist approach to our subjects and see whether there are any invisible connections buried just beneath the surface. One anagram of 'Herman Melville,

*Moby-Dick*' would be 'Hmm – a credible milky novel'. Shuffle the letters of 'Dan Brown's *The Da Vinci Code*' and we uncover this message: 'B. was a contrived, hidden con.' And rearranging 'Andy Miller – *The Year of Reading Dangerously*' proves what we have suspected for a while: 'I am only a greying fatheaded Surrey nerd – LOL.'

Dr Langdon may be onto something.


## 6. DAY JOBS

Because they need to feed and clothe themselves, many published authors have day jobs before, during and after their literary careers; Herman Melville was no exception. Prior to becoming a novelist, he was a sailor; while he was a novelist, he was also a lecturer and a journalist; and, as noted above, after the failure of *Moby-Dick* and *Pierre*, he became a customs official. Disturbingly, both he and Dan Brown also found paid work as English teachers. 'I didn't understand how funny this play *Much Ado About Nothing* truly was until I had to teach it,' Brown has said. 'There is no wittier dialogue anywhere.' It is a mark of Brown's commercial clout that an edition of *Much Ado About Nothing* was recently published with this quote stamped on the front cover – someone at the publishers clearly felt Shakespeare could do with the leg-up.

Before becoming a bestselling author, Brown hung around in Hollywood, teaching English and trying to make it as a singer-songwriter. He formed his own record company and self-released several unsuccessful albums. In 1993, *Dan Brown* contained a song entitled '976-LOVE' which, possibly catching a wave from Nicholson Baker's 1992 novel *Vox*, appears to be about phone sex. '*Now when I'm feeling small, you're the one that I call*,' sings Brown, with rudimentary symbolism. '*I see your face in my mind / I feel your love come pulsin' through my telephone line –*'

Ugh! Hang up, hang up!

As far as we know, Herman Melville never wrote a song about phone sex. But a glance at Chapter 94 of *Moby-Dick*, 'A Squeeze of the Hand', furnishes us with a hint of what a song it might have been. '*Squeeze! squeeze! squeeze! all the morning long; / I squeezed that sperm till I myself almost melted into it . . . / nay, let us all squeeze ourselves into each other . . . / Would that I could keep squeezing that sperm for ever*!' From which we conclude that, unlike Dan Brown, Herman Melville could have made a serious fist of it in LA.

## 7. CRITICS

As discussed, as Dan Brown's fortune has spiralled, so has the opprobrium of critics. The Catholic Church denounces him as a heretic; professors of literature lambast him; celebrities like Stephen Fry dismiss his books as 'arse gravy of the worst kind'.[3] He has to put up with spiteful parodies, online polls of his twenty worst sentences and a man with a Fatwa on his head calling him names. Brown tries to be sanguine. 'There are some people who understand what I do, and they sort of get on the train and go for a ride and have a great time,' he said on publication of *The Lost Symbol*, 'and there are other people who should probably just read somebody else.'

But if anything, Brown should count himself lucky. With sales of his books already dwindling, critics attacked Herman Melville with such venom that they effectively put him out of business. The bafflement which greeted *Moby-Dick* turned to outrage when *Pierre* appeared. On 8 September 1852, the *New York Day Book* ran a news story under the headline: 'HERMAN MELVILLE CRAZY'. The paper's correspondent

---

3 'The worst kind of arse gravy' is a tautology, unless Stephen Fry's books represent the best kind.

reported that *'a critical friend, who read Melville's last book, "Ambiguities" (sic.) . . . told us that it appeared to be composed of the ravings and reveries of a madman.'* He continues: *'We were somewhat startled at the remark, but still more at learning, a few days after, that Melville was really supposed to be deranged, and that his friends were taking measures to place him under treatment. We hope one of the earliest precautions will be to keep him stringently secluded from pen and ink.'* With press and public deserting him, Melville's publishers soon followed suit. Which is ironic, because . . .

## 8. BLOODY PUBLISHERS

Both Brown and Melville have good reason to blame their editors and publishers for at least some of the negative feeling directed towards them. *Moby-Dick* was first published in London by Richard Bentley, who made numerous cuts to the manuscript and forgot to include the book's epilogue, leading many already discombobulated critics to conclude that Ishmael had drowned with the rest of the *Pequod*'s crew, and was therefore unavailable to narrate the novel they had just read, an error for which they entirely blamed Melville and not his incompetent publisher.

Likewise, many of the factual and grammatical errors with which *The Da Vinci Code* is littered arguably could and should have been picked up before publication. As one of our friend Socrates' fellow correspondents notes, *'No self-respecting editor could have missed such blunders. Editors' jobs are to make the author look better (and more educated) than they are.'* Apparently, something went wrong with *The Da Vinci Code*. Or maybe it didn't. Perhaps no one ever thought Brown's mass-market thriller would come under such close, rigorous, critical scrutiny. Under normal circumstances, this would have been a reasonable expectation because, under normal circumstances, such a page-turner might be read exclusively by the audience Brown was writing for, readers who want to 'get on the train and go for a ride and have a great time'. True, someone could have gone over the train with a squeegee prior to departure – an editor, or Brown himself for that matter – but ultimately it has made no difference to the passengers. To stretch the metaphor to breaking point, Dan Brown's high-speed bullet trains run on farts but they get millions where they want to go. On Herman Melville's scenic, if slow, stopping service, meanwhile, there will always be seats available. But no thanks to the rail operator.

In Brown's novels, Robert Langdon has an editor called Jonas Faukman. A well-meaning soul, he works in Manhattan, has a goatee beard and over 'power lunches', listens patiently while Langdon burbles on about conspiracies and Mary Magdalene and the Priory of Sion like – well, like a character from a Dan Brown novel. In this regard, Brown is for once entirely accurate:

*'"Authors," he [Faukman] thought. "Even the sane ones are nuts."'*

## 9. THE PLANKTON FACTOR

Both *Moby-Dick* and *The Da Vinci Code* have spawned entire secondary industries of movies, merchandise, spin-off books and, in the case of the latter, lawyers' fees for plagiarism suits (always settled in Brown's favour, it should be noted). Some authors have even written entire books comparing and contrasting Brown's work with the complete canon of Western literature: a deplorable act. Both books have also attracted a high number of Internet geeks, conspiracy theories and obsessive crackpots. The *Moby-Dick* feeding pool has more academic bottom – the crackpots have PhDs and publish their ravings in quarterly journals – but the ecology is much the same. A Leviathan will always host its share of barnacles.

## 10. THE *ZELIG* FACTOR

In Woody Allen's movie *Zelig*, the eponymous hero involuntarily changes his appearance to physically resemble whoever he is talking to at the time – rabbis, doctors, Nazis, etc. Under hypnosis, he relates the childhood trauma that triggered this condition: 'At school . . . There were very bright people . . . Asked me if I read *Moby-Dick* . . . I was ashamed to say I never read it . . .'

*The Da Vinci Code* and *Moby-Dick* are both novels about which, in social situations, we might feel a Zelig-like pressure to adapt, to express a view, to employ phrases like 'I couldn't put it down!' or 'You wouldn't catch me reading that rubbish!' or 'I admired the author's use of symbolism!', even if we have not read either and have little intention of doing so. Ideally, it is a pressure we should resist but, as you will have realised by now, some of us find it hard to do so. As Zelig confesses, 'I want to be liked.'

*

Unlike Dan Brown, Herman Melville is not around to enjoy the recognition and fortune that was later afforded him. He died obscure and despondent, a failure in his own time and by his own standards. Fifty years on, he became a literary icon. Although there are signs that the Brown phenomenon may be burning itself out – British charity shops report that *The Da Vinci Code* is their most-donated book, although this may simply be because it has now been read by every man, woman and child in the country and there is no one left to buy it – he has become more famous, faster, than any other writer in living memory, with the possible exceptions of J.K. Rowling and the aforementioned E.L. James. Yet fifty years from now, it may well be that few people remember his name.

And this is really the point of this Love Match: implausible as it may sound, Melville and Brown were trying to write the same book – like Leonard Zelig, they both wanted to fit in and be liked. Dan Brown was not trying to write *Moby-Dick*, a key to all mythologies – that would be ridiculous – but at some level, Herman Melville was trying to write *The Da Vinci Code*. Had he succeeded, he would not have had to spend the rest of his life working as a customs officer. Like all writers, he hoped his books would engage, inspire and sell. Melville may not have desired riches in the way I think Dan Brown did – he was not trying to make it in showbusiness – but after the failure of *Moby-Dick*, he was not able to earn even a living wage from his writing. This fact blighted the rest of his days. And I do not believe he was so committed to art for art's sake that he would willingly have forsaken a modest but loyal readership in his lifetime on a promise of immortality. Because when he wants it to, *Moby-Dick* thrills and dazzles and tells a page-turning, exhilarating story. But it does everything else too.

When Herman Melville died, he was working on a novella called *Billy Budd, Sailor*. It was the first fiction he had written for many years. Tucked away by his widow Elizabeth, the manuscript was not found and published until 1924, by which time the Melville revival was well under way. Though it may be short, *Billy Budd, Sailor* is an unforgettable and extraordinary book. At the end of his miserable later life, its author's wayward genius had returned, inimitable and intact. It felt then, and feels now, like the fierce, pathetic proof of the clipping found glued to the inside of the desk on which Melville wrote his story:

'Keep true to the dreams of thy youth.'

# Book Eleven

*Anna Karenina* by Leo Tolstoy

'As a hungry animal seizes every object it meets, hoping to find food in it, so Vronsky unconsciously seized now on politics, now on new books, now on pictures.'

*Anna Karenina*, Part V, Chapter 8

'"You have a consistent character yourself and you wish all the facts of life to be consistent, but they never are . . . You also want the activity of each separate man to have an aim, and love and family life always to coincide – and that doesn't happen either. All the variety, charm and beauty of life are made up of light and shade."'

*Anna Karenina*, Part I, Chapter 11

At the National Gallery in London, Alex and I were standing at the feet of a tiger in a typhoon.

'Grrr!' said Alex, pointing up at the painting and giggling. 'Grrr!'

I tried to smile at the blazer-wearing attendant who was sitting next to the picture but she refused to look at us. My happy child threatened to disrupt the sombre mood of her gallery. What do I think this is, Tate Modern?

*Fig. 7:* Surpris! (Surprised!). *Henri Rousseau, 1891.*
*Tiger, bottom left.*

'You're right, Alex,' I told him. 'Grrr!'

It was the week after Christmas. The National Gallery was full of families, parties of tourists and shoppers taking a break from the sales. They congregated near the *Water-Lilies* or *Sunflowers*, before making a beeline for the Sainsbury's gift shop – sorry, the Sainsbury Wing gift shop – to purchase headscarves or jigsaws or, bizarrely, miniature ginger-haired, one-eared Vincent Van Gogh dolls you could stick to the door of your fridge.

Twenty yards away, through a set of heavy wooden double doors, on the south wall of the Harry and Carol Djanogly Room, at a height of approximately 440 centimetres off the ground (I feel the spirit of Dan Brown working through me) was a painting I wanted Alex to see. Georges Seurat's *Bathers at Asnières* is my favourite picture in the National Gallery. If I am passing, and I have time to spare, I will come to Room 44 and sit in front of it and rest like the boy in the straw hat. It measures 201 by 300 centimetres, which is irrelevant. Look at the picture, the haze of a summer's day by the Seine more than a century ago. Asnières was an industrial suburb of Paris; in the background Seurat has painted the smoking chimneys of the local factories. Should these youths be at work? Or is light industry intruding on their day off, contributing smog to a lazy blue sky? At these moments, such questions are irrelevant too. The painting is a pool of colour and light.

'What do you think?' I asked Alex.

'I like the doggy,' said Alex thoughtfully. 'Woof!'

*Fig. 8:* Une Baignade, Asnières (Bathers at Asnières). *Georges Seurat, 1884. Dog, bottom left.*

He was right again. The dog completes the painting; its tail, its alertness, its solidity. Everything else in the picture is infectiously drowsy and slow.

Seurat's elevation of such a humdrum scene and determinedly common people was considered rather ludicrous in its day. It always puts me in mind of Jacques Demy's 1964 film *Les parapluies de Cherbourg*, which takes the commonplace setting of a dingy Normandy fishing port and stages a winsomely pretty social-realist musical in it – an idea which, if you don't get it, must seem ludicrous too. But Seurat's painting and Demy's film, like William Eggleston's photographs or Ray Davies' songs for *The Kinks Are the Village Green Preservation Society*, frame 'ordinary' people in provincial situations and make them glow. Their gaze is not uncritical but it rarely patronises. I would like to call it magical realism but that term is already taken, having been registered at a sweltering Latin-American patent office in the early 1980s and usually signifying a mixture of the real and the surreal ('surreal realism' never caught on). Let's just say I like the doggy too, because Seurat has painted a real dog magically, not a fantastical dog with wings and a top hat.

In the gift shop, Alex and I bought postcards, a small hardback of Rousseau's animal pictures and a Monet phone-block for my mother. We left the magnetic Vincents where they were. Alex was old enough now to enjoy going to museums, galleries and cinemas, and their gift shops too. They were all parts of the same experience, and we liked visiting them together, together.

Outside, preparations were being made for the imminent New Year celebrations, when crowds of revellers would gather in Trafalgar Square and revel through the night. (Just as the word 'flotilla' has become tied to the phrase 'little ships', so 'reveller' only seems to come out on New Year's Eve.) I would not be doing much revelling myself this year but I would be having a marvellous time. I would be reading Tolstoy.

A few weeks earlier at a Christmas drinks party, I had met a gentleman from Louisiana who had gone into raptures over *A Confederacy of Dunces*, not because of its ferociously cynical worldview but because it offered a realistic social portrait of his hometown, New Orleans. I explained about the List of Betterment.

'Oh my God!' he cried. 'Have you read *Anna Karenina*? Tell me you're going to read *Anna Karenina*!'

Yes, I said. I am going to read *Anna Karenina*. It still felt audacious to say this and know it was true.

On Christmas Eve, I began Анна Каренина (*Anna Karenina*, though *Karenin* is more correct). On Christmas Day, between unwrapping presents, assembling a Noah's Ark and basting my first turkey, I read some more. By Boxing Day my priority was no longer my own family but the Oblonskys and their circle. At my mother-in-law's I stole away to the spare bedroom when the Pictionary came out. This was not just a great book; it was a great book I could love. Of course, I loved my family too, never more so than when in another part of the house, reading about someone else's family, long ago and far away.

Is it wrong to prefer books to people? Not at Christmas. A book is like a guest you have invited into your home, except you don't have to play Pictionary with it or supply it with biscuits and stollen. Tina and I were still getting used to the shape of Christmas now Alex was part of the family. When he was a baby, we had been appalled to discover that he would not even give us Christmas Day off. He was worse than Scrooge! No more lying around in bed, sipping sherry and blubbing at *Noel's Christmas Presents*. Now Alex was a few years older, Christmas was an enchanted time, not least for the grandparents who, having spent many years slaving over sprouts, spuds and turkeys for their own broods, could now sit back and watch us do the same for them. This is what is called 'the circle of life'.

When Alex was born, my aunt gave me a far-sighted piece of advice. 'Family life is wonderful, Andrew,' she told me, 'but you have to give in to it.' I think my aunt knew I might find this a challenge – and she was right. Having a child brought with it a new, unanticipated role I did not really want. I loved being Alex's dad but I could do without the secondary responsibilities to everybody else. It was hard, repetitive and often nerve-jangling work. Tina's mum and dad are long divorced; my mother lives on her own; my brother-in-law and his family emigrated to Australia a few years ago. So at Christmas, we don't just have to chop and shop and wrap and cook, we do it atop an emotional powder keg which might blow at any time between the first long-distance Skype call and the Queen's Speech.

'*All happy families resemble one another, but each unhappy family is unhappy in its own way*' reads the famous opening statement of *Anna Karenina*. Did Tolstoy give in to family life? Despite being married for nearly fifty years and having thirteen (legitimate) children, he did not. Instead, the great man bent family life to fit round him, thus ensuring that his family was not unhappy in its own way but in his. It was a domestic arrangement that was '*one of the most miserable in literary history*', according to one biographer.

Of course, for a while it resulted in great work. But the work proved not to be enough for the great man making it. With hindsight, the novel is testimony to its author's growing disenchantment not just with families but with art itself. '*The two drops of honey which diverted my eyes from the cruel truth longer than the rest: my love of family, and of writing – art as I called it – were no longer sweet to me,*' he recalled a few years later in the memoir *A Confession*. Shortly after *Anna Karenina* was published, Tolstoy publicly repented of his wasteful life to date, his youthful ambition, the compulsive womanising and novelising. *War and Peace* had been a mistake, so had *Anna*. Fiction itself was as sinful as lust unless directed to a higher purpose. Henceforth, he would turn away from anything that did not glorify Jesus' teachings – or Tolstoy's interpretation of them – and prepare His kingdom on Earth. It was one of the most masochistic midlife crises imaginable, but Tolstoy being Tolstoy, there was no turning back. For the next three decades he attempted to live as a Christian anarchist, a peasant, a holy man – anything but a writer of fiction or a father, though he could not quite suppress either impulse. The Countess Tolstoy had good reason to complain, which she did, incessantly.

I don't know what Christmas was like in the Tolstoy residence but there was probably some tension between celebrating the birth of Jesus and celebrating the life of Tolstoy. Abandoning art does not seem to have brought much peace to his titanic ego. He knew that his essays and his sermons, though pure in conception and execution, carried only a fraction of the authority of his damnable fiction – his transcendent later stories like *The Death of Ivan Ilyich* and *The Kreutzer Sonata* merely confirmed this. Nabokov relates the story of Tolstoy '*picking up a book one dreary day in his old age, many years after he had stopped writing novels, and starting to read in the middle, and getting interested and very much pleased, and then looking at the title – and seeing:* Anna Karenin *by Leo Tolstoy*'.

By now, I had been reading the List for nearly two months. Every book had had something extraordinary about it. Yet *Anna Karenina* was so grand, so all-encompassing, that it seemed to contain all those remarkable books within it. It was as elaborate as *Middlemarch*, as idiosyncratic as *The Sea, The Sea* and, every so often, as brutal as *Post Office*. Its climax was as moving as *Twenty Thousand Streets* . . . and as experimental as *The Unnamable*. It offered a working overview of nineteenth-century agricultural theory which was Melvillian in scope. It even had several characters standing around in wheat fields, leaning on ploughshares and arguing about communism. It had it all.

In other words, *Anna Karenina* made good on the promise I had divined in *The Master and Margarita*. This was the book, or the gap, I had been hunting from the beginning, from before the beginning. It was the perfect balance of art and entertainment – no, not a balance, a union of the two. One was indivisible from the other. The way in which Tolstoy framed his characters' choices was startlingly contemporary, their psychological dilemma, their suffering and moments of clarity; or maybe it was timeless and therefore always contemporary. Like people, they contradicted themselves. They changed their beliefs, their temper, their appearance. In a lesser writer this might seem like inconsistency but in Tolstoy's hands this changeability was completely lifelike. The scale of the plot and the Russianness of the names soon seemed inconsequential. And when he chose to create a set piece, such as the birth of a child or the lingering death of an invalid, one felt he was aiming to articulate the last word on the subject, so pristine was the detail and so forceful the character behind it. It could not be described as an easy read, and perhaps if I had not just finished Eliot and Melville and Beckett and Toole and Tressell, one after another, I would not have found *Anna Karenina* so beguiling or so straight-forward. But I was not intimidated by the book. Like Seurat's painting or *Les parapluies de Cherbourg* or my beloved Kinks records, *Anna Karenina* was like the real world, only better.

Of course, to a small child on Christmas morning, the real world is like the real world, only better. First Father Christmas and his reindeer, then Mummy and Daddy, and Granny and Granddad and Nanny – no, darling, Granddad doesn't live with Granny; no, he doesn't live with Nanny either – showering you with love and, more importantly, piles and piles of parcels containing toys and sweeties and books. It is a day of magical realism. And in a break from peeling vegetables and averting fights, my son and I sat and flicked the pages of a picture book, basking in it all together.

Early that morning, Alex had presented me with a shiny gold envelope containing my Christmas gift. Inside was a pair of tickets for a show called *Sunday in the Park with George*, a Sondheim musical I had never seen, which was at the time being revived in the West End of London. As its starting point, it took the paintings of Georges Seurat, in particular the pointillist masterpiece which followed *Bathers at Asnières* – the view from across the river, *Un dimanche après-midi à l'Île de la Grande Jatte* or *A Sunday Afternoon on the Island of la Grande Jatte*. It was the perfect present.

The attentive reader will have noticed that I love musicals. This, along with a deep-seated dislike of sport, barbecues and cars, is what has led my wife to refer to me as a flamboyant heterosexual. To some, the modern stage musical is hopelessly unserious, inherently camp or detestably bourgeois, like the novel or the family: 'Thatcherism in action' according to one respected critic. Certain shows struggle to defy the gravity of their source material – I refer you to the scathing reviews that greeted *Moby! A Whale of a Tale* and numbers such as 'Mr Starbuck' and 'In Old Nantucket'. But my parents adored Lerner and Loewe, Rodgers and Hammerstein, Frank Loesser *et al.*, and as a child obsessed by pop music and storytelling, I loved how their songs compressed wordplay and emotion and plot into three-minute tunes. Now I am a grown-up, I still do. This is not to say all musicals are good – when they are bad, they are disastrous – but I like the populism of these shows and their vividness and the fact that, when they work, they create more than the sum of many different disciplines and talents. I also love singing. Jacques Demy, speaking of his own musicals, once said singing was 'a way of communicating that I find more interesting. It can be more tender, more generous, more violent, more aggressive, more gentle, whatever.'

(Another coincidence: while watching the documentary *L'univers de Jacques Demy* again this morning to make a note of the above quote, I was amazed to see that in the mid-1970s Demy and his *Parapluies* . . . collaborator Michel Legrand planned a film musical adaptation of *Anna Karenina* called *Anouchka*. Demy, his wife Agnès Varda and their two children even moved to Moscow and started learning Russian. Demy and Legrand got as far as finishing the score before funding for the picture fell through.)

My *Sunday in the Park with George* tickets were for the end of the month, which meant I would have time to take Alex to see Seurat's painting in London, and show him why Dad was so pleased with his present. And by that time, I might even have ticked off the few remaining books on the List. After *Anna Karenina*, if I stuck to my original target, there were only two to go. Not that I was in any rush to finish it quickly. *Anna Karenina* really was better than Christmas.

I shall not attempt to précis the plot of *Anna Karenina*. The story is long, convoluted and utterly enthralling, and if you have not done so already, my every effort in these few pages is directed towards getting you to read it. But here is a summary of its central theme, taken from Lemony Snicket's *A Series of Unfortunate Events*: '*A rural life of moral simplicity, despite its monotony, is the preferable personal narrative to a daring life of impulsive passion, which only leads to tragedy.*' (*Book the Tenth: The Slippery Slope*)

In the middle of the novel, there is an interlude of sorts.

Anna has abandoned her husband and young son Seryozha – her duty – and is touring Europe with her lover, Count Alexei Vronsky. Tolstoy tells us they have passed through Venice, Rome and Naples and are now arrived in '*a small Italian town where they meant to make a longer stay*'. Their self-imposed exile from St Petersburg society is placing the relationship under some strain. Vronsky, an army officer, in particular is growing restless. For a while, he takes up painting. The couple make the acquaintance of a notable Russian émigré artist, Mikhaylov, whom Vronsky commissions to paint Anna's portrait. He cannot grasp why Mikhaylov's sketches of Anna capture her essence, '*that sweet spiritual expression*', so much better than his own efforts. Nor can he and Anna understand why Mikhaylov does not wish to cultivate their acquaintance as they wish to cultivate his: '*His* [Mikhaylov's] *reserved, disagreeable, and apparently hostile attitude when they came to know him better much displeased them, and they were glad when the sittings were over, the beautiful portrait was theirs, and his visits ceased.*'[1]

1 The extracts here are taken from Louise and Aylmer Maude's translation of *Anna Karenina*, which was approved by Tolstoy himself: '*Better translators . . . could not be invented.*' I cannot vouch for its fidelity to the cadences of the original Russian but it is a lyrical read and full of personality – though whether it is the author's is a moot point. Translation is a tricky and competitive business, partly because of the personalities of those involved. There can never be a right answer, yet academics and publishers are always pushing for fresh, 'definitive' editions. In recent years, another crack husband and wife team, Richard Pevear and Larissa Volokhonsky, have cornered the market in crisp new versions of works by Tolstoy, Dostoevsky, Gogol *et al.* Their *Anna* was selected as an Oprah Book Club choice and sold several hundred thousand copies. 'Tolstoy is not reader-friendly,' Pevear told the *New Yorker* in 2005. 'Tolstoy's style is the least interesting thing about him, though it is very peculiar.' So perhaps the lyricism I detected in *Anna Karenina* was the Maudes' and not Tolstoy's after all. But wait! Pevear '*has never mastered conversational Russian*', notes the *New Yorker*, and it is his wife who actually speaks the language. I tell you, it's a hall of mirrors.

Mikhaylov is a distant, more productive relation of Ignatius J. Reilly. We are introduced to him in his studio, working at his 'big picture', a giant canvas of 'Pilate's Admonition – Matthew, chapter xxvii'. He has just argued with his wife because she has failed to pacify their landlady, who is clamouring for the rent. '*He never worked with such ardour or so successfully as when things were going badly with him, and especially after a quarrel with his wife. "Oh dear! If only I could escape somewhere!" he thought as he worked.*' The painting may never be finished; Mikhaylov erases, reworks and chases inspiration as and when it comes to him. A stray grease spot fills him with joy because it suggests a new pose: '*Remembering the energetic pose and prominent chin of a shopman from whom he had bought cigars, he gave the figure that man's face and chin.*' In this setting, Anna and Vronsky are ill-educated and intrusive. Mikhaylov craves their opinion and their trade; having secured both, he cannot wait to be rid of them, especially Vronsky's dilettante trifling with art, which pains him dreadfully: '*One cannot forbid a man's making a big wax doll and kissing it. But if the man came and sat down with his doll in front of a lover, and began to caress it as the lover caresses his beloved, it would displease the lover. It was this kind of unpleasantness that Mikhaylov experienced when he saw Vronsky's pictures: he was amused, vexed, sorry, and hurt.*'

Shortly after the portrait is completed, Anna and Vronsky return to St Petersburg, and neither they nor we meet Mikhaylov again. But in four short chapters, Tolstoy sums up the never-ending transaction between the eternal values of art and the muddled world of the artist. Plus he makes you laugh. I had just finished this Mikhaylov interlude

Fundamentally, there is probably no substitute for the original Russian; but unless we accept a substitute we don't get to read Tolstoy at all.

when I took Alex to look at *Bathers at Asnières* at the National. Seurat's picture had long since escaped the shackles of Seurat's life but it still bore the imprint of his character. Although his technique of painting in thousands of tiny dots had been given a technical name – 'divisionism' or 'pointillism' – it remained the product of an individual's vision. And like Mikhaylov reluctantly courting Anna and Vronsky, an artist's posthumous reputation was still subject to the ebb and flow of public opinion and the readiness of galleries and institutions to popularise the image of his painting, and thus their own reputations, via mouse mats or jigsaws, ginger fridge magnets or big wax dolls. The picture was finished years ago but the rent is always due.

The same nagging tension lies at the heart of *Sunday in the Park with George* (which, it hardly needs saying, is a bit more complicated than *Jersey Boys*). As Seurat works on *Un dimanche après-midi à l'Île de la Grande Jatte*, we are first

*Fig. 9:* Un dimanche après-midi à l'Île de la Grande Jatte (A Sunday Afternoon on the Island of La Grand Jatte).
*Georges Seurat, 1886.*
*Never mind the dogs, here's a monkey, bottom right.*

shown the personal sacrifices that go into its creation and then, in the second act, the tricky negotiations with popularity that continue into the present day – the business of art. From my seat in the stalls, not five minutes from the *Bathers*, I watched as both painting and sacrifice were brought miraculously to life.

Sondheim and playwright James Lapine build the show around Seurat's real writings on pointillist theories of colour and light – design, tension, composition, balance, harmony – and apply them first to the imagined lives of the characters in the painting, then Seurat and his mistress Dot (their invention), then the modern art scene and the efforts of Seurat's great-grandson George to find inspiration and funding for his own artworks. Much of this is sung to a score whose staccato notes suggest the dots of paint from Seurat's paintbrush. The songs jump between the real world and the painting, and characters come and go from both. At one point, Seurat gives voice to the dogs in the park, which rise or fall from the stage at his command.[2] 'Finishing the Hat', 'Color and Light', 'Move On', 'Putting it Together': the metaphor should buckle under the strain but it never does. The refrain of the latter – art isn't easy – repeated by the younger George as he schmoozes a gallery of wealthy potential patrons, could be the theme tune of the last few months. I have rarely, if ever, been so moved in a theatre.

2 At the performance I attended of *Sunday in the Park with George*, we sat behind the novelist and intellectual Andrew O'Hagan, who bought an ice cream during the interval and appeared to enjoy the show. In 2010, O'Hagan published the novel *The Life and Opinions of Maf the Dog, and of His Friend Marilyn Monroe*, the narrator of which is a talking dog. Having proved he too could give voice to a notorious hound, O'Hagan's next project was ghost-writing the 'unauthorised autobiography' of Wikileaks founder Julian Assange. They say Sondheim has been approached to work on a musical adaptation.

For much of the second half, I felt like something enormous was trying to escape from my chest.

In Act II, Seurat's daughter, now in her nineties and confined to a wheelchair, reports one of her mother's favourite sayings. '*You know, there are only two worthwhile things to leave behind when you depart this world of ours – children and art.*' She then sings wistfully and delicately of '. . . La Grande Jatte', painted by her father long ago, as 'our family tree'. Great art is our family tree, just as children are a glimpse into the future and the past. Tolstoy came to view these essential elements of life, children and art as barriers to enlightenment, but surely he was wrong? When we find a painting or a novel or a musical we love, we are briefly connected to the best that human beings are capable of, in ourselves and others, and we are reminded that our path through the world must intersect with others. Whether we like it or not, we are not alone. Tolstoy realised this in *Anna Karenina* but after his conversion he spent much of his subsequent life trying to deny it or postpone it to the afterlife. Families and art, paintings and crowds, books and their troublesome readers: composition, balance, tension, harmony. It is our duty and our privilege to try to resolve these things here and now, with the help of a song or a decent book. Because they will not wait for later.

When we got home, I looked in at Alex, asleep. I was somebody's son and somebody's father. It had not been much consolation for Tolstoy but I was not Tolstoy.

I could do better.

# Books Twelve and Thirteen

*Of Human Bondage* by W. Somerset Maugham
*Pride and Prejudice* by Jane Austen

'"How despicably I have acted!" she cried. "I, who have prided myself on my discernment! – I, who have valued myself on my abilities! Who have often disdained the generous candour of my sister, and gratified my vanity, in useless or blameable distrust! – How humiliating is this discovery! – Yet, how just a humiliation!"'

*Pride and Prejudice*

'"That's all literature," she said, a little contemptuously. "You must get away from that."'

*Of Human Bondage*

It was a new year but the end was nigh. There were only two books left to read and afterwards I could go back to the *Standard* and spreadsheets and half-finished manuscripts and magazines. Except of course, I couldn't.

Reading is not an activity one associates with action. Yet as the end of the List approached, I found it difficult to accept that I had done nothing except look at words on the page. There had to be more to it than that. The last couple of months had made me ask serious questions about art, work, family, freedom, integrity and packed lunches. Now it was up to me to answer those questions. How was I going to move on? And what was I going to do when the List was finished?

These momentous decisions would have to be put off a little longer, however, while I wrestled with a new problem: *Of Human Bondage*. On the surface, this should have been an easy task. Although it was 700 pages long, Somerset Maugham wrote in a clear, plain style, and the novel recounted a straightforward rites-of-passage story in a series of appealing settings: the stretch of Kent coast where we lived, the Paris milieu of Seurat and the Post-Impressionists, and a London of pubs, poverty and omnibuses.

On day two, I sought advice from the person from whom I had borrowed the book. Her maiden name was written in blue on the title page; although her copy of *Of Human Bondage* had clearly been read, the blocky spine remained commendably unbroken. Its owner took good care of her personal library, a quality I found nerdily attractive.

'Tina,' I said, 'I'm not getting on with this at all. Does it pick up?'

'I can't remember much about it. Is that the one where he's got a club foot?'

On day four, precisely two hundred pages in and not a word more – I had in fact left off mid-sentence, just as Philip Carey, the novel's hero, claps eyes on a shrivel-breasted naked woman for the first time – I asked again. When might I expect a breakthrough?

'I don't know,' said Tina. 'It's ages since I read it. I liked it at the time. Is that the one with the waitress?'

'Not yet,' I said hesitantly. It did not augur well for the

remaining 500 pages that the two most memorable items were the club foot, which had first been alluded to on page two, and a waitress.

On day six, the waitress appeared. Her name was Mildred and she was common and anaemic. Philip Carey was ruinously obsessed with her, though not in any way which seemed very original or interesting. The story laboured on. It felt to me like an anaemic retread of *Twenty Thousand Streets Under the Sky*, which I knew to be unfair, because Maugham's novel had been published fifteen years before Patrick Hamilton's. But still.[1] As far as I could tell, Maugham seemed to think he was a terrifically astute judge of human character. He presided over the novel like a magistrate. Nothing anyone did or said seemed to come as a surprise. It was deathly.

After a week of *Of Human Bondage*, I felt confident enough to venture an informed opinion to my wife.

'This book is rubbish,' I said.

'Yes, I didn't think you'd like it,' she replied. '*The Razor's Edge* is good though.'

That decided it. What I did was, I gave up.

Giving up on a book was expressly against the rules of Betterment, but, oh, it felt wonderful. My problem with *Of Human Bondage* was not that it was too difficult or experimental or eccentric or trivial. It was none of these. The problem was that it was so excruciatingly boring.

How should we deal with books we do not like? This was the first time I had encountered this question in the List of Betterment and, strangely, I had not really expected it. I had assumed that all the classics I chose would have

1 In his article on Patrick Hamilton, Dan Rhodes calls *The Midnight Bell* 'a cover version' of *Of Human Bondage*.

something unambiguous to recommend them, a point of interest or excellence that would guide my reading. And so it had proved, until now. *Of Human Bondage*, for all its reputation, for all the elements that ought to have commended it to me – the plain, clear prose, the recognisable streets and cities, the enchanting seediness of it all – stubbornly refused to yield, well, anything very much. I could have carried on to the end but I knew it would not be worth the considerable effort. Halfway through, I had the measure of it – or I thought I did. So I stopped.

Although I had not anticipated this problem, I knew how to deal with it. For some years now, I had coped with any book I did not like by rejecting it, fast. Partly, this was professional expediency. As a bookseller and later as an editor, the sheer volume of incoming words could be overwhelming. These jobs often required a rush to judgement – form a decisive opinion, then act upon it. But I also subscribed to some vague notion of readers' rights: life is brief, time is precious, why waste either on doing something you do not enjoy, consumer choice, and so forth. Do you need to have read a book all the way through in order to have an opinion about it? Of course not. You do not need to have read a book *at all* and you can still let the world know how you feel, just as at the public swimming baths, you don't have to complete a length of the adult pool before deciding to take a wee in the deep end. That is between you and your conscience.

However, once you start to give up on books, you may lose the skill of finishing them – my early difficulties with *The Master and Margarita* and *Middlemarch* proved this. In addition, your opinion will automatically be worth less than that of someone who has taken the trouble to finish the book because, in at least one key respect, they know what they are talking about and you don't.[2] And little by little you may erode your integrity to a point where you sincerely believe the difference between saying you have read a book and actually reading it is little more than semantics. You come to believe that it doesn't matter anyway, because it's all a load of shit.

For a period in the mid-1930s, between more anthropologically prestigious engagements, George Orwell worked in a bookshop. He tired of it quickly. *'The real reason why I should not like to be in the book trade for life is that while I was in it I lost my love of books,'* he later wrote. *'A bookseller has to tell lies about books, and that gives him a distaste for them; still worse is the fact that he is constantly dusting them and hauling them to and fro.'* However, he was not merely alienated from the stock. *'The thing that chiefly struck me was the rarity of really bookish people. Our shop had an exceptionally interesting stock, yet I doubt whether ten per cent of our customers knew a good book from a bad one . . . Many of the people who came to us were of the kind who would be a nuisance anywhere but have special opportunities in a bookshop.'*

I do not know how true this is today but it was certainly the case twenty years ago, when I first started telling lies about books professionally. Often when a customer brought a book to the till and asked, 'Have you read this? Is it good?', the worst thing you could do was tell the truth. It was kinder, and cleaner, to answer all such queries with a 'yes'. The customer rarely wanted the honest opinion of a shop assistant anyway. At the moment of purchase, they were looking for their own discerning taste

2 'All opinions are not equal. Some are a very great deal more robust, sophisticated, and well-supported in logic and argument than others.' Douglas Adams, interview with *The American Atheist*.

to be confirmed by the approval of someone who was not in a position to disagree.[3]

And what if you had read the book in question? If you thought it was rubbish and said so, you satisfied no one. 'Have you read this?' enquired a middle-aged lady, holding up a copy of *The English Patient* by Michael Ondaatje. 'Is it good?' 'Yes,' I replied. 'It's awful.' (I had read some of it and I believed it was.) 'Oh,' she said, somewhat startled. At this point, another customer, a younger woman in her thirties, intervened. 'Oh no,' she said earnestly. 'It's beautiful.' She then turned to me and said: 'But it's not a *thriller* . . .' A heated discussion of the merits of *The English Patient* ensued. While the young woman and I argued, the older lady returned *The English Patient* to the shelf. The carefree moment of purchase had been spoiled. On the other hand, if you had read a book and really liked it, it could still turn out badly. I once inadvertently dissuaded a customer from buying Gordon Burn's *Alma Cogan* by recommending it with such boggle-eyed fervour that, smiling and nodding, they backed out of the shop and never came back.

No, it was better to conceal what you really thought. How much simpler, as yet another copy of *Captain Corelli's Mandolin* or *The Secret History* passed through your hands, to go with the flow of received opinion.[4] Yes, it is an excellent book, well done you for selecting it, a distinctive choice. In the era I worked in the shop, it sometimes felt like the only books we ever sold were the same half dozen novels,

3 One former marketing director of the book chain Waterstones once told me that he got round the problem of constantly being asked 'Have you read X or Y?' with the foolproof response: 'Not personally', a formulation I have utilised many times since.
4 For more on this topic, Pierre Bayard's *How to Talk About Books You Haven't Read* (Granta), is warmly recommended. NB. I have not read it.

over and over: *Captain Corelli's Mandolin, The Secret History, Perfume, Birdsong* . . . I personally recommended these titles hundreds of times, though I had only read one of them, and not thought much of it. But these were the books people wanted, even when they did not know they wanted them. 'I'm looking for a new novel, I can't remember the title, I heard something about it on Radio 4 . . .' 'Was it *Captain Corelli's Mandolin*?' 'Yes, that was it! How on earth did you know?' To which one could not reply, 'You are obviously from the same socio-economic group as everyone else who buys this one' or just 'You look the type'.

Books are different. You would not go into a greengrocer or a supermarket and announce, apropos of nothing, that you were looking for something to eat; or approach the cashier at B&Q and ask them to recommend some cutting-edge screws. ('Well, sir, what kind of screws do you usually enjoy?') It is a peculiarity of bookshops, and our relationships with books, that when we go browsing in them, or on their homepages, we feel we are – cough – 'joining an on-going conversation'. But for precisely this reason, we can find it hard to accept that Orwell's 'really bookish people' are the ones behind the counter. It is more flattering to all concerned to pretend otherwise.[5]

5 There are, of course, exceptions. You will have had the experience of asking for a widely-reviewed title by someone you consider a well-known author, only to be met with a blank stare or a request to spell 'Brown'. Fortunately, you have the humility to acknowledge that you are not the world – nor are you the sort to enjoy lording it over a poorly-paid shop worker. If only all customers were as patient and wise as you are.

I once worked alongside someone who, by her own admission, knew next to nothing about literature. She once asked me to recommend a book by Graham Greene. 'Why don't you try *The End of the Affair*?' I suggested. 'What, just the end? Not the whole thing?' she replied. But she was cheerful and well-spoken and many of the regular customers

Over time, I came to see that what a customer really wants from a bookseller is not a love of books *per se* but a love of selling books – not an unreasonable demand. However, for the whole business to run smoothly, the latter needs to masquerade as the former. If you love books more than you love selling them, then eventually that discrepancy will get the better of you. Let us suppose that you prize the novels of Tolstoy above all others. You imagine that, while working with books, you will have the opportunity to share your enthusiasm for Tolstoy with the public. How frustrated you will be, then, when you discover that the majority of the public are more interested in the novels of, say, Alan Titchmarsh. To them, your sincere passion for Tolstoy, if expressed openly, will seem like one-upmanship or hoity-toity elitism. So you repress it. But wait – not only do you have to deny your true feelings for Tolstoy, they want you to be overjoyed every time you sell another Titchmarsh. You try to do it because it is your job. But it is debilitating. And so, in order to protect your love of books, you start telling lies about them – inevitably. Orwell saw this and got out after a year or so; I was not so vigilant.[6]

Similarly, when, several years later, I became an editor and got the chance to publish books myself, I soon learned the value of the judicious fib. Most publishers receive their books from literary agents, either as finished manuscripts or sketched-out proposals with sample chapters attached. In the majority of cases, the editor will not like the manuscript

---

came to ask for her by name, and were sorry when she left to set up her own catering business. She is now a millionaire.

6 NB. One might swap round the names 'Tolstoy' and 'Titchmarsh' here without altering the thrust of the argument. If I loved the novels of Alan Titchmarsh but people insisted on buying that bloody *War and Peace* all the time, it would be equally infuriating.

or proposal and not wish to publish it. It then falls to the editor to telephone or email the agent and reject the book. However, when rejecting these non-starters, it can be necessary to invent excuses: not right for the list at this time, cannot see where such a book would fit into the market, and so on. An editor will rarely have the daring to say simply 'I didn't like it' for fear of appearing unprofessional or uninformed or, in due course, when the book becomes a bestseller and wins a prize or two, wrong. And when a manuscript or proposal is terrible, the same line of defence is usually followed. No one wants to be unkind; and besides, next week the same agent might have something far more prize-worthy or commercial to offer, perhaps both. To a good editor, the white lie is every bit as important as the blue pencil.

When I was a junior editor, one of my new colleagues was offered the first novel of an up-and-coming broadsheet journalist and reviewer, whom we shall call 'J'. 'J' was under thirty; his agent was highly regarded; and the novel was eye-wateringly atrocious. It was a lame, penile dog of a book. To complicate matters, my colleague was on drinking terms with the journalist and we had been offered the novel exclusively: it was ours to refuse. How might she reject it without causing offence to the agent, spoiling a friendship and jeopardising future positive reviews 'J' might pen for her books? 'I think someone younger needs to have a look at it,' she said. 'Maybe I'm not getting it. Would you mind . . .?' In my naivety, I was thrilled to help. I wrote an email in which I methodically detailed the novel's many glaring faults. 'Crikey,' she said. 'Look, I think you ought to let them know we don't want the book. I've told them I've passed it on to you.' So I copied and pasted much of my email into a letter and sent the manuscript back to the agent. 'Thank you for your candour,' said the agent, and never submitted anything to me again. Subsequently, the novel was picked up by another publisher and became a modest success, receiving positive notices in all those papers and magazines to which 'J' contributed, though noticeably less so elsewhere. It was an early lesson in literary *Realpolitik*.

So when, years later, I informed my wife *Of Human Bondage* was rubbish, it was the plain truth as I saw it; and when I decided to stop reading, it was freedom in action. So why did I feel guilty about it?

I had previous. When Tina and I were in the first flush of our courtship, we did as many young booklovers do and swapped favourite novels. She read mine, *Absolute Beginners*, from cover to cover. I only read the first three chapters of hers. Then, in a questionnaire in *The Bookseller* magazine, I went into print with a premature review of it. '*It is a truth universally acknowledged,*' I wrote, '*that if anyone in Jane Austen's* Pride and Prejudice *said what they thought, the whole novel would be over in an instant. I hated it.*' Looking at this now, I cannot believe she married me, not because I disliked *Pride and Prejudice* – I mean, she was lukewarm on *Absolute Beginners* – or because I was poking fun at it, but because I did not even do her or Jane Austen the courtesy of *finishing the book*.

Returning to *Pride and Prejudice* after a break of fifteen years, I felt a little warmer towards it. For a start, it was not *Of Human Bondage*. Compared with some of the huge books I had read recently, it was promisingly slender. And thanks to the TV and film adaptations, it was a known quantity. I was not leaping into the dark; all I had to do was put one foot in front of the other for a few more days. Besides, fifteen years was a long time ago. I was older, wiser. I had just read *Moby-Dick* and *The Sea, The Sea*. I had learned my lesson.

How strange to discover then that after only a few pages, my response to *Pride and Prejudice* was the same as ever: exasperation and impatience. It was as though I had put the book aside in annoyance and popped out of the room for fifteen years. God, it was irritating. Get on with it! I had expected to come back to Austen with a fresh sensitivity and understanding – a renewed sense and sensibility – but nothing had changed; it seemed like my reaction was almost an allergic one. If you don't like macaroni cheese, you don't like macaroni cheese. If eating peanut butter makes you feel sick and wheezy, eating more peanut butter will only make you sicker and wheezier. Regrettably, Austen seemed to act on me like macaroni-cheese-flavoured peanut butter and no amount of persuasion – or indeed, *Persuasion* – was going to alter that, no matter how delicious, organic or smooth the recipe was supposed to be.

You cannot like everything. These are the wise words of the critic Dominic Maxwell. However widely-read you may be, however educated and open-minded, you will probably always have intolerances or blind spots – and this is ok. Without them, you have no taste to call your own. This meant I might never get along with Jane Austen – I could accept that. It was not as if she needed my support. Unfortunately, having succumbed to the temptation of leaving *Of Human Bondage* unfinished, I was now looking at *Pride and Prejudice* and thinking: why should I finish this one? I knew what was going to happen in it; I knew what I thought about it; and what I said about it publicly would remain the same whether I plodded on to the bitter end or not. What, in other words, would be the difference between saying I had read *Pride and Prejudice* and actually reading it? Perhaps it would be more honest *not* to finish it; perhaps there was something noble in running the race and, at the last minute, refusing to cross the line, like Tom Courtenay in *The Loneliness of the Long Distance Runner*.[7]

But I completed the race and this is why. While such thoughts buzzed distractingly round my brain, I stumbled on. Momentum carried me forward. Beneath the veneer of *Pride and Prejudice* – the clockwork plot, the rapier wit, sharp to many but dull to me – lay a cold, hard fact of life: it was better to be married than to be poor. Poverty, and the fear of it, shaped the choices faced by Elizabeth Bennet and her sisters. The fate of the entire family was dependent on one or more girl making a 'good marriage'. Fear of poverty was the engine of the novel because, for millions in the era in which Austen was writing, it was the engine of their precarious lives. This was a truth universally acknowledged by the books I had read in the last few weeks and months – *Middlemarch*, *The Communist Manifesto*, even *Anna Karenina*. And moving into the twentieth century, it was the dread at the heart of *The Ragged Trousered Philanthropists*, *Twenty Thousand Streets Under the Sky* and *Of Human Bondage*: the ruin and degradation of poverty.

In such a world, books mattered. They were valuable and unique objects, a means of education or consolation or escape. In *Pride and Prejudice*, Austen shows what books mean to different characters. Elizabeth, as we might expect, loves to read nearly as much as she loves to tramp across fields and make quips. Her father, Mr Bennet, rarely ventures forth from his library; he hides in it to escape from his wife, who seems never to have read a book in her life. The unctuous parson Mr Collins never reads novels, preferring

7 I know the character's name is Smith and not Tom Courtenay. I am deliberately referring to the 1962 film adaptation rather than Alan Sillitoe's original novella because I have seen the former but not read the latter. So piss off.

tedious volumes of sermons. Their well-to-do new neighbour Mr Bingley has few books (*'I am an idle fellow, and though I have not many, I have more than I ever look into'*) and his shallow sister Caroline only reads because Mr Darcy does: *'At length, quite exhausted by the attempt to be amused with her own book, which she had only chosen because it was the second volume of his, she gave a great yawn and said, "How pleasant it is to spend an evening in this way! I declare after all there is no enjoyment like reading!"'*

It is Darcy, inevitably, who Austen presents as a perfect lover of books. His attitude is one of profound respect; the possession of them is a privilege. Darcy is always buying books and adding to the library at Pemberley, which he describes as 'the work of many generations': *'I cannot comprehend the neglect of a family library in such days as these.'* And when we are shown Darcy in the act of reading, he even does this correctly, never allowing himself to be diverted from the task in hand by a Bennet or a Bingley. Nor does he lie about books. Austen leaves us in little doubt that in reading, as in so much else, Mr Darcy has purpose and integrity; he always finishes what he starts.

I was still mulling this over when, without meaning to, I came to the end of *Pride and Prejudice* and, I suppose, the List of Betterment. I had successfully distracted myself into completing both.

I had read thirteen books – well, twelve and a half. It had been like a holiday to take one after another and do little more than appreciate them, to silently answer the questions 'Have you read this? Is it any good?' with an easy and wholehearted 'yes' – because it was the truth. I had rediscovered, or maybe discovered for the first time, the pleasure of sharing enthusiasm for a novel gratuitously, not as an exercise in social standing or a bid to feel part of *contemporary opinion*. It occurred to me that I had been extraordinarily fortunate to have grown up in a prosperous country in an era when, for pretty much the first time in its history, I could read whatever I wanted, whenever I wanted to. And what had I done with this freedom? I had slowly, though unintentionally, abused it. My reading life had become an accumulation of bad habits, short cuts and lies. I bought books I did not read. I started books I never finished. I expressed strong views I had not earned. And this had all become clear to me through the simple process of turning one page after another, faithfully, properly, for a few short weeks. If I kept going, perhaps I could change. But first I had to go back.

*Of Human Bondage* was waiting for me under a pile of socks.

'I thought you'd decided to give up on that,' said Tina.

'It's my penance,' I said.

You cannot like everything. But you owe it to yourself, and Mr Darcy, to try.


In *Of Human Bondage*, the young Philip Carey picks up what Maugham calls *'the most delightful habit in the world'*:

'He could think of nothing else. He forgot the life about him. He had to be called two or three times before he would come to his dinner. Insensibly he formed the most delightful habit in the world, the habit of reading: he did not know that thus he was providing himself with a refuge from all the distress of life; he did not know either that he was creating for himself an unreal world which would make the real world of every day a source of bitter disappointment.'

What a miserable sod; a pity he is entirely correct.

Last night, as usual, my son Alex went up to bed early so he could read. His love of books is uncomplicated and all-consuming. Should we tell him that, after *Captain Underpants*, the rest of his life may well prove a bitter disappointment? Should we warn him off reading altogether, or push him outdoors and get him kicking a football about before it's too late? Or perhaps we should give him his own List of Betterment, the better to prepare him for the awfulness of what awaits him. Ten pages of *The Unnamable*, son, and then lights out.

When I was a boy, I loved reading in just the way Alex does now. But life had separated me from that boy; books had got in the way. Because if I had learned one thing from the List of Betterment, it was that a love of reading and a love of books are not necessarily the same thing.

A few weeks after finally completing *Of Human Bondage*, I was caught late one night in London. Locking up the office at about nine, I grabbed a couple of manuscripts and my copy of Homer's *Odyssey*. In the glow of victory, I had resolved to extend the List from a dozen great books to fifty – to keep moving forward. Betterment was continuing.

It was raining as I set off for the station. When I arrived at Victoria I discovered that all train services to the coast had been cancelled. Great. I was standing on the concourse, dripping and wondering what to do next when I heard someone calling my name.

'Andy Miller! How are you? Come for a drink!'

It was an old colleague of mine called Patric. Raincoat, attaché case, rolled-up *Sporting Life*. Patric seemed rather drunk. I kept him company for an hour, matching his drinks, then caught the last train home. It was several years since we had worked together. A few months earlier, he told me,

147

his partner had died suddenly. Days at the office were bearable but he did not know what to do with the evenings. The prospect of retirement, for which they had both prepared so diligently, now filled him with dread.

'I ought to be angry,' Patric said. 'I am angry. But you'll understand that.'

'What do you mean?'

'You always struck me as a very angry person,' he said, as we propped up the station bar. 'I don't know why. Sooo angry. I think you are one of the angriest men I have ever met.'

I put him on his train and then, reeling a little from the drink, went to find mine. As we pulled through the usual stops, I could not concentrate on *The Odyssey*. I was too tired and fuzzy, and Patric's words kept coming back to me. Angry? Really? I did not think of myself as especially angry, no more than anyone else on the threshold of middle-age. And yet, in recent weeks, whenever I thought about my life and the path it had taken so far, along avenues lined with books, one image kept pushing itself to the front of my mind: John Goodman, rampaging along the hotel corridor in *Barton Fink*, fire exploding at his back, his face transfigured with outrage, roaring in fury:

'I'LL SHOW YOU THE LIFE OF THE MIND!
I'LL SHOW YOU THE LIFE OF THE MIND!
I'LL SHOW YOU THE LIFE OF THE MIND!'

And I shall.

II

'The books one reads in childhood, and perhaps most of all the bad and good bad books, create in one's mind a sort of false map of the world, a series of fabulous countries into which one can retreat at odd moments throughout the rest of life, and which in some cases can even survive a visit to the real countries which they are supposed to represent.'

George Orwell, 'Riding Down from Bangor'

'We tried but we didn't have long.'

Hot Chip, 'And I Was A Boy From School'

It is a Thursday morning in May, a few days before my thirty-ninth birthday. I am on a train to Bournemouth where I shall be attending a conference. I am reading a book: *One Hundred Years of Solitude* by Gabriel García Márquez. I feel like I am going out of my mind.

It is four months since I staggered to the end of *Of Human Bondage*. Since then, I have finished off a dozen more great books of varying lengths and difficulty. Seated in this train carriage on a May morning is someone who has read not only *The Master and Margarita, Middlemarch, Post Office, The Communist Manifesto, The Ragged Trousered Philanthropists, The Sea, The Sea, A Confederacy of Dunces, The Unnamable, Twenty Thousand Streets Under the Sky, Moby-Dick, Anna Karenina, Pride and Prejudice* and *Of Human Bondage*, but also *Catch-22, Lord of the Flies, Frankenstein, The Odyssey, Crime and Punishment, The Unfortunates, Fear and Loathing in Las Vegas, The Heart is a Lonely Hunter, Vanity Fair, Jane Eyre, Everyman* and *Absolute Beginners*. When I shut my eyes, this list scrolls across the inside of my eyelids like the Times Square news ticker. I shut my eyes a lot. I am exhausted.

For this and other reasons, I am finding it hard to concentrate on *One Hundred Years of Solitude*. I resent having to spend a night away from home on a junket. I am listening to *The Warning* by Hot Chip and while it is a really good record, it is also distracting me from Márquez. I have not been to Bournemouth since I was a teenager, on a short family holiday, and I am apprehensive about the feelings that might be dredged up by returning there. The train does not smell like my train. Also, the book is terrible.

A week ago, I re-read *Absolute Beginners* by Colin MacInnes. For many years, this was my favourite book; it was disconcerting, in the midst of Betterment, to realise it still might be. It spoke to me when I was sixteen, seventeen, twenty-five. Somehow, it speaks to me now, urgently and without apology. This cannot be right.

Anyway, it has been a heavy anti-climax to turn back to Literature. I am finding it tough to establish common ground with *One Hundred Years* . . . When it first appeared in English, thirty years ago, this novel was hailed as revolutionary, romantic, a firework display of the imagination – but this is not how it strikes me. To me it seems like one initially amusing trick repeated again and again, a chimp in a small room riding a tricycle, puffing on the stub of a cigar, going round and round in circles. I don't want to feel like this about *One Hundred Years of Solitude*, which I know is special to readers around the world – I am trying not to have these unworthy, chimpish thoughts – but I cannot help it. The trouble with magical realism for me, as I suggested earlier, is that it is neither realistic nor magical. I press on, uptight and bored.

The best track on Hot Chip's *The Warning* is called 'And I Was A Boy From School'. It is an electronic lament, full of yearning for something just out of the singer's grasp. *'And I was a boy from school, helplessly helping all the rules . . .'* It seems to be a very nostalgic song, or maybe it is about nostalgia? Either way, with its bubbling analogue keyboards, it speaks to me. I especially like the song's gorgeous middle eight, where, to an accompaniment of celestial electric harps and Casiotones, Alexis and Joe, Hot Chip's two singers, absent-mindedly squabble with each other.

Joe (*mournfully*): I got, I got lost . . .
Alexis (*sweetly*): You said this was the way back . . .

The train pulls into Bournemouth station and I pick up a taxi to drive me to the hotel. From the back of the cab, parts of the town seem briefly familiar but then fall away. It has been twenty-five years. Mum and Dad and I stayed here for a week in successive Easter holidays, 1983 and 1984. Every single day I walked the length and breadth of the town, combing the shops for interesting paper and vinyl: a tie-in novelisation of The Beatles' film *Help!* by someone called Al Hine,[1] two early issues of *The Face* magazine, *(Keep Feeling) Fascination* by the Human League. I still think about those two weeks often, on my own at childhood's end. I have probably never been happier.

After checking in at the hotel, I am supposed to make my way to the conference centre and attend a keynote speech or breakout working party or some piece of nonsense, but instead I skive off. I lie on the bed and finish reading *One Hundred Years of Solitude*. I watch the chimp ride the trike round the room until the chimp and I have both had enough. And then the chimp grows magical wings and flies away, like his father, and his father's father before him. Meanwhile, I make a cup of tea and eat a shortbread finger and think: that's that. At this moment, I cannot conceive of picking up another book. Betterment is over.

1 I still have Al Hine's book *The Beatles in Help!*. I can see it on the shelf from here. Of course, I have never read it.

It is four o'clock, too late to join my fellow delegates, but not too late for a melancholy stroll. So I leave my room and go down into the streets and sure enough break my heart, as I always knew I would, trying and failing to find the boy from school who came here with his mum and dad, a lifetime ago.

(Let's pretend that I left *One Hundred Years of Solitude* lying open on the bedside table, and that you, like a camera, have panned from the closing door to the table, and that, as my retreating footsteps echo down the stairs, you focus on these words . . .)

*'Aureliano did not understand until then how much he loved his friends, how much he missed them, and how much he would have given to be with them at that moment . . . [He] wandered aimlessly through the town, searching for an entrance that went back to the past.'*

One evening at bedtime, Alex and I were reading *The Tiger Who Came to Tea*.

'Hey!' I said, surprised. 'That's where I grew up!'

We were looking at a double-page illustration of Mummy and Daddy and Sophie walking along the street in the early evening. *'So they went out in the dark,'* ran the text in the bottom left-hand corner, *'and all the street lamps were lit, and all the cars had their lights on, and they walked down the road to a café.'* The street was somewhere in London; a 72 bus is pulling away in the background, its conductor perching on the rear platform, peering into the oncoming traffic. A blue car drives past – a Ford Escort? A Morris Marina? Across the road, an older woman is walking a white dog. Nearby, a couple seem to be turning into a restaurant called H. Pether. Other businesses line the street: Harding, a florist; Rudman, a fishmonger; TOY SHOP; a children's outfitters called Melinda. The shops are shut, but above several of them, lights in the flats are on and curtains pulled. The street lamps glow yellow in the dusk.

'You grew up there?' asked Alex.

'Sorry, I don't mean that,' I said. 'I mean I was a boy there, or somewhere like it. It looks like the place I lived with Granny and with Granddad Mick when I was a little boy.' And it really did, in spirit as well as substance – a suburban English high street of the late 1960s or early 70s, rendered as a child of those years might like to remember it. I wanted to fall into the book.

In the foreground of the picture, Sophie and Daddy and Mummy walk arm-in-arm, laughing and chatting. They are dressed in raincoats and boots and Daddy is wearing a hat.[2] On the pavement behind them, they have just passed a smiling marmalade cat and another pedestrian. But something is not quite right. The cat is arching its back, its tail pointing straight in the air. Is it stretching? Yawning? Perhaps it is getting ready to leap at something or someone, hissing, claws extended – perhaps it has been disturbed by the other pedestrian. He is a curiously unsettling figure. We cannot see his face; his back is turned to us, his hat pulled down, his jacket wrapped around his shoulders as he leans into a biting wind *only he can feel*.

'Who is that?' asked Alex, pointing at the hunched figure.

'That is Death,' I replied. 'Night night.'

I wonder what *The Tiger Who Came to Tea* is really about – is it a colourful metaphor for Mummy's marital infidelity

2 Daddy has not had time to get changed out of his office clothes: pork-pie hat, brown brogues, blue tartan suit, bright red tie and socks. In fact, Judith Kerr never actually tells us that Daddy goes to an office, only that he is out for much of the day and he would never knock because he's 'got his key'. Dressed like that, I think Daddy is either a small-time gangster or working the halls.

or addiction to shopping? Is it a critique of the fiscal underpinning of the traditional nuclear family, where there are three consumers but only one breadwinner? Or is it about the suppression of female desire, the Tiger a wish-fulfilment personification of the id, rampant, unleashed? Look again at the figures that walk arm-in-arm down the road. Mummy and Sophie are laughing and chatting but Daddy seems preoccupied, an impression reinforced by the tableau which follows: the family is in the café now, smiling and enjoying *'a lovely supper with sausages and chips and ice cream'* – paid for by Daddy – but none of them are looking at one another. Daddy holds a half-pint barrel-glass of beer but he is not drinking, and the look on his face is one of sadness, wistfulness, regret. Perhaps he blames himself for the Tiger that ran amok while he was out. Or perhaps he is daydreaming the story we have just read, and the Tiger is his fantasy, not Mummy's or Sophie's, an irrational explanation of the life his wife and only child lead when he is not there.[3]

'What do you think this book is about?' I asked Alex this morning, a few years later.

'It's about a tiger,' he said.

*Fig. 10: Sausages and chips and ice cream.*

3 For lots more in-depth analysis of *The Tiger Who Came to Tea* by frustrated English graduates with too much time on their hands, check the numerous discussion threads archived at Mumsnet.

That's the problem with tigers. What immortal hand or eye can frame their fearful summit tea? Yeah?

I think I must have read *The Tiger Who Came to Tea* at primary school, when it was still a new-ish book (it was published the year I was born). I have a memory of a hardback copy lying in the book box in the corner of the classroom. If it wasn't there, then it was at the library in the town. Actually, there were two libraries nearby, one a large red-brick building on the main shopping street, and another smaller lending library, octagonal or circular in shape, next door to my school in the old town. I know we didn't own a copy. My parents, though both dedicated readers, rarely bought books; but every Saturday morning they borrowed them, three tickets each, from the big library, and I went with them.

How I loved the municipal libraries of South Croydon. They were not child-friendly places; in fact, they were not friendly at all, to anyone. They were large, dark, wood-panelled rooms full of books, in which visitors were expected to be silent, and the only sound was the clicking of school shoes on polished parquet floor. The larger building in the town had its own children's library, accessible at one end of the hall via an imposing door, but what lay behind that door was not a children's library as we might understand it today, full of scatter cushions and toys and strategies of appeasement; it revealed simply a smaller, replica wood-panelled room full of books. And this – the shared expectation of respect, the solemnity, the shelves crammed end-to-end with books, no face-outs or yawning gaps – is what I loved about these places and what I found inspiring. The balance of power lay with the books, not the public. This would never be permitted today.

The smaller, octagonal library on the hill was lighter and

brighter – but it too was bursting with books, politely demanded silence, and had a polished parquet floor. Forty years later, that tang, the heady perfume of parquet, affects me like Proust's sacred madeleine. I am transported back to those rooms whose *raison d'être*, whose heart, was the books they housed. I have probably been trying to get back there ever since.

Of course, we had books at home but my parents were not bookish. They read for pleasure but I cannot recall them re-reading. There was little fiction and almost nothing in the way of classics, ancient or modern – no Eliot, no Dickens, definitely no French authors or Russians; no Iris Murdoch, John Fowles, Robert Graves; nothing published by The Bodley Head. That kind of literature was another country; we definitely lived on the outskirts of Croydon. Instead, we had *Alistair Cooke's America*, *The Moon's a Balloon* by David Niven, two AA motoring atlases, a *Reader's Digest Guide to Home Maintenance*, and David Wallechinsky and Irving Wallace's *The People's Almanac*, by some margin the most fascinating book in the house.[4]

My parents' books were kept in two places. The first was a massive multi-purpose shelving unit Dad had hammered together in the garage and installed in the dining room, incorporating a drinks cabinet, on which stood a blue metallic soda siphon, Poole pottery, smoked glass ornaments, my plaster-cast models of characters from Beatrix Potter

---

4 *The Moon's a Balloon* is terrific, obviously, but *The People's Almanac* (1975) is an extraordinary 1500pp repository of whatever information its compilers found colourful, revelatory or entertaining, the useful and useless side-by-side – the Wikipedia of its day. It was with *The People's Almanac* that I first scared myself stupid with the doomsday prophecies of Nostradamus, studied the inconsistencies of the Warren Report into the assassination of President Kennedy and, at the age of twelve, convinced myself that I had somehow contracted syphilis. What a book.

books and *The Muppet Show*, and all the atlases and instruc-
tion manuals. The second was a wooden cabinet with a
sliding glass front. This cabinet stored a set of uniform
editions of novels by the likes of Ngaio Marsh and Alistair
MacLean: *Ice Station Zebra*, *Final Curtain* and so on – the
results of a subscription to the Companion Book Club some
years before I was born. These were certainly never read
in my lifetime. All the dust jackets had been thrown away.

Nonetheless, my parents were always reading, whatever
had been borrowed from the library, or paperbacks on
holiday. My mother enjoyed, and still enjoys, historical
romances set in Cornwall or at a royal court. When I was
a boy, her favourite authors were Jean Plaidy (*The Captive
of Kensington Palace*, *The Thistle and the Rose*) and Victoria Holt
(*Bride of Pendorric*, *My Enemy, the Queen*). She slightly favoured
Holt over Plaidy, but there was little to choose between
them, not least because Jean Plaidy and Victoria Holt were
the same person writing under different pen names.[5] These
days, she reads Philippa Gregory, Dick Francis and Alan
Titchmarsh, again all the same person, probably Victoria
Holt.

To make use of a cliché, my mother does not know much
about art but she knows what she likes. Actually, no, that
is not quite correct. My mother knows enough about art
but she prefers what she likes. Thus, in her late seventies,
inspired by a trip to Castle Howard in Yorkshire, she read
*Brideshead Revisited* and found it underwhelming. It was,
she informed me, markedly inferior to Alan Titchmarsh's
most recent novel. When I begged to differ, she pointed
out that I had not read it and suggested I was simply being

5 Eleanor Hibbert, 1906–1993, sold more than 100 million books in her
lifetime. Jean Plaidy and Victoria Holt were just two of her bestseller
*noms de plume*.

a snob. 'He has written some really super books, Andrew,' she said. She thinks I could learn a thing or two about being a successful writer from Alan Titchmarsh; undeniably true.

My father, for his part, liked to read about the First World War, the Second World War and/or the Cold War, either as fiction or fact, and so read the novelists everybody's dad read in the 1970s: Frederick Forsyth, Len Deighton, John le Carré. He had been sent out to work at fifteen, up to the City every day while German bombs fell on London. In his early twenties, he developed severe diabetes and the pattern of his adult life was fixed. If Dad was bitter about these events, he never showed it to me, nor did he harbour thwarted academic ambitions, although he was well aware of the advantages and confidence such an education bestowed. 'You always know when a person has been to Oxford or Cambridge,' he used to say, 'because they always tell you.' This too has proven to be undeniably true.

Is it redundant to say I loved my parents? My father was wonderful company, intelligent, articulate, argumentative, and my mother was patient and talkative and loving. They were older parents with one cherished child, and we were undoubtedly an old-fashioned family, Dad taking the train to town every day while Mum stayed behind and made a home for us. My father's ill-health meant he needed stability and routine; my mother worked hard to provide him with these things. The upheavals of the 1960s passed them by or they chose to ignore them – we knew no war, and my father continued to wear a bowler hat to work well into the next decade. There may not have been any Tolstoy in our house but what I want to say is that I did not care then and I do not care now. We were happy, and we were happy in our own way.

But then I had to go to school, the catastrophe of my childhood. I stood in the playground on the very first morning, while all around children ran and shrieked and laughed, and though I did not yet know the word, I thought to myself: oh shit oh shit oh shit. And these first impressions proved to be correct. There was not a single school day for the next thirteen years when I did not think: oh shit. From the moment I arrived, I was waiting to leave.

Books became more important to me then. For the first few weeks of school, I spent as much time as I could sitting inside, reading, until my teacher, Miss Twitchit, told me gently that I was banned from the classroom during break times and I had to go outside and play with what she called 'your friends'. And though I did make friends eventually, I always preferred indoors to outdoors because indoors was where the books were kept.

Although I was predictably inept at PE, and average at most other subjects, it is correct to say I was exceptionally good at reading. What rewards did this bring? The good opinion of Miss Twitchit, on the one hand, and, on the other, the bemusement and contempt of 'my friends'. In the summer term, the advanced readers in the class were allowed to take their little chairs out onto the grass, form a circle, and talk about what they had been reading. I was the only boy in this group. Every week, the little girls would be furious that their book club had been infiltrated by a boy – and a girly boy at that. Every week, the clever girls would make me cry and run indoors, establishing the pattern of my relationships with women into my adult life, up to and including when I met my wife, the cleverest girl of all.

What was it I got from reading as a child? It fired my imagination and provided me with an escape – that much is corny but true. Everything in the world of stories was harmonious and fair and I often found it easier to spend time there than in the muddy, idiotic, confusing world of other people.[6] However, what I really got from reading was this: it was the one thing at which I truly excelled. It was my natural talent, my golden voice, my prodigious goal-scoring gift; and although it did not carry the same institutional prestige or heroic status as football skills and virtuosity on the descant recorder, it was enough to be good at something – not just good, better than *you*. By my penultimate year, I had exhausted all the books in the school and my parents were asked to send me in with new books from home or from the library nearby. Did I really read every single book in the school? My mother maintains I did. Maybe I just told the teachers I had and they all believed me. Maybe this is where the lying about books really began. Where were the checks and balances? I blame the authorities.

So, my parents gave me a love of reading; Croydon Borough Council, via its libraries, gave me a love of books; and schooldays ensured I became emotionally dependent on both. But only one person taught me how to collect books, how to covet them and hoard them, how to buy them. That was all me, autodidact, infant bibliolater. From the age of seven, it was my dearest wish to build a library of my own, all donations greedily accepted; and every Asterix or Tintin book that came home, every Dahl or Blyton or Fisk taken out on loan, was never returned without

6 'Those who love life do not read. Nor do they go to the movies, actually. No matter what might be said, access to the artistic universe is more or less entirely the preserve of those who are a little *fed up* with the world.' Michel Houellebecq, *H.P. Lovecraft: Against the World, Against Life*.

regret and a mental note to acquire a copy for the collection when funds permitted. I wanted to possess all the books I had already read, as well as all those I had not – every book in the whole wide world, in other words. Where did this mania come from? It was the tiger who came to tea and never left.

I also wanted to be a palaeontologist.

I read a piece in a magazine recently which rated book tokens as one of the most disappointing Christmas presents of the 1970s, just below home-knits and any bicycle which wasn't a Chopper or a Tomahawk. This was not my experience. I liked receiving toys as much as the next tank-top-wearing kid but, in my eyes, book tokens were every bit as 'skill' as, say, Evel Knievel or Ker-Plunk!. A book token was a golden ticket to a land of pure imagination, and also the big branch of WHSmith in Croydon's Whitgift Centre.[7]

And what did I spend my book tokens on? *Asterix* and *Tintin*, Roald Dahl, Nicholas Fisk and *Littlenose*. *The How and Why Wonder Book of Dinosaurs*. *Mr Men* books (original set, pre-*Little Miss*). Beatrix Potter. *Winnie-the-Pooh* and *The House at Pooh Corner*. *Now We Are Six* and *When We Were Very Young*. *The Dinosaur Encyclopedia*. Selected adventures of *Alfred Hitchcock and the Three Investigators*. *I-Spy* books. Pop-up books by Jan Pieńkowski. *The Guinness Book of Records*. *Fattypuffs and Thinifers*, *Fungus the Bogeyman*, *Masquerade* by Kit Williams. Spike Milligan, the Rev. W. Awdry, *How to be Topp*.

---

7 A certain sort of reader might expect me to renounce Croydon, Smiths and even book tokens but I won't do it. I loved all three. The same reader might expect me to report that my love of books was nurtured by an independent children's bookshop, a magical cavern of storytelling, etc. etc. etc., but it wasn't, because there wasn't one. We can't all live in Muswell Hill.

The Secret Seven and the Famous Five (I did prefer the Secret Seven). *Emil and the Detectives*. *Stig of the Dump*. *Blue Peter* annuals, *Beano* annuals, *Rupert* annuals – jumble sales were good for old annuals. *Arabella's Raven*. *The Wind in the Willows*. *How to Be a Junior Palaeontologist*. Sir Arthur Conan Doyle, *The Lost World*.

Essentially, provided it had nothing to do with football, war or girls, I liked everything. I read the *Radio Times* and 'The Robins' in my mother's *Woman's Weekly*. I read the four-panel cartoons in the *Daily Express* and flicked through the *Croydon Advertiser* in search of more. I was addicted to comics, the jokey comics like *Whizzer and Chips*, *Buster*, *Cheeky Weekly* and *Whoopee!*, or the 12p American imports of Marvel and DC titles: *The Amazing Spider-Man*, *The Uncanny X-Men*, *The Mighty Thor*, with their action-packed advertisements for Sea Monkeys, Hostess Twinkies and *GRIT*, '*America's Greatest Family Newspaper Since 1882*'. To a British child growing up in the 1970s, these adverts were every bit as amazing and uncanny as the adventures of the adjectivally-endowed superheroes.[8] My parents indulged me in all of the above. My mother took an uncharacteristically liberal 'as long as they're reading' approach, though there was one notable exception: I was not allowed to bring *Look-in* (aka *The Junior TV Times*) into the house.

At school, reading won me my first and only prize, for

8 An unfulfilled hankering for Sea Monkeys and Twinkies stayed with me for years. In 1998, I begged the author Shawn Levy, visiting the UK to publicise his new book, to bring with him a box or a packet or a bag of Twinkies, however they damn came, so I could finally discover what the legendary enchanted sweetbreads tasted like. When Shawn told his two young boys what the Englishman wanted, they looked at him in amazement. 'But Dad,' they said. '*Why??*' And with good reason, as it turned out. Twinkies are horrible. (I note this more in sadness than anger. At the time of writing, Hostess has just filed for Chapter 11 bankruptcy protection.)

which I received a certificate and, fortuitously, a book token. In the cubs, though the swimming and athletics badges were beyond me, I could earn the readers' badge by talking about a book I had enjoyed and explaining how a library works – dur. And, inevitably, I was a member of the Puffin Club, with a shiny enamel pin, my Puffineers' codebook and a pink plastic binder for back issues of *Puffin Post*. In 1976, I pleaded with my mother to take me up to the ICA for that year's Puffin Exhibition, the Club's annual jamboree. We queued in the Mall for ages to get in but it was worth it; we saw Quentin Blake and Bernard Cribbins and Fat Puffin. I would not set foot in the ICA again for ten years, not until an *NME*-sponsored gig by The Wedding Present, The Servants and a pre-ecstasy Primal Scream. This seems fitting because, with its badges and its cryptic messages, the *NME* in that period operated like a Puffin Club for students. And I would not meet Fat Puffin again until 1991, when Penguin loaned one of their Fat Puffin costumes to the shop I was working in and I volunteered to wear it and some youths in the street told Fat Puffin to fuck off and punched him in the stomach. But I digress.

A few books and authors stand out as my absolute favourites from childhood. Both *Winnie-the-Pooh* books, of course. Tove Jansson's Moomin stories, which have undergone a kind of merchandised revival over the last few years, were fabulous (as in fable) and reassuringly unsentimental; I liked the dark, windswept *Moominpappa at Sea* the best. *The Eighteenth Emergency* by Betsy Byars, with its Quentin Blake cover, whose hero Benjie 'Mouse' Fawley must learn to take a beating from the school bully, Marv Hammerman. And thirty or so thin Coronet paperbacks of *Peanuts* strip cartoons by Schulz called things like *You Can't Win Them All, Charlie Brown* and *You're On Your Own, Snoopy*, which I read, and read again, and still read today, whose sheer brilliance is all the more apparent now I have a child of my own.[9]

The above does not represent an editorial sampling, these really were my favourites. Or perhaps these are the books that have stayed with me most vividly from that time, both in imagination and in reality. I carry the impression of them in my head – but I also still have physical copies of most of them somewhere in the house.

*Fig. 11: 'From the library of Andrew Miller':*
*Puffin Club bookplate, circa 1977.*

I loved the humour in these books, of course, but they are a melancholy bunch. Eeyore spoke louder to me than Tigger;

---

9 Fantagraphics Books' ongoing publication of every *Peanuts* strip cartoon in attractive hardback volumes, with introductions by fans like Matt Groening and Jonathan Franzen, is one of the most welcome publishing programmes of recent times. It is to be hoped that the project, which commenced in 2004, reaches completion before printed, hardbound books become obsolete – I fear it will be a race to the finish.

I think I instinctively felt this was *realistic*. Life could be fun but mostly it wasn't, and between times there was an awful lot of hanging about in gloomy places, '*rather boggy and sad*'. In these books, children like Linus and Lucy, Mouse and Hammerman, Little My and Moomintroll, all seemed to behave like children really behaved, even the ones who were Moomins, beagles or piglets: playing, bickering, watching TV, feeling sorry for themselves and 'slugging' one another. These characters got bored and frustrated and scared; sometimes they laughed so hard they fell off their doghouse. And they had wild imaginative lives and alter egos. In their heads, Mouse and his friend Ezzie know precisely how to deal with Crocodile Attack (Emergency Four) or Seizure By Gorilla (Emergency Seven), but not the Eighteenth Emergency – how to defeat the school bully. In *Peanuts*, Charlie Brown often appears depressed and withdrawn ('*I can't stand it . . .*') but his dog is irrepressible, Snoopy the World War I Flying Ace; the World-Famous Astronaut, Attorney or Author; Joe Cool.

And what did life have in store, according to these guide-books? In the Marvel universe, this angst intensified in adolescence, with girlfriends and fighting and general turmoil, but so did the alter egotism. The trick was to get bitten by a radioactive spider, be a billionaire playboy, etc., and then your alter ego was empowered to act out its, and your, fantasies: dressing up in a homemade costume, slugging all-comers and eating nothing but Hostess Twinkies. Sok! Zap! Barf! Etc!

When you grew to adulthood, you ceased to be a super-hero and turned into a fretful Fillyjonk or a pompous Hemulen or a Grandpa-Grumble. If you became a parent, you were invisible like the adults in *Peanuts* or *Pooh*, an unseen presence just outside the frame. And as life dragged on, you grew mystifyingly captivated by work or chores or gardening, until even the appeal of these fell away and you found yourself stranded like Moominpappa in the opening lines of *Moominpappa at Sea*:

> 'One afternoon at the end of August, Moominpappa was walking about in his garden feeling at a loss. He had no idea what to do with himself, because it seemed everything there was to be done had already been done or was being done by somebody else.'

And eventually the freezing, friendless, lonesome Groak would catch up with you and that would be the end of it. *Moominpappa at Sea* is a chronicle of mid-life crisis foretold, for readers of nine and over. Looking back, I wonder that I bothered growing up at all – if indeed I did. It was all too true.

Were Mum and Dad aware that, like Nostradamus in the pages of *The People's Almanac*, I was reading these runes and determining a bleak future – a self-fulfilling prophecy of doom? Ought they to have steered me away from such morbid, introspective fare to healthy, sunny *Swallows and Amazons* or *Just William*? Well, thank God they didn't. I was a child with a morbid, introspective streak and it comforted me to see this streak reflected back at me in fiction, where it could be treated with compassion and laughter.

In fact, *Look-in* aside, my parents seemed happy to let me follow my own path through the bookshelves of our libraries and stationers. There was no one in my life pushing the canon of children's literature, no one waving a proto-List of Betterment in my face. No one tried to improve me with C.S. Lewis or *A Child's Garden of Verses*. Though I grew to appreciate it later, I can remember trying out *Alice's Adventures in Wonderland* at the age of eight and being tremendously disappointed; it was *so* much better on TV.

The biggest influence on my burgeoning taste was probably television, which could have been a bad thing had I not had the extreme good fortune to be living in Britain in the 1970s. In the first instance, this meant *Jackanory* on BBC1, a programme whose format was cheap, simple, educational and entertaining: point a camera at an actor like Alan Bennett or Judi Dench or Mai Zetterling or Kenneth Williams and at teatime every day they read to you from a good book. It was via *Jackanory* that I and millions of other impressionable children were given a chance to discover the Moomins and *The Eighteenth Emergency*, and treasure like *The Eagle of the Ninth* by Rosemary Sutcliff, *Ludo and the Star Horse* by Mary Stewart, *Black Jack* by Leon Garfield; the magic of reading itself.

But our generation was fortunate twice over. The huge captive audience and empty schedules meant that programme makers frequently turned to books from an earlier era as dramatic source material. You need not have read E. Nesbit to know *The Railway Children* or *The Phoenix and the Carpet* or *Five Children and It*, or Pamela Brown, Frances Hodgson Burnett or John Masefield to know *The Swish of the Curtain*, *The Secret Garden* and *The Box of Delights*, respectively. By modern standards, these adaptations were daringly sedate and wordy. Because I loved *Doctor Who*, I also loved the Target series of novelisations of the Doctor's adventures – I think *Doctor Who and the Brain of Morbius* by Terrance Dicks was probably the first book I ever read from cover to cover in one go, glued to the back seat of our Morris Marina. And on Sundays, the BBC broadcast the Classic Serial, dramatisations of Carroll or Swift or Dickens for the family to watch together. I know this all sounds very worthy and middle-class and paternalistic but my point is this: if you were a child who liked books, who actually was much of a reader, there were books in libraries, books in bookshops, books at school and books on TV. You'd never had it so good; and, arguably, nor would you again.[10]

My parents gave me their love of reading, as I have said, but they were not snobs, inverted or upright, who favoured books over other forms of entertainment. There were few cultural neighbourhoods that were *not for the likes of us*; we watched *Coronation Street* and *3-2-1* like everyone else. But my parents were not modernists. What preconceptions they did have were reserved for 'modern art' and pop in its post-Beatles form, which Dad in particular thought was one gigantic racket, monetary and musical. When we traded the Morris Marina for a car with a cassette player in it, my tape of *Dare* by the Human League was barred, along with all my other tapes – XTC, Skids, the lot. The only albums we could listen to without an argument were original cast recordings of songs from the shows: *Oliver!*, *Kiss Me Kate*, *My Fair Lady*, all of which we were word-perfect in. I consider myself lucky. These were my introduction not only to Lionel Bart, Cole Porter and Lerner and Loewe, but also Dickens, Shakespeare and Bernard Shaw, not to mention Oliver Reed,

10 I did say arguably. There are still many fantastic programmes being made for children in the UK but few of them are based on books, and definitely not vintage books. Classic children's drama of this sort has almost entirely vanished from the schedules, except at Christmas when the BBC or ITV will dramatise *The Borrowers* for the umpteenth time. The spirit of *Jackanory* survives more in the bedtime story on CBeebies, or Stephen Fry's readings of *Harry Potter*, than it does in the current incarnation of *Jackanory* itself, *Jackanory Junior*, which treats its young viewers as though every single one of them is suffering from chronic attention deficit disorder, such is the bombardment of sound effects, animated inserts and green-screen overload. These days, decent adaptations of English literature, classic or contemporary, are more likely to come to us via Hollywood, e.g. *The Lion, the Witch and the Wardrobe*, *Nanny McPhee*, *The Secret Garden* and the *Harry Potter* movies, often made in the UK with American money.

Ann Miller and Audrey Hepburn (and CinemaScope, and Bob Fosse, and Cecil Beaton, et cetera, et cetera).[11]

Our number-one tape for long car journeys was the Broadway cast recording of *Guys and Dolls*. The last time I had been to Bournemouth, it had been in the car with Mum and Dad, sitting in the back seat, singing along to 'Luck Be a Lady' and 'My Kind of Town', and making a better fist of it than Marlon Brando.[12] And here I was again in solitude, a hundred years later. I wandered the streets, missing my family – my families – and wanting to be with them.

When I returned home, I could not bring myself to start a new book. The List of Betterment seemed to have reached a dispiriting conclusion. I kicked about the house, went to work and fell back into bad habits on the train: crosswords, paperwork, magazines. The gap between the agony of *One Hundred Years of Solitude* and the ecstasy of *Absolute Beginners* seemed too wide to bridge.

Looking back, *Absolute Beginners* is perhaps the only book I can truthfully say has changed my life – I mean actually changed it, as opposed to a sort of media-friendly shorthand for 'a book I really like and would be willing to talk about for money'.

11 Pedants, I know Marni Nixon replaced Audrey Hepburn's vocal tracks on the *My Fair Lady* soundtrack, and CinemaScope movies were only ever shown pan-and-scan on television. Have a heart! In fact, technically speaking none of these films qualifies as true 'Scope: *Oliver!* is Panavision, *My Fair Lady* is Super Panavision 70 and *Kiss Me Kate*, though announced as CinemaScope, was filmed and released in 3-D.

12 Again, I am well aware Marlon Brando was not in the original Broadway cast of *Guys and Dolls* and that he only played Sky Masterson in the movie. There was no commercial release of the film soundtrack available at this time, owing to a contractual dispute about which record company owned the rights to Frank Sinatra's vocal performances. I merely wished to make a cheap jibe at the expense of the late Marlon Brando, while drawing your attention to my own bell-like singing voice. Don't miss the audiobook! P.S. *Guys and Dolls* was shot in CinemaScope.

Teenage boys of my generation graduated to adult reading through the gory horror thrills of James Herbert or the thrilling Nazi gore of Sven Hassel. I, on the other hand, mooched about in my customary gloomy place, sometimes with humour – Douglas Adams, David Nobbs – and sometimes without – Graham Greene, George Orwell. *The Hitchhiker's Guide to the Galaxy*, *The Fall and Rise of Reginald Perrin*, *Our Man in Havana*, *Coming Up for Air*. Jokes or not, these were my comfort and my maps, one middle-age meltdown after another.

I first came to *Absolute Beginners* in 1984, when the book was probably at the peak of its popularity. Paul Weller was its most famous advocate, and his group The Jam had released a single with the same title.[13] A film was in production. It was one of those cult novels which, if you were sixteen as I was, you needed to have read.[14] I raced through it in a day, whilst on holiday with my parents in Scotland. Yeah! My body may have been on the car deck of a Caledonian MacBrayne ferry between Oban on the mainland and the historic Isle of Iona but my heart was in the jazz joints of 1950s Notting Hill – or Napoli as MacInnes had rechristened it. Dig!

I remember finishing it while sitting up on deck on the return crossing, oblivious to the Scottish summer gale that battered the boat. I had never been grabbed by a book in quite the way *Absolute Beginners* grabbed me (not even *Doctor Who and the Brain of Morbius*). It engaged me intellectually,

13 Paul Weller, like Morrissey, is someone with a single-minded loyalty to his teenage self. When he appeared on *Desert Island Discs* in 2007, aged 49, he chose *Absolute Beginners* as the book he would take with him to the desert island.

14 A British teenager's reading list in 1984 might typically consist of Orwell, *Brighton Rock*, *Brave New World* and the plays of Joe Orton, as well as the unofficial American set texts like *Catcher in the Rye*, *On the Road* and *Catch-22*.

emotionally – completely. I felt it spoke *to* me and *for* me. I have a photo of Mum and Dad I took on Iona that afternoon, standing in front of its medieval abbey. It is the last photograph of my childhood, my parents as I saw them when I was still the junior member of our small family (my father died the following year). When we got home, I was not the same. I was at long last a teenager; no, not a teenager – a young adult. I could see a path out of childhood.

So *Absolute Beginners* gave me an exit strategy, a teenage identity I could relate and aspire to. In the process, it liberated and liberalised me – awakened in me the nervous excitement of being young, on the brink, in the same way that great pop music does. At a stroke, it made me more tolerant towards difference of many kinds. It made me feel all right. It changed my life.

I read the book over and over again in late adolescence. Its spell never diminished. And then I went out into the world and forgot about it, let it become a memory. So when, in the dying months of my thirties, I re-read the book for the first time in twenty years, it turned me upside down all over again. Variously, I felt: homesick, elated, angry, exhilarated, righteous and all right. I felt vindicated. When I was sixteen, I knew where it was at.

I was working in West London. I had made a life in books. The company's office was in Ladbroke Grove, exactly where the novel is set; until recently, we had lived nearby with our young son. In the week I read the book again, the British National Party made significant gains in London at the local council elections. It was depressingly easy to transpose the 1950s race riots of the novel to the streets around me; their names, after all, had not changed. But the book didn't just draw a line between the present and the past (*my* present and *my* past), it made me feel they were happening simultaneously – a superimposing of the 1950s (the events of the book), the 1980s (me when I first read it), and my life in the twenty-first century, its likely future, a telescoped view of the whole ambiguous relationship between me and London and books.

'Every job I get, even the well-paid ones, denied me the two things I consider absolutely necessary for gracious living, namely – take out a pencil, please, and write them down – to work in your own time and not somebody else's, number one, and number two, even if you can't make big money every day, to have a graft that lets you make it sometime. It's terrible, in other words, to live entirely without hope'.

What, I asked myself, was the point of reading these books if all it was going to achieve was a succession of ticked boxes? What was it for? What was dangerous about reading dangerously unless you acted on it?

Albert Camus once wrote '*A man's work is nothing but this slow trek to rediscover through the detours of art, those two or three great and simple images in whose presence his heart first opened.*' The quote is emblazoned on the gatefold cover of Scott Walker's 1969 LP *Scott 4*, which is where I first encountered it. Walker is an artist who has moved forward incrementally, his bursts of noise and activity punctuated by ten-year silences while he waits for something new to say. In an interview published at the time of his last album, Walker was asked why he had so dramatically changed the style of his music in the late 1970s:

'I suddenly woke up . . . I'd acted in bad faith for so long I'd lost my heart for the world, sort of. I had to discover my life again, to just do it for me alone. So I made the decision: no more bad faith.'

Bad faith is what had happened to *Absolute Beginners* – the film turned out to be such a disaster it killed off interest in the book. Perhaps I was a victim of bad faith too. I had nearly killed the thing I love. I had forgotten the parquet floor, the boy sitting in the back seat or stretched out on his bed on a summer's day, lost and found in a good book. I needed to keep faith with those 'two or three great and simple images' and I needed to discover them again. I had to keep reading, wherever that took me. I had to move on.

Open your heart and dare to keep feeling fascination. See, Dad? I told you the Human League were good.

The following Monday morning, I boarded the 6.44am train with a renewed sense of purpose. In its own tiresome way, *One Hundred Years of Solitude* had reminded me, as *Absolute Beginners* had done, that we never know where inspiration might strike next nor in what guise. So far the List of Betterment had offered me glimpses of something bigger and better. It was up to me to keep looking for it, to push reality aside until I relocated the magic of reading – and no lousy magical realists were going to stand in my way.

I took off my coat and sat down. From my bag, I pulled *Don Quixote* – book twenty-seven. I had started reading again. This time I would not stop until the train came off the rails.

In 1979 we moved house, to another town and a new school. Our new library was acceptable, I suppose, despite being more welcoming and user-friendly than the old ones. There were still plenty of books in it, and not just books. This library contained a small selection of LPs for hire. The week after we moved into our new home, I borrowed *Sgt.*

*Pepper's Lonely Hearts Club Band* and the double blue album, the one that went from 1967 to The Beatles' break-up, and while Dad was at work, I played 'Strawberry Fields Forever' and 'I am the Walrus' over and over again, utterly enthralled in a way I did not recognise; whatever it was, these songs were alive and they spoke to me. Our new town also had a bookshop in it and, more significantly perhaps, a record shop. But that is another story.

The town where I live now has, for the time being, a bookshop, a record shop and a library too: use them or lose them, as the phrase goes. Of course, technology, cuts and supermarkets will ensure we lose all three eventually but we carry on using them regardless. The bookshop is a good one, the record shop can order what I want and although the library is more like a drop-in centre than a *sanctum sanctorum*, at least it is there, serving the community and its children. In Croydon, at the time of writing, to save a bit of money the local authority is trying to shut permanently the branches where my love of books flourished. If they succeed, presumably the council will heave the remaining stock into a skip and take a hammer to the precious parquet flooring, which they can then sell off block-by-block to incurable nostalgics like me. I do not want any of this to happen but life flows on, within you and without you.

My son likes books and we indulge him just as much as my parents indulged me. It is easy to do when you have a child who loves reading and when there are so many amazing new books out there: Michael Morpurgo, Jacqueline Wilson and *Wimpy Kid*; the absurd adventures of Mr Gum; *Harry Potter* and *His Dark Materials*; Varjak Paw, the mystic warrior cat; Patrick Ness and Philip Reeve; and the series I would have adored as a child, the morbid, hilarious and linguistically punctilious *A Series of Unfortunate Events* by Lemony

Snicket. Let's not be snotty about the gleeful boogerism of *Captain Underpants* or the fighting fantasy heroics of *Beast Quest* either. Alex polishes off each new instalment in the never-ending saga like I polished off *Doctor Who* books, stretched out on the bed or sitting in the back seat of the car while Mum and Dad go about their grown-up drudgeries. And, overlooking the part it played in her son's downfall, his grandmother has enrolled him in the rejuvenated Puffin Club, who will be delighted to receive yet another plug in a book that is not even published by Penguin.[15]

*Fig. 12: 'From the library of Alex Miller':*
*Puffin Club bookplate, circa 2012.*

15 Unbeknownst to Alex's grandmother, the rejuvenated Puffin Club was being operated by the Penguin Group, who had quietly outsourced it to the mail-order company The Book People on a three-year contract. In late 2012, this arrangement was abruptly terminated, with the result that the Puffin Club is once again on 'indefinite hiatus' while Penguin decide what to do with it. I tried to explain to a heartbroken Alex that the reason he wouldn't be receiving any more special bookplates, Puffin Posts or new books was because of the differing financial aims and expectations of the various parties involved in running the Puffin Club franchise in a rapidly-evolving marketplace. But he cried anyway.

As a child, reading is something you do while you are waiting for life to begin. As a parent, however, if you are lucky and you seize your chance, you can be part of it too. Last summer, while his mum was ill, Alex and I read *The Hobbit* together. Sometimes he read to me, mostly I read to him. I did Gandalf as Sir Ian McKellen and Bilbo as a sort of bouncy Roy Kinnear. My Gollum was a whispered triumph, *my precious - ss - ss*, while the dwarves seemed to hail from somewhere near Bristol via *Treasure Island* – it was difficult to pinpoint. And Smaug, the terrible dragon under the Lonely Mountain, the Great Worm coiled on his dragon-hoard of gold, spoke loudly and languorously in the unmistakable, rich baritone of the best Doctor Who, Tom Baker: *'I am armoured above and below with iron scales and hard gems. No blade can pierce me.'*

Thus, while it lasted, we held the world at bay. And we were sorry when it had to come to an end.

# III

'Mais ne lisez pas, comme les enfants lisent, pour vous amuser, ni comme les ambitieux lisent, pour vous instruire. Non, lisez pour vivre.'

'But do not read, as children read, for fun, or like the ambitious read, for training purposes. No, read for your life.'
Gustave Flaubert, letter to Mademoiselle Leroyer de<br>Chantepie, June 1857

We shall not cease from exploration
And the end of all our exploring
Will be to arrive where we started
And know the place for the first time.
T.S. Eliot, 'Little Gidding'

# Books 28, 29 and 31

*Beyond Black* by Hilary Mantel
*The Diary of a Nobody* by George and Weedon Grossmith
*The Mystery of Edwin Drood* by Charles Dickens

'April 27.–Painted the bath red, and was delighted with the result. Sorry to say Carrie was not, in fact we had a few words about it. She said I ought to have consulted her, and she had never heard of such a thing as a bath being painted red. I replied: "It's merely a matter of taste."'

*The Diary of a Nobody*

'Nutmeg graters. Toby jugs. Decorative pincushions with all the pins still in. She had a coffee table with a glass top and a repeat motif of The Beatles underneath, printed on wallpaper – it must have been an heirloom. She had original Pyrex oven dishes with pictures of carrots and onions on the side. She had a Spanish lady with a flouncy skirt that you sat on top of your spare loo roll. I used to run to her house when I wanted to go to the toilet because there was always some bloke wanking in ours.'

*Beyond Black*

'"I have no objection to discuss it. I trust, my dear, I am always open to discussion." There was a vibration in the old lady's cap, as though she internally added: "and I should like to see the discussion that would change *my* mind!"'

The Mystery of Edwin Drood

On a beautiful day in late June, the sun sparkling on the lively breakers of Viking Bay, my companions and I followed the Grand Parade from the Pierremont War Memorial to Victoria Gardens on the seafront. Ahead of us strolled Little Nell, Oliver Twist, Mister Micawber and a fierce-looking dog in an England football shirt, for this was the gala opening of the annual Broadstairs Dickens Festival and all were welcome.

According to my souvenir programme, Dickens visited Broadstairs regularly from 1837 until his extended stay in 1851 when he christened the town 'Our English Watering Place'. In 1936, the centenary of *The Pickwick Papers*, an adaptation of 'Pickwick' was staged by local residents. The following year, 1937, it was repeated as the centrepiece of a small festival celebrating the centenary of Dickens' first visit to the town. '*Under the guidance of Gladys Waterer and Dora Tattam who lived in Dickens House,*' continued my programme, '*the Festival grew and with the exception of the war years has been held annually ever since. In the 1950s costumed Dickensians around the town added colour to the Festival.*' Now football-shirted dogs had been admitted to the Grand Parade, as they have been to all public events in England in the twenty-first century, lining up beside the Queen at the Cenotaph on Remembrance Sunday and, memorably, in 2012, carrying the Olympic Torch on the final leg of its journey, like a juicy, flaming bone. This is what Gladys Waterer and Dora Tattam might have wanted, and if they didn't, they should have done. All right?!

'*Come to Broadstairs*!' urged Dickens in letters to his friends. '*Come to Broadstairs! Come now*!' As Claire Tomalin makes clear in her recent biography, being a friend of Dickens could be exhausting. He was a demanding and irrepressible host, perpetually summoning members of his entourage to dine alongside him, listen to him read, stage impromptu theatricals, play billiards till dawn, stride with him for miles across the Kentish fields, campaign vigorously for constitutional reform, tour the workhouses, inspect the morgues, laugh uproariously, weep unrestrainedly and, if they were still breathing, come to Broadstairs.

Broadstairs was still showing its gratitude 150 years later, not just for one week in June but all the year round, in the names of the shops and businesses which lined the route of the parade: the Dickens House Museum, of course, but also Peggoty's Café, Copperfields Restaurant, The Old Curiosity Shop (bric-a-brac), Plate Expectations (crockery), Tidy Tim (barber), Gamps (pre-school nursery) and Barnaby Fudge (fudge). We passed all these – all save the ones I have just made up – as the procession wound its way down the hill to the bandstand on the seafront. There we were heartily welcomed by a town crier and, on a makeshift stage in front of a marquee selling arts and crafts, treated to two short extracts from *Hard Times*, that year's Festival Play. And then a rather diffident 'Charles Dickens' stood up from his writing desk at the side of the stage and asked if there was anyone here present from his various books, from *Great Expectations* or *A Christmas Carol* or *Nicholas Nickleby*, at which point 'Miss Havisham' and 'Jacob Marley's Ghost' and 'Smike' made themselves known, each expressing a few words of appreciation to their creator, seemingly oblivious to the desperate lives or afterlives he had bestowed on them. The sun shone, the audience applauded, ice cream was endemic. It was the best of times.

It was hard to think of another author British people might celebrate in this manner; Shakespeare certainly, perhaps Austen or the Brontës, but that was about all. The British still love Dickens, even if they have never read him.[1] No writer has ever produced such a cornucopia of archetypes and oddballs, so many of whom endure in the popular imagination. His characters are larger than life and so was he, to the extent that here in Broadstairs, it seemed natural for 'Charles Dickens' to share a stage with Mr Pickwick, Scrooge, the Artful Dodger and all the rest. As a writer-celebrity, Charles Dickens was as much his own creation as they were, the hero of his own life and beyond, and the public cannot forget him.

Inevitably, however, some characters loom larger than others. There seemed to be no one in the crowd representing the less cherished works like *Martin Chuzzlewit* or *Barnaby Rudge*, and there was definitely nobody standing up for Dickens' final, unfinished novel *The Mystery of Edwin Drood*. Unless you counted me. This was where Betterment had led me: back to Broadstairs and back to Boz. I was currently in the thick of *The Mystery of Edwin Drood*, the only Dickens novel I had never read. It was, as expected, fantastic.

Since the stumble over *One Hundred Years of Solitude*, Betterment had proceeded steadily and without serious incident. I had started keeping a blog, noting my thoughts and impressions of the books as I went. The decision to read *Drood* at this point was, I admit, partly inspired by forthcoming

1 'The Dickensian thing is to us what the Western is to America. Just as it's their brave new frontier which defines America culturally, for England it's the Victorian era. And since that time we've been kind of relegated and degraded and decaying.' Russell Brand, interview, *Daily Telegraph*.

events in Broadstairs but also, having successfully completed thirty books, I wanted to try something more obscure by a writer I already liked and whose work I was fluent in. Dickens seemed an obvious candidate. I had read nearly all the major novels and had studied him at university. He was a local author. And I approved of his populist streak – no one will ever take to the streets of Hampstead dressed as their favourite character from Margaret Drabble.

(I say I had chosen *Drood* because it was the only Dickens novel I had never read. Of course, this is not entirely accurate. It was the only Dickens novel with which I was *entirely unfamiliar*. In truth, I could not remember if had read *Martin Chuzzlewit* and *Barnaby Rudge* or not; if I had, it was a long time ago; equally, the little I knew of those books might have been gleaned from academic hearsay or the Sunday teatime classic serial. But I definitely knew nothing of *Drood*, if only because, being unfinished, it defied easy TV adaptation.[2] So there was that. And although I felt confident I had never lied directly about having read *Drood*, at some point I had almost certainly expressed genuine enthusiasm for Dickens by claiming to have read 'everything' by him, as one does – as one tries not to.)

The populism of Dickens – by which I mean not only his shameless playing to the gallery as a novelist and performer but also the fact that he was so successful at it – has long represented a kind of barrier to his reputation as a first-rate writer. Can someone so populist *and* popular really be as good as all that? Certain critics cavil at his humour, his sentimentality, his didacticism, his grotesquerie, his *'chaste lovers and his puritanical heroines in their all-concealing draperies,*

2 The BBC finally produced a solid adaptation of *The Mystery of Edwin Drood* in 2012 to mark the bicentenary of Dickens' birth.

*sharing ethereal passions and just fluttering their eyelashes, blushing coyly, weeping for joy and holding hands'.*[3] Virginia Woolf, while acknowledging his greatness, classed him with Tolstoy as 'the preachers and the teachers', in contrast to Austen and Turgenev, who were 'the pure artists'. To some, Dickens represents something regrettably provincial, suburban and middlebrow in the English cultural identity. And certainly, the Broadstairs Dickens Festival could be regarded as all these things; but it was also sincere and welcoming and unpretentious. It was a world away from Bloomsbury.

The festivities were drawing to a close for the time being, so we decided to repair to the nearest public house, the Charles Dickens (*'Visit us during Dickens Week and your "Great Expectations" will become reality!!'*). Inside, the Australian bar staff were all dressed up in period costume, bustles and stovepipe hats. They did not appear perturbed by this, probably because all Australians enjoy being hot.

'What can I get ya?' asked a cheerful barman in gaiters and cardboard sideburns.

While I sipped at my pewter tankard of foaming porter – all right then, half a cider – I considered two of the books which had preceded *The Mystery of Edwin Drood* in my reading. Hilary Mantel's *Beyond Black*, an idiosyncratic alliance of ghost story and black farce, was located in the middle England where most people live yet which is seldom written about sympathetically by the literary novelists, whose minds are on higher planes and more rarefied places:

'Colette joined Alison in those days when the comet Hale-Bopp, like God's shuttlecock, blazed over the market towns and dormitory suburbs, over the playing

3 J.-K. Huysmans, *Against Nature*.

fields of Eton, over the shopping malls of Oxford, over the traffic-crazed towns of Woking and Maidenhead: over the choked slip roads and the junctions of the M4, over the superstores and out-of-town carpet warehouses, the nurseries and prisons, the gravel pits and sewage works, and the green fields of the home counties shredded by JCBs.'

Suburbia, in other words; my heartland. So *Beyond Black* had had a head start.

The other book represented something of a dilemma. It too was a book about suburbia, perhaps the most influential book about suburbia – *The Diary of a Nobody* by George and Weedon Grossmith.[4] Its hero, Charles Pooter of the Laurels, Brickfield Terrace, Holloway, was so amusingly sketched, so palpable, that his name is in the dictionary representing an entire class of suburban, small-minded bore: '**Pooterish**, *adj., characteristic of or resembling the fictional character Pooter, esp. in being bourgeois, genteel, or self-important.*' Novelists, newspaper editors and sitcom writers from *The Good Life* to *Peep Show* owe the Grossmiths a profound debt of gratitude, and probably royalties.

What was the dilemma? It was this: I could not decide if it was acceptable to like the book or not. I knew I liked it but I was not sure if I ought to. On the one hand, *The Diary of a Nobody* is riddled with the authors' snobbery and class-hatred – I am referring to the Grossmith brothers, not Pooter. On the other, the book is funny, humane and true. But is its longevity wholly due to the latter fine qualities? Are we laughing at Charles Pooter and his successors or

4 *The Diary of a Nobody* is generally thought to have been written by George Grossmith alone, with his brother contributing ideas and the illustrations.

with them?[5] Personally, I rarely use the term 'Pooterish' unless I am applying it to myself. It only ever seems to be deployed as an insult.

*The Diary of a Nobody* first appeared in instalments in the humour magazine *Punch*, where it was swiftly and widely acclaimed. On one level, the Grossmiths had minted an instant cultural icon, the original Alan Partridge or David Brent. On another, though, they were simply putting a comic spin on one of the prevailing themes of late nineteenth and early twentieth-century arts and letters: the sheer awfulness of the plebs. As lovingly described by John Carey in his book *The Intellectuals and the Masses*, several generations of writers and artists, from H.G. Wells and E.M. Forster to modernists like T.S. Eliot or Virginia Woolf, even Orwell, were horrified by the swarming middle-classes, the jumped-up clerks and opinionated shop girls with ideas above their station, and pursued the topic at length in their essays, novels and poetry. How they loathed us, with our little patch of garden, our packed commuter trains, our despicable, belching crematoria – even when we die, they must suck our greasy ashes into their plutocratic lungs. The intellectual's distaste for suburbia persists. We are *middle England*; we live in laughable towns like Surbiton, Slough and Croydon; we are literally sub-urban.[6]

5 This distinction may be demonstrated by two differing adaptations of *The Diary of a Nobody*. The 2007 BBC TV series is a definite case of 'laughing at' the character: Hugh Bonneville's Pooter comes across as vulgar and risible. Compare this with the sublime reading given by Arthur Lowe for BBC radio in the 1970s. His Pooter is pompous, hilarious and a recognisable human being to boot. We may recall that Arthur Lowe was not only famous for playing the Pooterish – excuse me – Captain Mainwaring in *Dad's Army* but also worked with left-ish filmmakers like Lindsay Anderson (*The White Bus, If . . ., O Lucky Man!*) and Peter Medak (*The Ruling Class*). 6 Clever wording, cheers. I think I may have stolen this phrase from Simon Munnery's comedy sloganeer Alan Parker, Urban Warrior; he intended it as satire. Perhaps we should move to reclaim the word Pooter

In Chapter 20 of *The Diary of a Nobody*, Mr and Mrs Charles Pooter are invited to a dinner in Peckham in honour of Mr Hardfur Huttle, *'a very clever writer for the American papers'* with, Pooter observes, *'an amazing eloquence that made his unwelcome opinions positively convincing'*:

'I shall never forget the effect the words, "happy medium," had upon him *[i.e. Huttle]*. He was brilliant and most daring in his interpretation of the words. He positively alarmed me. He said something like the following: "Happy medium, indeed. Do you know 'happy medium' are two words which mean 'miserable mediocrity'? . . . The happy medium means respectability, and respectability means insipidness. Does it not, Mr Pooter?"

I was so taken aback by being personally appealed to, that I could only bow apologetically, and say I feared I was not competent to offer an opinion.'

I recognise Pooter's hot flush of panic at being ambushed like this. When Huttle brashly concludes that the *'happy medium . . . will spend the rest of his days in a suburban villa with a stucco-column portico, resembling a four-post bedstead'*, his suburban captive audience takes the only available course of action: *'We all laughed.'*

Three brief observations. Firstly, this is meticulous comic writing, perfectly balanced and socially acute. Secondly, people with unwelcome opinions – journalists like Hardfur Huttle – will always be with us. Finally, these people expect

from the anti-suburban haters. Might it be possible for sneered-at suburbanites to start referring to themselves with pride as 'Pootaz With Attitude'? *Straight Outta Croydon*, it takes a handful of people to hold us back, etc.

us to laugh at ourselves, and we usually oblige them. We are nothing if not polite.

Happy medium, middle England, middlebrow: all names for the same unfortunate tendency. *'The middlebrow,'* wrote Virginia Woolf, *'is the man, or woman, of middlebred intelligence who ambles and saunters now on this side of the hedge, now on that, in pursuit of no single object, neither art itself nor life itself, but both mixed indistinguishably, and rather nastily, with money, fame, power, or prestige.'*[7] She must be turning in her family plot. According to academic commentators like David Carter, the middlebrow is undergoing an unprecedented 'contemporary resurgence', evidenced by the booming popularity of festivals, literary prizes, online discussion and, yes, lists of the greatest books of all time. By sheer weight of numbers, the plebs appear to have gained the upper hand at last. And nothing exemplifies their triumph more than the irresistible rise of the reading group.

Sitting in the Charles Dickens pub with my cider, I set aside my copy of *Edwin Drood* and pulled the local paper out of my bag. On the train on the way over, one story had caught my eye. Under the headline **Book group will avoid the highbrow chat**, it ran as follows:

IF YOU have ever been tempted by the idea of joining a book club but put off by the thought of highbrow discussions, the town's latest group could be for you. A club meets at the Umbrella Centre each month to discuss literature – but you don't even have to read the book to take part. Organiser Liz W. said the idea was to have fun and make new friends. 'We choose books that are easy to read, and that have been made

7 From 'Middlebrow', *The Death of the Moth* (Hogarth Press, 1947).

into films so you don't even have to read if you don't want to,' she said. 'It should be fun and it's as much about socialising as it is about the books.' The group was set up after people complained they felt intimidated by groups held in people's houses. It particularly welcomes male members.

At the end of the piece there was a contact phone number. Fortunately, I was already a member of a book group otherwise I might have been tempted to join. It sounded mind-boggling yet somehow inevitable: a book group where you didn't have to read the book. Wherever she lies, Virginia Woolf must be punching herself in the face.

I had decided to join a book group after the crisis of confidence brought on by *Absolute Beginners* and *One Hundred Years of Solitude*. It might do me good to be more outward-looking, contemporary and sociable in my reading, I thought. A friend in the town told me that his group had just lost someone and a vacancy had come up. This group was almost the opposite of the one described in the local paper – it met once a month in people's houses, the chat aimed to be serious and, in an old-fashioned way, members did actually have to read the book. It may not have been everyone's idea of fun but it was certainly mine. The group was called Sparta B.C. (book club), which reflected both a sense of discipline and asceticism, and also its founder's enthusiasm for The Fall's 'Theme From Sparta F.C.'.

'We mostly read modern fiction,' said my friend. 'Last month we read *Atomised* – you know, the Houellebecq book. Some people *hated* it.'

Houellebecq's on my list, I said. Count me in.

Unusually for a book group – for anything called Sparta – there were as many female Spartans as there were male, which appealed to me. A fraternity was not what I was seeking.[8] They were a friendly bunch, enthusiastic and opinionated, comprising a solicitor, a creative-writing student, a carpenter, a singing teacher and three psychotherapists.

I was fortunate to have stumbled on a mixed group. The majority of reading groups are all-female – according to some surveys, perhaps as many as 90 per cent. Correspondingly, there is a measure of snobbery directed against them as both intellectually feeble and the modern equivalent of coffee mornings or knitting circles, what the academic Beth Driscoll calls the 'feminized middlebrow'.[9] It is demonstrably sexist to define all reading groups as dumb and girly and little more than an excuse to sit around gossiping about kids, schools, shopping, etc. And yet how can we square that with the group advertising for members in my local paper – *you don't even have to read the book* – or with this tweet which was posted yesterday by one local mum?

---

8 Why do so many men yearn to spend time with one another exclusively – lads' nights, down the pub, up the steam-baths? When I look back on my life, I wish I had spent more time in the company of women, not less.

9 Driscoll cites several examples of the 'gendered ridicule' of book groups, from the nineteenth century through to *Desperate Housewives*: '*The reading practices of contemporary reading groups are particularly susceptible to characterization as middlebrow. Book clubs are middle-class institutions, part of the middle-class package of values that includes education and self-improvement . . . These members are overwhelmingly women.*' ('*Not the normal kind of chicklit'? Richard & Judy and the Feminized Middlebrow* by Beth Driscoll, in *The Richard & Judy Book Club Reader* edited by Jenni Ramone and Helen Cousins.) It should be noted that although the word 'middlebrow' retains many of its pejorative connotations in everyday usage, it is a respectable term in the groves of academia. Please see the rather marvellous Middlebrow Network (www.middlebrow-network.com) for numerous examples from across the spectrum of opinion, not least this 1925 definition of the term from *Punch* magazine, home of Mr Pooter: '*The BBC claim to have discovered a new type, the "middlebrow". It consists of people who are hoping that some day they will get used to the stuff they ought to like.*'

*Book club tonight = quick chat about book + long chat about school / children / work / family / gossip + wine, yipee!* (sic) Or, more generally, with the graffito scribbled in marker pen on the wall of the nearest bookshop: **BOOK ARE FOR WIMPZ**? (To which the reply must be, yes, but at least we can string a sentence together.) That's the trouble with stereotypes: they are not wholly disconnected from the truth.

The first few Sparta meetings were agreeably Spartan, in a twenty-first-century middle-English kind of way. There was red wine; the crisps were burnished with paprika and sea-salt. There was small talk about schools and children. And there was gladiatorial combat governed by an ancient and binding set of rules of behaviour. It was terrible and civilised and *all terribly civilised* – an all-in orgy of all-out passive aggro. You needed to keep your wits about you. In the beginning, I enjoyed it.

However, disenchantment crept in during a discussion of *Cakes and Ale* by Somerset Maugham. This was not the one with the waitress but a different book entirely. In *Of Human Bondage*, the lower-class strumpet who turns the hero's head is called Mildred, and you will recall that she is thin and anaemic. But in *Cakes and Ale*, the lower-class strumpet who turns the hero's head is plump and rosy-cheeked; Maugham dug deep for a name and came up with 'Rosie'. Mildred is younger than the protagonist of *Of Human Bondage*, who in later life leaves his small Kent town to become a successful author rather like Somerset Maugham; whereas in *Cakes and Ale*, Rosie is older than the protagonist, though this does not materially affect his decision to leave his small Kent town and become a Maugham-ish author in later life too. There was one major difference between the books, however. Although *Cakes and Ale* shared many of the themes and preoccupations of *Of Human Bondage*, it had the considerable advantage of being hundreds of pages shorter. But when I expressed this opinion to the group, I was taken aback that several people – gulp – disagreed with me. Specifically, two of the women of Sparta felt I had completely misjudged 'her', i.e. Rosie. They seemed offended, as though it was the character itself, and by extension all women like 'her', that was causing me problems, rather than the patronising way in which 'she' had been written by the chauvinistic Maugham. I'm on your side, I wanted to say, but I seemed unable to make myself understood. I went home fuming – as, I'm sure, did they.

After a sleepless night and several days of running through the contretemps in my mind, I concluded that the fault was entirely mine. I had not wanted to read *Cakes and Ale* and had probably done so in bad faith, with the result that I had channelled all my petulance into expressing a dislike for the book, a dislike which of course had been inevitable, with a vehemence that must have seemed like exasperation with the person who had chosen it. Inadvertently, I had made it personal. The alternative explanation was simply that I had been wrong about *Cakes and Ale*. But that was absurd.

When my turn came to make a selection for the group, I decided I needed a book about which I could be entirely positive and eloquent and which could not be misconstrued in any way. I chose *Beyond Black*. The story was strong, the subject matter was accessible, if a little quirky, the setting was familiar and the quality of Hilary Mantel's prose was beyond reproach. I could vouch for all this because I had read the book for Betterment, but if my fellow Spartans did not entirely trust me, they could always take the word of Philip Pullman, Helen Dunmore, Fay Weldon or any of the twenty or so rave reviews reproduced on the paperback cover and across several fly pages – *'wonderfully funny'*, *'laceratingly observant'*, *'pins elusive Middle England to the page'*, *'an illuminating study of what can happen when you try to confront the past with honest choices made in the present'*.[10] And if none of that worked, at the back was a brief explicatory interview with Hilary Mantel and a set of notes for reading groups. I eagerly awaited the next meeting when everyone would thank me for introducing them to such a wonderful novel and I would be forgiven for whatever it was I had misunderstood about *Cakes and Ale* – i.e. nothing.

What actually happened was this. I could not get back from London in time for the meeting, so I missed it. A few days later, I bumped into one of the psychotherapists in the high street. Sorry I couldn't make it, I said, work stuff. How did it go?

The psychotherapist rubbed his chin. I think we needed you to be there, he said.

Why? I asked.

No one could understand why you'd chosen it, he replied. There didn't seem much to it.

And before I could stop him, he told me everything they felt was wrong with the book. It seemed rather lightweight. It wasn't funny. The plotting was obscure, the characters unsympathetic. And wasn't the author sneering at suburbia? It just seemed strange that you would choose a book like that.

Right, I said. I see.

Well, see you next month, said the psychotherapist cheerfully. And off he went.

The first and second rules of Fight Club should also

10 *Spectator, Independent, Observer* and *Time Out.*

apply to Book Club, I know that. However, I must speak out. *Beyond Black* quickly became a Sparta running joke. Whenever it came up in conversation, people rolled their eyes or tutted and chuckled. Every month, however ponderous the choice of book, however po-faced or flimsy it might be, there was always one quality to recommend it: it wasn't *Beyond Black*. But I never wavered in my belief that *Beyond Black* was, and is, a *glorious* novel, and that all the other members of my reading group were wrong. To Hilary Mantel, I apologise; I hope repeatedly winning the Man Booker allows you to put this unfortunate incident behind you. To my fellow Spartans, I do not apologise; I hope Hilary Mantel repeatedly winning the Man Booker goes some way to showing you the error of your ways.

The flawed logic at the heart of the book group process runs as follows. Everyone is entitled to their opinion. All opinions carry equal weight. But opinions will invariably differ. Of these, some will be judged to be wrong. Yet if all opinions carry equal weight and everyone is entitled to a wrong opinion, what is the use of being right? The best that one can hope for is a happy medium. Or to express that as an equation: book club = quick chat about book + long chat about school / children / work / family / gossip + wine. Yipee! (sic).

Let's say I was wrong about *Cakes and Ale*, which I wasn't, and they were wrong about *Beyond Black*, which they were. What had either party gained from having their enjoyment in these books challenged? An argument and a sleepless night. Worse, the pleasure each had taken in their book had been diminished by the experience of discussing it with people who didn't enjoy it – in the case of *Beyond Black*, for months to come. No committee was going to change that.

When it came down to it, where was our common

ground? We were not academics. We were not friends. Our jobs allowed occasional professional insights into the books – our group was especially adept at psychological profiling – but these were usually more anecdotal than illuminating. Where we came together was in how the books made us feel, which characters we identified with, and so on: the feminised middlebrow in action. But I did not join a book group to talk about my feelings. I wanted to talk about books: how they fit together, why they worked, the occasional miracle of fiction. This is not the perspective of an emotionally-repressed male. I love talking about my feelings, as my wife will wearily attest. However, I did not require a book group to help me do it, even one with three psychotherapists in it.

I came to the conclusion that I was probably not cut out for the reading group experience. It was not the fault of the solicitor, the creative-writing student, the carpenter, the singing teacher or any of the three psychotherapists, not even the Jungian. It was me. As an editor and writer, I was overqualified.

I did not reach this conclusion immediately and it may surprise the reader to learn that I remained a proud Spartan for almost three years, longer than some marriages, though no less bloody. There were happy times. There were bad patches. I learned to spot the types of story each member liked and tried to tailor my views so as to cause the minimum of offence. When the break came, we remained on good terms. I enjoyed hanging out with them. They became my friends, *dammit*. But the truth is I never once changed my mind about a book because of anything said in one of our meetings. I looked at *Cakes and Ale* again before writing this chapter. I still think it's rotten.

On a sunny day in Broadstairs, however, I saw no shadow

of a parting. At the Charles Dickens, I finished my drink, shouldered my bag and stepped out into the afternoon sunshine. The Dickensians had fanned out through the town and were standing on corners or promenading by the bandstand. Up ahead, Mister Micawber had fainted in the heat and was being attended at the roadside by the St John's Ambulance. I wonder how my lot would get on with *Edwin Drood*, I thought, as I climbed the hill back to the railway station. A novel without an ending; that could be fun.

So when my turn came around again, I nominated *The Mystery of Edwin Drood*. And although there was a smaller turnout than usual, the singing teacher was there and the carpenter and one of the psychotherapists, and they had all managed to finish the book just as much as its author had. We interrogated Drood's unexplained disappearance, the true nature of John Jasper's guilt, the incongruousness of Dick Datchery's mismatched white hair and black eyebrows. We marvelled at Dickens' spectacular, grandiloquent sentences and opioid, elephantine imagery – '*white elephants caparisoned in countless gorgeous colours, and infinite in number and attendants*'. We speculated as to the identity of the murderer, or if a murder had even been committed. We found little or nothing we could relate to our day-to-day lives, which was fine. We drank a lot and we laughed a lot. We had a great time. All we talked about was the book.

The following day, head still pounding, I wrote it all up on my new blog. The blog was partly a rolling progress report on the List of Betterment and partly, like the book group, an attempt to be outward-looking, contemporary and sociable – communal reading with people I did not know and planned never to meet. If all went well, I thought, my diary might become as widely read and admired as that of my suburban ancestor – *Hypocrite lecteur, – mon semblable, – mon frère!*

Why should I not publish my diary? I have often seen reminiscences of people I have never even heard of, and I fail to see – because I do not happen to be a 'Somebody' – why my diary should not be interesting. My only regret is that I did not commence it when I was a youth.

CHARLES POOTER

The Laurels,
   Brickfield Terrace,
      Holloway.

# Books 41 and 42

*The Essential Silver Surfer, Vol. 1* by Stan Lee, Jack Kirby, John Buscema

*Krautrocksampler: One Head's Guide to the Great Kosmische Musik – 1968 Onwards* by Julian Cope

'AND YET . . . WHAT IS **THAT** . . . AHEAD OF ME . . ? . . . WHAT FANTASTIC **RELIC** OF A BYGONE AGE HAVE I STUMBLED ONTO?'

*The Silver Surfer #1*

'"Father Cannot Yell" was a fascinating and fruitful exercise that T.S. Eliot would have been proud of. In his essay "The Metaphysical Poets", Eliot chided the establishment for always seeing similarities between artists as negative. Why, he asked, was it not possible to return to the ancient bardic perspective that happily accepted the apprentice's use of his master's blueprint? Only in acceptance of what had gone before could he himself truly move on. Can certainly proved this on *Monster Movie*.'

*Krautrocksampler*

The summer passed in a haze of *Jane Eyre, Wide Sargasso Sea, On the Road, American Psycho, Under the Volcano, The Epic of Gilgamesh* . . . I persevered and as I persevered, I blogged.

I showered some books with superlatives and others with brickbats. Occasionally, someone out there would respond to one of my posts with a superlative or brickbat of their own. I would try to reply in an easy, chatty manner but my heart wasn't in it. The more time I spent writing the blog, the less there was for reading. Also, I wasn't being paid.

In early September, shortly after summarising *Paradise Lost* in two words which weren't even mine – *'mostly harmless'* – I came across the worst sentence from the worst paragraph from the worst great book on the List of Betterment so far:

> 'Three feet from me rocked two young men engaged
> in a passionate, deep-throated kiss. I felt as if I had
> been half-slammed, half-caressed in the belly with a
> slippery bagful of wet cunts.'

The book was *The Dice Man* by Luke Rhinehart. Why, I asked myself, was I stopping to gawp at the phrase *I felt as if I had been half-slammed, half-caressed in the belly with a slippery bagful of wet cunts*? What was the purpose of interrogating the total ugliness of this sentence publicly? It was transparently, self-evidently terrible. Just reading it made me feel as if I had been half-slammed, half-caressed in the brain with a gratuitously offensive and ineptly articulated metaphor. It would be better to turn the page and hurry swiftly along – nothing to see here. So I suspended the blog.[1]

Maybe for some readers keeping a blog expedited the

1 Edited highlights of this blog are available to read via my website at mill-i-am.com or as 'bonus content' in the ebook edition of *The Year of Reading Dangerously*. I am told my thoughts on *The Epic of Gilgamesh* represent a strong 'incentive to purchase'. Hmm.

thought process. I'm sorry to say I found it a distraction and, as time went on, a chore. Once again, it was something that was almost, but not quite, entirely unlike reading. You stayed alert for the dominant themes, the telling phrases, about which you could opine wittily but, once you'd found the hook, engagement with the text went no further than it needed to in order to produce copy on time and in good order. Take *American Psycho*, for example. It occurred to me quite early on that it could be read as a critique of the type of alt. consumerism I had enjoyed pinning on *On the Road* a few weeks earlier. As a result, I focused not on the book *as a whole* but on applying my initial conception of *American Psycho* to what remained, i.e. the bulk of it, and on how best to make this observation on the blog. But the pleasure lay in the thought rather than the expression. Also – and this bears repeating – I wasn't being paid.

No one but a blockhead ever wrote except for money, said Doctor Johnson, and for centuries this held true. But in the Internet age, where comment is free and everyone is entitled to a wrong opinion, blockheads write zealously, copiously and for nothing. They have a platform unprecedented in human history. The problem faced by 'old media', and professional critics in particular, with their years of experience and their skill in fine phrase-making, is that their opinions now carry little more worth than those of the individual with a laptop who has never read any books and who would not recognise a pleasing and insightful cadence if it half-slammed, half-caressed them in the belly with a slippery bagful – well, you know how it goes by now.

You might think I would be happy at the rise of bloggers, non-professional critics beholden to no one. But haven't you got it yet? I'm never happy. Somebody once described the Internet as a library where all the books have been taken off the shelves and dumped in the middle of the floor. Disorganisation, however, is not the issue. The Internet is the greatest library in the universe; unfortunately someone has removed all the 'no talking' signs.

Happily, the next title on the List was *The Essential Silver Surfer, Vol. 1*. With the blog on hold, here was a book I could enjoy without having to worry about what I might write about it later or what anybody else might think. There were lots of exciting pictures to look at too. *The Essential Silver Surfer, Vol. 1* was a compilation of issues #1 to #18 of the 1960s Marvel comic. Bibliographically, it qualified as a graphic novel, in as much as it told an evolving story and was bound between paper covers, but like *The Mystery of Edwin Drood*, *The Essential Silver Surfer, Vol. 1* was a novel without a conclusion – Marvel had abruptly cancelled the comic after issue #18.

*The Silver Surfer* has all the hallmarks of the so-called 'Silver Age' of comic-books with which Marvel is synonymous: iconic heroes and villains, spectacular draughtsmanship, dynamic story-telling. As a child, I had always liked the character of the Surfer. With his cosmic powers (aka the Power Cosmic), his sleek, space-age appearance and his zippy, surfboard-like mode of transportation, the Silver Surfer – *SKY-RIDER OF THE SPACEWAYS!* – was a regular guest in other Marvel titles like *The Amazing Spider-Man* and *The Fantastic Four*. I had a few of the original *Silver Surfer* comics in my collection but I had never had an opportunity to enjoy an uninterrupted run of his solo adventures until now.

As a book, however, *The Essential Silver Surfer, Vol. 1* proved a bit of a letdown. It was printed in cheapo black and white when the original artwork had been in colour; and the vintage advertisements had been left out, so there were no

Hostess Twinkies, Sea Monkeys or pictorials for BB rifles *'just like Dad's'*. Also, read as chapters in a book, one after another in quick succession, the underlying formula of *The Silver Surfer* comics showed through rather too plainly. Norrin Radd, aka the Silver Surfer, has been exiled to Earth by his former master and creator Galactus.[2] He zooms around feeling sorry for himself on a flying surfboard powered by cosmic self-pity. Sometimes he tries, and fails, to break through the invisible barrier Galactus has placed around the Earth. Typically, he encounters some big-headed maniac who intends to destroy the planet. The Surfer battles and defeats them, often at considerable risk to his own life, but is mankind grateful? It is not. Mankind makes existence yet more intolerable for our argentine hero by shooting at him with rifles, missiles, etc. Cue much soliloquising from

*Fig. 13: The wrong type of Silver Surfer.*

2 If *FANTASTIC FOUR #50* PASSED YOU BY, YOU'LL HAVE TO TAKE MY *WORD* THIS IS WHAT HAPPENED! THE TALE IS TOO *TWISTY* TO RE-TELL HERE! NUFF SAID! – ANFRACTUOUS ANDY.

the Surfer, who at such moments likes to refer to himself in the third person and shunt his verbs to the end of each clause, about how much happier on his home world Zenn-La would the Silver Surfer be, how much his girlfriend Shalla Bal the Silver Surfer misses, and generally how by no one is the Silver Surfer understood. With the benefit of hindsight, the Silver Surfer was less a sky-rider of the spaceways and more a syntactically-confused adolescent with a martyr complex, which is probably exactly why he so strongly to the young Andy Miller appealed.

As Norrin Radd rediscovered in every issue of *The Silver Surfer*, you can't go home again. Reading these comics as an adult was an act of nostalgia. They were overwrought to the point of kitsch. And yet, and yet . . . there was still something magical about them. The kinetic artwork had lost none of its impact and the stories were ambitious to a fault. Across forty hand-inked, incident-filled pages, plus ads, they dealt with topics such as the arms race, the black power struggle, the fundamentals of metaphysics and the descent of man. On several occasions, the Surfer is pitched against Satan himself (e.g. issue #9, October 1969, *TO STEAL THE SURFER'S SOUL!*), although for reasons of religious sensitivity and copyright-infringement, Satan goes by the name Mephisto, Monarch of Evil. It was a pop-art *Paradise Lost*.[3]

---

3 Co-creator Jack Kirby's original vision was of the Surfer as the Fallen Angel and Galactus as an Old Testament Jehovah. Under writer Stan Lee's direction, the character more closely resembles another religious archetype, the Wandering Jew. The pioneers of the comics industry, many of whom were Jewish, are the subject of Michael Chabon's novel *The Amazing Adventures of Kavalier & Clay* and Chabon has said that the character of Joe Kavalier was partly inspired by Jack Kirby. I must read that book, it sounds every bit as fascinating as I keep telling people it is.

Perhaps because I could still relate to the character of a troubled loner with special powers, I was able to forgive *The Silver Surfer* a lot. He could be mawkish and gauche, and clumsily did the Surfer himself express, but this was how I'd felt as a child and occasionally still felt as an adult. Whatever their flaws, I had found the comics at the right moment in life and they had stayed with me, in the same way *Absolute Beginners* had. Perhaps if I had encountered Dean Moriarty – another restless wanderer with grammar issues – at an impressionable age I could have been more forgiving of *On the Road*. But that moment was long gone and, with no choice but to read *On the Road* as a grown-up, with a grown-up's fears and preoccupations, Kerouac was not selling the kind of trip I could use. I needed a new beat, not the old ones.

There were relatively few books on the List left for me to read, but the answer I was looking for, the answer to life, the universe and everything, still seemed remote and unknowable. I was not even sure what the question was. I had to believe that the next book might tell me but, with the best will in the world, it looked rather improbable.

Book #42 on the List of Betterment was Julian Cope's *Krautrocksampler*, a highly personal monograph by the former singer of new-wave group The Teardrop Explodes on the subject of German progressive rock in the late 1960s and early 1970s, bands like Tangerine Dream, NEU!, and Amon Düül II.[4] It was the sort of cosmic music I imagined

4 For the uninitiated, 'Krautrock' is a xenophobiasm (see below) coined by British music journalists in the 1970s to define this wave of German progressive music. Some prefer the term 'Kosmische Musik', denoting the genre's deep-space/inner-space connotations. To complicate matters, several German groups subsequently adopted the K-word themselves, e.g. 'Krautrock', the *sehr kosmische* opening track of Faust's fourth album, *Faust IV*. However one labels it, this music has remained a touchstone for experimental and alternative musicians for over forty years. No two

211

the Silver Surfer might hear as he flew between planets or listened to alone in his bedroom after another row with Galactus. Like the Surfer, Julian Cope was a hero of mine from way back; his music had been the soundtrack to my own rites of passage and still featured occasionally on my commute or around the house; at a young age, Alex had learned to bang his bowl on the kitchen table in time to 'World Shut Your Mouth'. I had no expectation that *Krautrocksampler* would be a great book in the way that *Don Quixote* or *Anna Karenina* were great books; and the impulse to read it now was, like the impulse to read *The Essential Silver Surfer, Vol. 1*, backward-looking and self-indulgent. But so what? I had earned the right to a little rock'n'roll fun.

But there was a hitch. I had owned *Krautrocksampler* ever since its publication in 1995. Now that the time had come to read it, however, the book seemed to have vanished into thin air. I could not find it anywhere. It was not with the row of music biographies on the sitting-room bookshelves, nor the stack of Cope LPs in my office, nor in our bedroom with the first editions of Cope's other books, *Head-On*, *Repossessed* and *The Modern Antiquarian*, nor lurking at the bottom of one of the still-unpacked cardboard boxes in the

---

groups sounded exactly alike but one could expect to hear some or all of the following on their records: long, experimental pieces filling the entire side of an LP; wailing, distorted electric guitar; unfathomable and often improvised vocals and chanting; a metronomic drumbeat referred to as 'motorik' or 'apache'; slow, glacial drones played on the only Moog synthesiser in West Germany. The author of *Krautrocksampler*, in the introduction alone, defines it as, variously, '*the German pre-punk self-awareness trip of all time . . . a substantial artform with considerable stamina . . . a whole Youth-nation working out their blues . . . some of the most astonishing, evocative, heroic glimpses of Man at his Peak of Artistic Magic*'. Julian H. Cope: never knowingly underwhelmed.

'Xenophobiasm' is a neologism coined by me to define a xenophobic neologism, rather than an orgasm of racist origin, e.g. one brought on by reading the *Daily Mail*.

loft or orange crates at the storage unit up the road. Oh well, I thought with pleasure, I'll have to buy another one.

*Krautrocksampler*, however, was out of print and no longer available in the shops. The cheapest secondhand copy I could find via the Internet was priced at almost £100. *Scheiße!* I liked buying books but I wasn't mentally ill. Frustrated, I decided to move ahead to the next titles on the List, which were *Beowulf*, *The Portrait of a Lady* and *The Handmaid's Tale*, until the safe place in which I had carefully stashed my copy of *Krautrocksampler* revealed itself.

But the book's sudden inaccessibility nagged at me like a neurosis. I needed to read it now, I decided, not after *Beowulf* or *The Portrait of a Lady* or *The Handmaid's Tale*, but right now, otherwise the project would not be following its proper course – perhaps I was mentally ill. I looked up *Krautrocksampler* in the British Library's online database. If I took a day's holiday, theoretically it should be possible to read the nation's copy from cover to cover at a desk in the St Pancras reading rooms. The prospect of this actually rather thrilled me, in a viscerally geeky sort of way. I had certainly had worse holidays.

Scanning down the Google page of search results for *Krautrocksampler*, however, my eye latched onto something else. It was a link to the blog of a Julian Cope fanatic whose owner had posted the whole of *Krautrocksampler* as a PDF file, cover scans and all. I clicked and downloaded the PDF to my hard drive immediately, where it has lived illegally ever since. It is open on my desktop right now as I sit typing these words and listening to Faust. Bloggers, please forgive me. It seems I owe you an apology.[5]

5 My original copy of *Krautrocksampler* has never turned up and, as the owner of the blog noted, this PDF looks like it was scanned by someone in a hurry. Pages 98 and 99 are missing, which means I may never know

Rock star, Gnostic, field researcher, peace warrior, astral traveller, cartoon character: if Julian Cope did not exist, Marvel comics would have to invent him – the Wandering Julian. As a matter of fact, The Teardrop Explodes had taken their name from a panel in a *Daredevil* comic. After The Teardrops' split, Cope ingested mythological quantities of LSD and recorded three sublime solo albums: *World Shut Your Mouth*, *Fried* and *Saint Julian*. Throughout this period he always had, and understood the importance of, Great Hair. In December 1989, he experienced a series of 'powerful and extremely positive' Visions, the effects of which were to prove life-changing. Cope declared himself as a mystic and a shaman – the 'Arch-drude'. He has pursued this idiosyncratic path ever since, following the Muse wherever She leads – mapping the megalithic sites of Britain and Europe, issuing collections of vocal mantras, 'meditational grooves' and 'ambient metal' via his Head Heritage website, delivering three-hour lectures at the British Museum in full Odin-inspired face paint, engaging in direct political and ecological protest across the British Isles and, whenever and wherever possible, staying in Travelodges. Latterly, for reasons of both artistic and follicular expediency, the Great Hair has been surmounted by a Great Hat: 'Actually, it's 1955 Luftwaffe; it's not Nazi,' he told Jon Savage. 'I put the braids on 'cos I thought it made it look heavier. I thought, I've got to be really careful here, because I'm not a Nazi.'[6]

---

how Cope feels about the two Amon Düül II albums, *Carnival in Babylon* and *Yeti*, '*the Ur-Kraut album of All*', though I can hazard a guess. Do you have these stray pages? Do you know someone who does? Get in touch, please. OCD's kickin' in pretty bad, man!

6 Of his preference for the Travelodge experience, in 2000 Cope told a BBC film crew: 'After about six or seven years of travelling I started realising that I was staying more and more in Travelodges and people were asking me why. "Why are you staying in Travelodges all the time?

Cope approaches everything he does with, in Savage's phrase, 'a curious kind of ludicrous rigour'. It was in the late 1980s, around the time he received his Visions, that Cope happened to read *The Master and Margarita* by Mikhail Bulgakov. '*[It] devoured me and immersed me,*' he later wrote. '*It was startlingly individual and like nothing else, yet its language spoke across the ages and called out to me as a Universal of Experience. It lay inside me forever and I knew that the rock'n'roll which I was forever seeking out also did precisely that.*' Well, exactly. He continued to expand his mind by reading Gurdjieff and Jung, Lester Bangs and John Sinclair; and books in turn shaped the music Cope was now making. 1992's Krautrock-leaning *Jehovahkill* LP came with a subtitle – *That'll Be the Deicide* – and a booklet that featured a title page, poetry, photographs of stone circles, diagrams and quotes from writers as diverse as William Blake, George Bernard Shaw and Philip K. Dick.

But the fire sparked by *The Master and Margarita* fanned out beyond music. '*1989 had seen a change come over me which was utterly consuming and coupling me with the cosmos,*' Cope remembered ten years later. '*I had never been a writer or keeper of neat notebooks, yet I now needed to write continuously.*' This compulsion found its outlet in the four extraordinary books Cope published over the next decade: two volumes

They're totally characterless, they're totally anonymous, they're always the same." I said, Precisely. I said, I'm just getting fed up with travelling for seven hours, being exhausted after a full day's fieldwork, and then having to listen to, you know, some sweet biddy who says, "Ooh, you know, this is the porch that we built two years ago." And I just feel like, Gimme me the keys, Bitch! . . . Is "Gimme me the keys, Bitch!" too compassionless? I think it's probably more rock, isn't it?' Inspired by Cope, I stayed exclusively in Travelodges while conducting fieldwork on Britain's crazy golf courses for my first book *Tilting at Windmills*; likewise, every word of *The Year of Reading Dangerously* has been written while wearing shades and a misinterpretable hat. I regret nothing, *Mein Führer*.

of gonzo autobiography, *Head-On* and *Repossessed*, his best-selling gazetteer of Britain's stone circles and burial mounds, *The Modern Antiquarian*, and, somewhere in the middle, *Krautrocksampler: One Head's Guide to the Great Kosmische Musik – 1968 Onwards*.

*Krautrocksampler* is many things – a memoir, a history module, a fan letter, an exegesis, a checklist of records – but to me, reading it off a laptop in the third millennium, it was a revelation. It seemed to me that what Cope was attempting in the book was almost superheroic. Utilising the tools and language the 37-year-old author had at his disposal – a passion for the music, a willingness to dig down and research, his raging infatuation with Bangs and Sinclair, his mission as a self-proclaimed 'Shamanic Rock'n'Rolling Inner-Space Cadet', plus a devotional belief in the transformative power of all of the above – he had taken the awe he felt as a teenager '*lying in a caravan in Tamworth in Staffordshire*' listening to John Peel spin 'Hallogallo' by NEU! and transubstantiated it into a sacred text of his own devising, a work of righteous, riotous prop-aganda, which was intended to speak to Modern Man, right here and right now. And as Cope would say, it fucking Achieved!!! *Krautrocksampler* was not *Beowulf* or *The Handmaid's Tale* or *The Portrait of a Lady* but it would not be denied. It was unquestionably a Great Book.

'*I was a teenage Krautrocker*,' Cope stated in his introduc-tion. '*I wrote this short history because of the way I feel about the music, that its supreme Magic & Power has lain Unrecognised for too long.*' I had thought reading *Krautrocksampler* to be a backward-looking and self-indulgent act; actually it was neither. As I scrolled through the PDF, I realised that Cope had indeed fucking Achieved!!! Out of his past, Cope had alchemised something Powerful and NEU! and never, ever Düül.

I finished *Krautrocksampler* in a little under three hours. Then I read it again, this time to the accompaniment of *Monster Movie* by Can, *Affenstunde* by Popol Vuh, and Walter Wegmüller's double LP *Tarot*: in Cope's persuasively unscientific analysis, 'THE SOUND OF THE COSMOS!!!' Why, I asked myself, was this incredible book unavailable to buy? Surely there was a readership for it? I subsequently learned that Cope himself had taken it out of print. Obeying the law of unintended consequences, what he had initiated as a spontaneous act of fandom had inadvertently brought about a Krautrock revival, which had in turn led to criticism from 'Kosmische Musik' buffs that *Krautrocksampler* was not merely incomplete and unreliable but also offensive in its use of the term 'Krautrock'. In a statement posted on his website, Cope responded thus: '*I don't feel like really updating the book much – it's a period piece written at a time when no fucker was interested and now all these neo-Krautheads are at me saying it's out of date. Fuck them! . . . Krautrock is about enlightenment, not complete-ism for some bourgeois record-collector to get purist about.*'[7]

Now *Krautrocksampler* passed from hand to hand on the Internet, from Head to Head, like *samizdat* or those bootleg editions of *The Master and Margarita* fifty years earlier. Perhaps Cope preferred it that way. Decoupled from the commercial realm, tantalisingly unavailable yet absolutely free, the book could renew its mission of enlightenment. Abandoned, it drifted through cyberspace, a monolith beaming an evolutionary message to any ape capable of receiving it.

That ape was me.

7 Plenty more where that came from at: www.headheritage.co.uk/julian_cope/qa2000ce/krautrock.

It was about now that I experienced a life-changing Vision of my own. *Krautrocksampler* was not the best book in the List of Betterment – that book was still to come – but it proved to be the most inspiring over the long haul. The book you are reading now would not exist without it.

As I said earlier, turning out reviews for the blog had been fundamentally unsatisfying. After all, a series of blog posts was unlikely to become more than the sum of its parts, just as a set of *Silver Surfer* comics doesn't add up to a real book simply because you print it as one. I felt, though, that the cumulative effect of all this dangerous reading was propelling me towards something ominous and inevitable and unmistakably like a new book of my own. The writer in me was stirring again, pushing the editor aside.

*Krautrocksampler* showed the way. If Cope could turn a teenage inspiration into something amusing, audacious and useful, surely I might do the same? Obviously, my life was nothing like the Arch-drude's nor did I have his gift for heroic overstatement; any book I wrote would draw from a more mundane pool of experience and utilise fewer CAPITALS!!! and Exclamation Marks. But *Krautrocksampler* certainly proved it was possible to go back to the past, to 'those two or three great and simple images in whose presence his heart first opened', and in doing so, revitalise both the present and the future. And if a list of fifty Krautrock records could do that, then why not fifty books?

So, improbable as it may seem, *Krautrocksampler* did offer me some kind of an answer – if not to life, the universe and everything, then to my long dark tea-time of the soul. If you squinted, you could just about make out the COSMOS.

Around the time he conceived *Krautrocksampler*, Cope recorded a shimmering version of Roky Erickson's 'I Have Always Been Here Before', adapting the original lyrics to encompass his recent shamanic Visions, the long barrows of Wiltshire and an essay by Carl Jung, no mean feat in four and a half minutes.

'The childish man shrinks back from the unknown world
And the grown man is threatened by sacrifice.
Whosoever protects himself from what is new and strange
Is as the man who is running from the past.'[8]

Here, hiding in plain hearing, was the lesson not just of *Krautrocksampler*, but of the entire List of Betterment. Do not fear the present or the past; use them both to face the future.

Perhaps the time had come, if not to put away childish things, then to share them with the child who lived in the room next door. I gathered together my stray comics and annuals and *The Essential Silver Surfer, Vol. 1* and left them in a pile in the corner of Alex's bedroom. Let him find them for himself when he's ready, I thought. They'll give us something to talk about when he's older.

8 Compare with Jung's essay, 'The Stages of Life': *'Whoever protects himself against what is new and strange and thereby regresses to the past, falls into the same neurotic condition as the man who identifies himself with the new and runs away from the past. The only difference is that the one has estranged himself from the past, and the other from the future . . . Just as a childish person shrinks back from the unknown in the world and in human existence, so the grown man shrinks back from the second half of life. It is as if unknown and dangerous tasks were expected of him; or as if he were threatened with sacrifices and losses which he does not wish to accept; or as if his life up to now seemed so fair and so precious that he could not do without it.' Modern Man in Search of a Soul* (1933), pp104–108. 'I paraphrase his [Jung's] stuff all the time,' Cope told Simon Reynolds in 1991. 'He's incredible.'

## Postscript: Be careful what you wish for . . .

*I am sitting at my desk, trying to think of a good way to tie up this chapter, when there is a knock at the office door.*

'Dad?'

'Yes, Alex, what is it?'

'Can I ask you something?'

'Go ahead.'

'Dad, when you were a kid, who was your favourite *Spider-Man* villain?'

'Oh I can't really remember. Name a few.'

'Mysterio, Master of Illusion.'

'Yes, I liked him.'

'The Vulture.'

'He was all right.'

'The Kangaroo.'

'I don't remember him. Was there really one called the Kangaroo or have you just made that up?'

*Alex goes into his bedroom and returns a moment later to show me the cover of* Amazing Spider-Man #81, 'The Coming of the Kangaroo!'

'He does massive leaps, look.'

'I can see. Does he carry a little version of himself around in a pouch too?'

'Dad! Was Galactus your favourite villain in *Spidey*?'

'I suppose so. But he wasn't really in the *Spider-Man* comics much. He was more in *Fantastic Four* or *The Silver Surfer*.'

'Who was your favourite in *Spidey* then?'

'Er . . . I liked the Green Goblin.'

'The first one or the second one?'

'Um, look, sorry, can I just get on with this?'
'Oh sure.'

*Later . . .*
'Dad?'
'Alex?'
'In *The Silver Surfer*, is Mephisto the Devil?'
'Yes. Well, no. Sort of. It's tricky to explain.'
'Is Son Of Satan the son of Mephisto?'
'No, I don't think so.'
'Is he really the son of Satan, then?'
'Er . . .'
'Do Mephisto and Satan ever meet?'
'Alex, I just need to finish this bit.'


*Later . . .*

'Alex, you know you were asking earlier if Mephisto and Satan ever meet? Well, I texted Stewart to ask him because it's the sort of thing he would know. He says, "*Ah. I believe that Satan and Mephisto are two separate entities. Satan is definitely a character and I remember a line that said he is 'but one of many rulers of various pocket dimensions known as hell' or something. Hope this helps.*"'

'Dad, when you were a kid, what were your favourite Marvel comics?'

'*Spider-Man, X-Men, Silver Surfer. Fantastic Four. Avengers.* I liked them all. I really got into them when I was about your age. They're one of the things I think of when I think about my childhood. I wonder what you'll think about when you look back on your childhood.'

'You writing your book for ages and ages and ages and then saying you'd finished it and then writing it some more for ages after that.'

'Oh . . . '
'But I got to see you a lot, so I don't mind.'
'Thanks, Alex.'

*And, not for the first time during the writing of this Greatbooksampler, I close the door behind me and weep like Norrin Radd.*

Happy Birthday,
Andy.
You Bloody Sod.

Julian Lennon
x x '91

# Book 45

*Atomised* (*Les Particules élémentaires*) by Michel Houellebecq

(Supplementary Books Three to Ten – *Whatever*; *Platform*; *Lanzarote*; *The Possibility of an Island*; *The Map and the Territory*; *H.P. Lovecraft: Against the World, Against Life*; *The Art of Struggle*, all by Michel Houellebecq; *Public Enemies* by Michel Houellebecq and Bernard-Henri Lévy)

'One of the readers' emails that gave me the most pleasure in my life was one where some guy started relating (not without talent) different anecdotes from his personal life; then he realized that that wasn't enough, that he should have sketched out his main themes, set out his principal characters, marked out the social boundaries, a whole bunch of things that he was happy for me to do in his place, and concluded with this sentence, which was exactly what I had wanted to hear for a long time: "Thanks for all the hard work."'

*Public Enemies*

## Another Word of Explanation

Do you recall how, at the beginning of this book, way back in the introduction, there was a long quotation from the author Malcolm Lowry about a book being like 'a sort of machine'? It started like this: '*It can be read simply as a story which you can skip if you want. It can be read as a story you will get more out of if you don't skip.*' And you read that paragraph and thought, 'What? What's that got to do with anything?' Well, the chapter that follows is what it had to do with. It's rather weird and confusing and you may want to skip it. Were I the editor of this book, I would have omitted it entirely. But I am not the editor, I am the author. For a little while yet, the author is the one controlling the machine.

What follows is a fan letter that Andy Miller wrote to the writer Michel Houellebecq shortly after finishing his novel *Atomised*. Like most fan letters it is garbled and gushing and a bit of an embarrassment but it catches something a more elegant or considered appreciation might not: the rush of excitement, the absolute surrender, that occurs just a few times in our lives, when we read a book for the first time and think: yes, the world is like *that*.

Before *Atomised*, Andy Miller had read a great many great books; recently, he had even been inspired to start writing a new book of his own. What this letter to Houellebecq captures, however, is the heady intoxication of reading for its own sake. Of course, when we're intoxicated, we sometimes do things we later regret. In the course of the communiqué, Miller bangs on about Neil Young and muses at length on subjects as diverse as hero-worship, the writer Douglas Adams, the function of art, etc., culminating in a knowingly obtuse 'cryptographic puzzle', which the author suggests contains the key to this entire book! As if.

If you do decide to proceed from here, I must remind you of another of the author's statements from the introduction: '*I am not urging you to read all the books in this book.*' From its first page, Andy Miller felt that *Atomised* was a great book, the greatest he had read for years, as you will learn if you choose not to skip this chapter. I agree with him. But you do not need to feel the same way. Like the members of Andy Miller's book group, you may have read *Atomised* a few years ago and hated it; or, based on what you have seen in newspapers and magazines, you may feel you know all you need to about its controversial author – *tant pis!* Try not to let it obscure the point of this bit, which is: never abandon the possibility that, however old you are, there might still be a book out there that will make you gush and garble and do something you might regret. It means you're still alive.

Now let's get this over with.

*M. Michel Houellebecq*
*Somewhere in Ireland, I believe*

Dear Michel Houellebecq,

My name is Andy Miller. No, not that one. You do not know me. We have never met and, after you have read this letter, let's pray we never do. As Mark E. Smith says, 'You should never meet your heroes, know what I mean? And vice versa.'

I am writing to you from the lobby of the British Library in London. The St Pancras facility, which consists of reading rooms, galleries, cafés and a shop, was designed by the architect Colin St John Wilson and opened to the public in 1997. It is the largest public building constructed in the United Kingdom in the twentieth century, requiring approximately ten million bricks and 180,000 tonnes of concrete to complete. In the middle of the building is a four-storey glass tower containing the King's Library, with 65,000 printed volumes along with other pamphlets, manuscripts and maps collected by King George III between 1763 and 1820. The main collection, which is comprised of more than 150 million items, expands at an average rate of three million items per year, like bacteria or metastasising cells in a cancer patient.

*Fig. 14: Bill Woodrow,* 'Sitting On History'.

I am seated near the entrance of the Library on a piece of sculpture by Bill Woodrow entitled 'Sitting On History'. The sculpture takes the form of an enormous unfolding book, cast in bronze, tethered to a ball and chain. The book is lying 'open' so as to permit simultaneous public functionality as both artwork and bench. Woodrow intended the piece to symbolise 'the book as the captor of information we cannot escape', which seems like a downbeat message to proclaim at the doorway to a library. But perhaps I am reading it wrong.

The basements beneath me extend to a depth of 24.5 metres. Like you, I am indebted to Wikipedia.

Michel, I selected this spot because I thought the irony might appeal to you, also because there is nowhere else to sit today. When I started coming here fifteen years ago, few people had laptops. Notes were taken on paper, in pencil, as per the Library's strictly enforced regulations; personal computing was still done in the home. Today the landings and walkways are full of Wi-Fi enabled visitors, bent over screens or sitting cross-legged on the floor. As a result, the Library has been forced to review its policy on the use of power sockets in the Entrance Hall and other public areas. There have been numerous incidents of people trailing adaptor leads across walkways, causing others to trip and injure themselves; furniture gets moved around, blocking access to disabled toilets and fire equipment. According to the 'Abuse' section of the bl.uk website, many people use the Library's power supply to charge not only their computers but also their MP3 players, mobile phones, even electric toothbrushes. Please note: multi-socket extension cables are not permitted in the Library.

Of course, I am symptomatic of this metabolic change. I write you this letter on my silver Sony Vaio notebook, with its 15.5in screen, its Intel® Core™ 2.53 GHz Processor, four gigabytes of RAM, 500 gigabyte hard drive and DVD SuperMulti Drive, using a piece of proprietary word processing software which keeps flashing adverts for related products at me – *OneNote™ Mobile – You need it. Sharpen your Excel skills – Get video training now!* – but which I lack the technical ability to disable. This Vaio is not a bad machine but the battery life is poor, a deficiency of the model which has been noted by several users online. Presently I shall have to get up and move to find a power socket. Also, 'Sitting On History' is proving to be a pain in the arse.

Ok. I have moved upstairs to the Rare Books & Music Reading Room where I can sit comfortably on a normal, monopurpose chair and plug this laptop into the desk-mounted power unit, permitting me to carry on with this letter while neutralising the risk to those who walk past without looking where they are going. This is desk 294. It was in this room, at this desk, that we became acquainted – though, as I said above, we have never really met. I had booked a day's holiday to read Graham Greene's novel *The Name of Action*. Greene hated this book, his second, and after its initial publication in 1930, effectively suppressed it; it has never been reprinted or appeared in paperback; original editions sell for many hundreds of Euros. At my request, a copy had been retrieved from one of the temperature-controlled storage units and delivered to the Reading Room. I receive twenty-three days annual leave as part of a package of benefits in my job with a London book publisher. Better to spend a little of it here than in some fucking gîte in the Dordogne, being ripped off by the local farmer and his greedy offspring who, once the old man starts dying, will move him into a nursing home and never visit.

Several years ago, while researching a book on The Kinks, I spent two weeks up at the British Library's newspaper and magazine facility at Colindale, North

London. Unlike the glossy, futuristic St Pancras reading rooms, Colindale still seemed like something one might find in a Boulting Brothers comedy from the 1950s, with disobliging library technicians presiding over a cataloguing system only they understood and dark cupboards where solitary men leafed through old issues of *Picture Post*, mumbling to themselves. There was no cafeteria or restaurant at Colindale, just a bare room with red plastic chairs and an automatic vending machine. At lunchtime, my fellow researchers and I would try not to make eye-contact and eat our packed lunches with the same idea: I hope they're not thinking about me what I am thinking about them.

The atmosphere in Rare Books & Music, by contrast, does not make one feel as though one is being indulged in an embarrassing vice. People here read exemplarily. There is something uplifting about the conspicuous contemplation that seems to be taking place all around, so that even if one has come to do no more than *read for pleasure* – if such a thing is still possible – one feels oneself joining a noble communal endeavour. Much has been written about the barely suppressed erotic charge of this environment. Are there attractive, bookish, large-breasted young women here? Do they periodically retire to the toilets for extended bouts of graphic lovemaking? No, because this is a library and not a Michel Houellebecq novel. It's a *ménage* of the mind.

At the time these events took place, I was nearing the end of a year-long effort to read fifty great books which, at one time or another, I had lied about having read before – mostly fiction, classics, a couple of politics and philosophy titles. Some of the choices were obvious: *Moby-Dick*, *Pride and Prejudice*, *Jane Eyre*, the manuscript of which resides in a glass case several floors below where I am now. It had also taken in quite a few cult books: Americans of course, some *Silver Surfer* comics, *The Ragged Trousered Philanthropists* by Robert Tressell, if you know that novel in France. It was only reading books, yet in my head I seemed to be engaged in a heroic struggle, rather like the quasi-Nietzschean depiction of Neil Young you contributed to Michka Assayas' *Dictionnaire du rock*: 'A man advancing, on a difficult and rocky road. Often he falls bloodied to his knees; he gets up again and keeps going.'

Throughout this uphill struggle, I had been hoping for the *coup de foudre*, the lightning flash which might illuminate the muddy track ahead of me. I had been moved and inspired and humbled by the books I had read – who could read *Anna Karenina* without experiencing all of these? – but I had yet to be shocked by something utterly unexpected and new. *The Master and Margarita* had come close; so too, if you can believe it, had Julian Cope's *Krautrocksampler*. But I was still waiting for that bolt from out of the blue.

Take the two books I had just completed, Toni Morrison's *Beloved* and Huysmans' *À rebours*, which I read in Robert Baldick's translation under the title by which it is best known in England, *Against Nature*. Morrison's novel was magnificent, a model of technical accomplishment, a super-refined product like the Canon Libris laptop-printer combination or the Camel Legend parka. And what is there to say about Huysmans that has not already been said a thousand times? Ludicrous, overripe, decadent yet somehow indestructible; I could fill the pages of this letter with quotes from *Against Nature*, entire paragraphs, which struck me as uncanny in their wit and modernity. It is a bad, wicked novel but a great one. But although I had devoured and appreciated *Beloved* and *Against Nature* for their literary qualities and cultural significance, and gained pleasure from doing so, they were only books; perhaps it was unreasonable to expect them to be anything more. They were like 1994's *Sleeps with Angels* and 1982's *Trans* respectively, two fine Neil Young albums, one the mature statement of a master, the other an experimental flop championed by a significant minority, but both chiefly understood in relation to other Neil Young albums and appreciated almost exclusively by fans of Neil Young. Or so I felt at that time, though perhaps not in those exact terms.

I was nearly forty years old, a married man, a father and, however much I wriggled, a mature adult. Midway on life's journey, it was probably unrealistic, if not a little pathetic, to expect books to be anything more than books.

On my way out of the house that morning, then, I had grabbed my copy of *Atomised* off the shelf because *Atomised* was the next book on my list and I needed something for the train. It was the same copy I had bought in the late twentieth century but never read. At the station, I succumbed to a magazine instead, a habit it was proving hard to break. As the autumn countryside sped past, I flicked through the magazine and gazed out the window, conserving my energies for *The Name of Action*. When I arrived at the Library, I was glad to observe Library protocol by depositing my belongings in a downstairs locker, save for a pencil, a notepad and your novel. I rode the escalator to Rare

Books & Music, found Desk 294, retrieved *The Name of Action* from the Issue Desk, sat down on this excellent chair and began to read.

*The Name of Action* was terrible. It was as though someone had concocted a malicious novel-length satire of a Graham Greene novel. No wonder Greene had tried to bury it. This was not like Neil Young's obstinate refusal to issue *Time Fades Away* (1973), one of his most important albums, on CD or via Spotify or iTunes – or maybe it was, except that *Time Fades Away* is a masterpiece and *The Name of Action*, which lacked anything in the way of a convincing setting, theme, character or plot, was a piece of crap. Either way, as a book, it could only be of interest to Greene completists. My pilgrimage was meant to be about enlightenment, not completeism for some bourgeois record-collector to get purist about, to paraphrase another of my old heroes.

I picked up your book, Michel, and opened it. Like *The Name of Action*, it was a first edition; and its publisher was William Heinemann, the same windmill logo embossed in gold leaf on both spines, seventy years apart. After successive corporate takeovers during the 1980s, William Heinemann is now part of Penguin Random House, the conglomerate which employs 10,000 people across five continents and comprises nearly 250 'editorially and creatively independent imprints'; in the UK, its most admired authors are probably you and the late Michael Jackson. Only half-concentrating, I cast my eye down the opening paragraph of the Prologue:

'This is principally the story of a man who lived out the greater part of his life in Western Europe, in the latter half of the twentieth century. Though alone for much of his life, he was nonetheless closely in touch with other men. He lived through an age that was miserable and troubled. The country into which he was born was sliding slowly, ineluctably, into the ranks of the less developed countries; often haunted by misery, the men of his generation lived out their lonely, bitter lives. Feelings such as love, tenderness and human fellowship had, for the most part, disappeared; the relationships between his contemporaries were at best indifferent and more often cruel.'

Ha! That was very good.

I read a little further. A biologist called Michel Djerzinski has organised his own leaving drinks to mark his departure from the research institution where he has worked for seven years. The party is a dismal failure; by 7.30pm it has broken up. Djerzinski walks one of his colleagues back to her car, a Golf. He smiles, they shake hands. He has remembered to smile, preparing himself mentally, but in retrospect wonders whether they could have kissed on both cheeks, *'like visiting dignitaries or people in show business'*. When his now ex-colleague does not immediately start her car, Djerzinski sits in his Toyota and wonders what she can be doing. *'Why had she not driven off? Was she masturbating while listening to Brahms?'* Djerzinski drives back to his Paris apartment, feeling like a character from *'a science-fiction film he had seen at university'*. He discovers his pet canary has died. He eats a ready-meal from Monoprix's Gourmet range *'washed down with a mediocre Valdepeñas'*, and dumps the dead bird in the rubbish chute: *'What was he supposed to do? Say mass?'* Djerzinski goes to bed, has a terrifying nightmare about giant snapping worms, old coffee filters and ravioli in tomato sauce, swallows some sleeping pills and passes out. '*So ended his first night of freedom.*'

That was it. I gathered up my stuff, returned *The Name of Action* to the Issue Desk, retrieved my bag from its locker and, without giving 'Sitting On History' a second glance, sprinted out onto the Euston Road and jumped on a number 390 bus heading for Archway. The longed-for *coup de foudre* had finally occurred.

While reading Huysmans a few days earlier, I had scribbled down the following passage from *À rebours*, which seemed to capture what I was still searching for: '*However much a reader wants to rid himself of prejudice and refrain from passion, he naturally prefers those works which correspond most intimately with his own personality . . . He wanted, in short, a work of art both for what it was in itself and for what it allowed him to bestow on it; he wanted to go along with it and on it, as if supported by a friend or carried by a vehicle.*' Now here I was, carried along both with *Atomised* and on it; similarly, the 390 bus to Archway. If this were a book, it would be almost too perfect.

I was making for the Archway Tavern, the pub in North London where The Kinks were photographed for the gatefold cover of their 1971 LP *Muswell Hillbillies*. I felt myself drawn to the place like a spawning salmon or a dying elephant or, more accurately, an ageing, sentimental Kinks fan. As with *The Unnamable* by Samuel Beckett, which I had listened to in a pub – it's a long story, Michel – I wanted to be out in the world, with a drink in my hand, surrounded by fruit machines and Irish alcoholics. I knew intuitively that *Atomised* was a vital book and, for that reason, I did not need to read it in a library; the library I needed was inside me.

Here is what I liked most about *Atomised*: it was brutally, bitterly, appallingly funny. I sat in that pub and sniggered so hard and so often that I frequently had to stop reading and put the book down to pause and metaphorically rub my disbelieving eyes. Yes, it was bleak. Obviously it was filthy, monotonously so. But more than anything, *it was alive and it spoke to me*. I was so taken aback that all I could do was laugh.

I am not sure I could ever truly love a book I didn't find funny, at least a little. This may be a failing on my part but if the writer offers no palliative, nothing to manage the pain, ironically I find it hard to take their work seriously. Perhaps it's because I'm English. Near the end of *Atomised*, there's an English character who says this:

'People often say that the English are very cold fish, very reserved, that they have a way of looking at things – even tragedy – with a sense of irony. There's some truth in it; it's pretty stupid, though. Irony won't save you from anything; humour doesn't do anything at all. You can look at life ironically for years, maybe decades; there are people who seem to go through most of their lives seeing the funny side, but in the end, life always breaks your heart. Doesn't matter how brave you are, or how reserved, or how much you've developed a sense of humour, you still end up with your heart broken. That's when you stop laughing. After that, there's just the cold, the silence and the loneliness. You might say, after that, there's only death.'

Was it wrong to find even this amusing? I don't mean to suggest that *Atomised* was *only* funny – it was shocking and cerebral and heart-breaking and all the things I said above – nor that it was *merely* funny. For someone approaching his fortieth birthday, it was a far from reassuring read. Every character in the novel who had achieved their fifth decade was either depressed, alienated, sexually tormented, haunted by the sense of their own encroaching obsolescence, riddled with cancer or dead. But the view of modern life it proposed, and the manner in which you expressed it, seemed so truthful to me, so fastidious and brave, I could only laugh in grateful recognition. It was existence broken down to its elementary particles: work, desire, ageing, death and the Monoprix's Gourmet range of ready-meals. On that particular day in the Archway Tavern, however, with a pint of Guinness in front of me and The Kinks on the jukebox, *Atomised* did not feel like the sequel or prelude to other books. It felt like life.

You know Neil Young and Crazy Horse's 1979 album *Rust Never Sleeps*? You must do; in an email to Bernard-Henri Lévy, you write: '*If there is an idea, a single idea that runs through all of my novels, it is the* absolute irreversibility of all processes of decay *once they have begun.*' Why use three words when thirty will do, eh Michel? Now I have read your other work, the novels, the poetry, watched the movies you've directed, even listened to *Présence humaine*, the CD you recorded with Bertrand Burgalat – you know I love you but, sorry, it's shit – I can confirm the veracity of this statement. But I admire the repetition in your books: the assiduous cataloguing of correct brand names, the references to film and music which, unlike most literary novelists, *you get right*, the recurring portrait of a society in which everything is commodified. I'm not bothered by the ridiculous amounts of sex your characters have or the sub-porno scenarios you describe; they are of a piece with the minutiae of package holiday arrangements in *Platform*, the mechanics of the cartographic process in *The Map and the Territory* and, for that matter, the vocabulary of science, those long chains of genetic code whose effect in *Atomised* is mesmerising to the point of boredom. It is the method by which you interrogate, over and over, that single, recurring idea of irreversible decay. Or, to quote the toiling Neil Young once more, from his fifth live album *Year of the Horse*: 'It's all one song.'

Where were we? Oh yes.

Here at the British Library – which, if you recall, is where I have been writing this letter today – people around me are shutting down their laptops and disconnecting their electric toothbrushes. Rare Books & Music will be closing soon and I need to pack up and go home too. But I have enjoyed sitting here, Michel, talking to you like this. It's been a lot of fun.

I am lying, of course. It's not been fun; I am not even in the British Library. In reality, I left Desk 294 over a week ago, shortly after comparing *Against Nature* and *Beloved* to a couple of obscure Neil Young albums thinking, what the hell, I can always take that out later. This letter, which will never be sent, has taken days of work: on the train, in my office, in a café, on the sofa while watching multiple episodes of *Oggy et les Cafards* with my son. Currently I am at home at my desk, thinking about what to eat for lunch. However, to sustain the beautiful illusion a while longer, let us pretend that, *after writing more than 4000 words in a day, ha ha ha ha*, I have quit the British Library and am once again sitting in the Archway Tavern with a pint, bashing this out on a phone or something. Yeah, that sounds plausible.

When I was a kid, my first literary hero was Douglas Adams. There were other writers whose books I loved in childhood, of course, but Adams was the first one who I thought of as a writer, sitting in front of his word processor, being spontaneously clever and hilarious, coming up with the goods. Even when he wasn't coming up with the goods, which was often, he was an inspiration: heroic accounts of missed deadlines, long baths and Bovril sandwiches. At the age of twelve, I remember being terribly impressed by the dedication from *The Restaurant at the End of the Universe*: '*To the Paul Simon album* One-Trick Pony *which I played incessantly while writing this book. Five years is far too long.*' Wow. Here was an occupation that allowed you to stay at home, eat sandwiches and listen to records as much as you liked. In my experience, these remain the chief perks of the job; the work itself, as you note, brings scant relief.

An imaginary sip of Guinness to accompany this unimaginative ham sandwich.

Has anyone ever told you how much your work reminds them of *The Hitchhiker's Guide to the Galaxy*? I shouldn't think they have. If there were two words inscribed on the cover of *Atomised*, they wouldn't be **DON'T PANIC**. But hear me out. You and Douglas Adams both weave stories out of high-concept scientific theory and philosophy. You portray the individual at the mercy of an absurd and hostile universe. The futuristic neo-humans who figure in *Atomised* and *The Possibility of an Island* regard their forebears in much the same way Zaphod Beeblebrox regards the hapless Arthur Dent: a talking monkey. And there is the sense of humour, of course, though obviously yours is blacker and more savage than Adams'. I have no idea whether you would be flattered or appalled by this comparison but I lay it before you like a cat dropping a dead bird at its owner's feet.

In *The Restaurant at the End of the Universe*, Adams invented the Total Perspective Vortex, an infernal machine which extrapolates the whole of existence from a small piece of fairy cake: '*When you are put into the Vortex you are given just one momentary glimpse of the entire unimaginable infinity of creation, and somewhere in it a tiny little marker, a microscopic dot on a microscopic dot, which says "You are here"*.' I must have read this sentence a thousand times over the last thirty years; it never fails to make me smile. Your hero H.P. Lovecraft built his supernatural horror stories on a similar concept – the struggle of the human mind to comprehend what he called '*the terrifying vistas of reality*'. Eliot's famous line from 'Burnt Norton' frames the same notion as poetry: '*human kind cannot bear very much reality*'. What I see in your books, Michel, is a combination of all three approaches – the comedy, the horror and the poetry of our day-to-day existence. And what Adams once meant to me, I now see in you. Enjoy your bird.

When I was seventeen, my father died. One morning, before getting up to go to work in London, he had a massive heart attack. I watched as it happened. The ambulance took him away, then I went to school; he died in hospital a few days later. He was alone when he died. Over a number of years, I either got over the shock or I didn't – it's still too soon to say. But it seems to have frozen my reaction to culture at that dramatic, bittersweet moment, forming an unquenchable emotional need to regain that *intensity of feeling*; as an adult, I am still not sure how else to do it. Isn't there something inescapably adolescent about this desire even in middle-age for heroes, about still seeking the encouragement and guidance of people we have never met and, with any luck, never will? Yet you have never abandoned yours – not just Lovecraft and Neil Young but Baudelaire, Dostoevsky, Pascal, Schopenhauer; the Great Texts of pessimism to which you refer again and again in your books. You and I turn to our heroes for the same reason: they will always tell us the truth.

I met Douglas Adams several times, four IIRC. My hero came face to face with me and vice versa. The details of these regrettable encounters will have to wait for another occasion though. They are calling last orders at the Archway Tavern – HURRY UP, PLEASE, IT'S TIME! – and I have a train to catch or something. I reach out and drain my imaginary pint.

Two final anecdotes before I go. A few months ago I happened to be in New York when Neil Young played a couple of dates at Madison Square Garden. We had tickets for the opening night, way back in an upper balcony. As the house lights dimmed, two guys in the seats in front of us whooped and raised their paper cups of beer in salutation. Neil and his band launched at full tilt into a succession of his greatest, loudest songs: 'Hey Hey, My My (Into the Black)', 'Powderfinger', 'Cinnamon Girl', 'Cortez the Killer' . . . It was like they were getting the encores out of the way first – which, as it transpired, they were. Looking across to bassist Rick Rosas and drummer Chad Cromwell, the author of *Ragged Glory* and *Comes a Time* nodded his head and the band ploughed into a brand new song, a song no one other than the musicians on stage had ever heard before. When it finished, few in the crowd seemed impressed; the new song was greeted with the wettest smatter of applause. After three further unfamiliar songs, the two guys in front of us grew restless. 'HEY NEIL!' shouted one. 'PLAY SOMETHING WE FUCKIN' KNOW!' His buddy, who was wearing a Neil Young t-shirt he had just bought from the merchandise stand, agreed. 'YEAH NEIL, YOU FUCKIN' ASSHOLE!' he yelled. 'NO MORE NEW CRAP!' At this, Neil approached the microphone and cleared his throat. 'Hey,' he said. 'We're auditioning for our old record company. The president, the CEO, they're all here tonight, Madison Square Garden. So when you hear those new songs, you make a shitload of noise whether you like 'em or not. OK?' And with that, he counted off another brand new disappointing song. 'ASSHOLE!' screamed our neighbours. Everyone was happy.

Similarly, in his short story 'The Vane Sisters', Vladimir Nabokov – a virtuoso I gather you do not hold in high regard, Michel – plays a subtle game with the reader. He conceals a message from the eponymous girls, both deceased, as an acrostic puzzle, unpicked by taking the first letter of each word in the final para-graph to form a Ouija board-like communiqué from the hereafter. This is not cryptography for the sake of it. Nabokov wants to investigate how our view of the world is shaped and articulated by forces *beneath the surface*: memories, stories, games. But when he submitted 'The Vane Sisters' to *The New Yorker* for publication, it was rejected for its elaborate obscurity. And when it finally appeared in *Encounter* eight years later, the magazine was obliged to tip off its readers to the story's veiled rationale because no one, including the author, was sure it could be deciphered otherwise. *'This particular trick can be tried only once in a thousand years of fiction,'* Nabokov later wrote. *'Whether it has come off is another question.'*

Michel, as a concluding 'thank you', I have incorporated a different sort of cryptographic puzzle into the closing stanzas of this letter. It is intended as a joke to be appreciated only by you and maybe a handful of others. Whether it has come off is another question.

Why do our heroes need us? To worship them? To foot their bills? To make a shitload of noise? If a tree falls in a forest and no one is there to hear it, should the tree be pulped to print a story no one can understand? If Neil Young plays new songs in a forest, are the squirrels entitled to throw acorns and squeak irately for 'Rockin' in the Free World'? These are not easy questions to answer. But without heroes to point the way, we stumble around, lost in the fog, alone.

Time fades away, Neil once sang in that 'unmanly' voice, *'un peu de la femme, du vieilliard ou d'enfant'*. We journey through the past, searching for the two or three great and simple images in whose presence our heart first opened. We do not know where to look, only that we must keep looking; absolute stillness is death. We hear other voices, preachers, teachers, the pure artists, but they seem distant, indistinct. Yonder stands the sinner, speaking a truth others find unpalatable, and it stops us in our tracks. The voice may come to us from Moscow a hundred years ago or LA in the 70s or Paris not far from now or the Laurels, Brickfield Terrace, Holloway. It speaks to us and we move towards it up the difficult and rocky road. We fall bloodied to our knees but it calls us on. Its message is an old one: keep love in mind; keep going; don't be denied. It is the bridge from their history to ours, the song that will accompany our future, the remainder of the journey, our last dance.

Michel, it doesn't matter anyway, because it's all a load of shit: here is the phrase with which I planned to end this letter. But now the moment has come, I find I can't do it. It might be funny, if only to me, but it would no longer be true. Your disgraceful books, for all their ridicule and despair, their disregard for contemporary society, their obsession with the inevitability of bodily decay, their ingrained and bitter pessimism, offered me what I now realise I had been searching for all along: hope. I could go on living in the world, as long as there were books like *Atomised* in it.

Please – *je vous en prie!* – have the last word:

'It's the voice of a human being, with a naïve and important thing to tell us: the world will always be the way it is, that's its affair; it's not any reason for us to give up trying to make it better.'

Sincerely yours,

A. Miller

## A Final Word of Explanation

Well, there it is. Don't say you weren't warned.

Readers who have made it this far may be curious as to the nature of the Nabokov-like 'cryptographic puzzle' mentioned by the author on page 244. On the next page, please refer to the neighbouring paragraph beginning '*Time fades away, Neil once sang . . .*' Hidden within it are the names of all the songs on Neil Young's album *Time Fades Away* in the sequence in which they appear on the original LP: the title track, 'Journey Through the Past', 'Yonder Stands the Sinner', and so on. This passage also contains certain images and phrases from *The Year of Reading Dangerously* that it would be impossible for anyone except the author to recognise – anyone, perhaps, except the attentive reader of this book who hasn't already skipped ahead to *War and Peace*.

What the author is trying to say – fuck it, what *I* am trying to say – in this paragraph is surprisingly simple, though the way I have articulated it is deliberately puzzling and playful. It's the most ornate expression of an idea that loops through this book like a double helix. We are creatures made as much by art as by experience and what we read in books is the sum of both. And if Michel Houellebecq is correct and life always breaks your heart – once they have begun, *the processes of decay are absolutely irreversible* – art is the equal and opposite reaction to that inevitable heartbreak, whether as a great book or a forgotten Neil Young album.

Time fades away, in other words; it's not any reason for us to give up trying to make it better.

# Books 49 and 50

*War and Peace* by Leo Tolstoy
*The Code of the Woosters* by P.G. Wodehouse

'Above him there was now nothing but the sky – the lofty sky, not clear yet still immeasurably lofty, with grey clouds gliding slowly across it. "How quiet, peaceful, and solemn; not at all as I ran," thought Prince Andrew "– not as we ran, shouting and fighting, not at all as the gunner and the Frenchman with frightened and angry faces struggled for the mop: how differently do those clouds glide across that lofty infinite sky! How was it I did not see that lofty sky before? And how happy I am to have found it at last! Yes! All is vanity, all falsehood, except that infinite sky. There is nothing, nothing, but that. But even it does not exist, there is nothing but quiet and peace. Thank God!. . ."'

*War and Peace*, Book One, Part III, Chapter XVI

'I braked the car.
"Journey's End, Jeeves?"
"So I should be disposed to imagine, sir."'

*The Code of the Woosters*

A twenty-minute drive along the coast from where we live now stands the ruin of a medieval monastery. On overcast days, with rain in the air and the salt sea crashing on the rocks below, there is no more romantic destination. The sky is vast, the light supernal, the prospect blustery and dramatic. This, you say to yourself, is the sort of scene captured by Turner in one of his elemental seascapes, the kind of view which inspired Debussy to the grandeur of *La Mer*.[1] The closer you study that view, however, the harder it becomes to maintain the impression of a limitless horizon. Industrial wind turbines cut across the natural spectacle. In the distance, through the ozone haze, your eye registers the concrete tower blocks of Southend-on-Sea and the Isle of Sheppey. You remind yourself that this is not the wide open sea of Melville or Murdoch but the Thames estuary, into which thousands of gallons of human effluent are pumped every day. And you recall that it is in the middle of this sewage-filled inlet that, a few years hence, the Mayor of London hopes to float an airport. You buy two coffees from the vending machine in the Visitor Centre with a heavy heart.

'Happy birthday,' I said to my wife, as I placed the coffees on the table and wiped away the sugar, crisp packets and paper napkins left by the table's previous occupants.

Tina's nose was running and her cheeks were red from being stung by hailstones. 'I needed that tissue,' she said.

Next to us, Alex was asleep in his pushchair. We drank

1 Oh, bad luck! Turner painted many remarkable canvases along this particular stretch of the Kent coast; but the majority of *La Mer* was composed in a sea-facing room at the Grand Hotel, Eastbourne, which is, of course, on the south coast, not the east. So you only get half a point. Yes, the footnotes are back. Did you miss them? I left them out of the previous chapter because it took the form of a letter or email and not even I annotate my own emails.

our coffee in what relationship counsellors refer to approvingly as 'companionable silence'.

It was early October, the season of mists, mellow fruitfulness and my wife's birthday. It was almost a year since the trip to Broadstairs which had accidentally started the List of Betterment. We were all a year older, at least. Over that time, I had completed forty-eight great books. It had not been painless, trouble-free or fun but as the finish line came in sight, I had no intention of not crossing it; there would be no insolent gestures of defiance in the manner of *The Loneliness of the Long Distance Runner*. After nearly coming a cropper over *Of Human Bondage* and *Pride and Prejudice*, way back before Christmas, I had stuck doggedly to one guiding principle: run the race to its end. I had atoned for taking short cuts in previous events, deepened my knowledge and appreciation of the landscape and rekindled a flagging enthusiasm for fresh air and exercise, by which I mean the precise opposite of fresh air and exercise, i.e. sitting indoors with my nose in a book.[1] Most rewardingly, perhaps, I had learned from past mistakes. With forty-eight great books behind me, and one by Dan Brown, I had trained myself to be good at reading again. Now I was operating at the peak of my fitness. I wasn't about to let it go to waste.

On the way back to the car from the Visitor Centre, the wind and rain whipping round our heads, I tapped Tina on the shoulder.

'I want to pack my job in,' I said. 'I think I can make a go of it as a freelancer.'

'Right,' she replied from inside the hood of her blue Regatta wet weather anorak, the same one she had bought on our honeymoon in the Western Isles of Scotland, one

1 Metaphor! What is it good for? Absolutely nothing!

half of a matching pair of anoraks which, when we wore them together, made us look like we were on a special day out from sheltered accommodation – which, in a sense, we were.

'Also,' I said, 'I need to write another book.'

'Is this news meant to be my birthday present?' Tina enquired as she unlocked the door of our oceanic green Volkswagen Polo, the same car which, when we bought it two years earlier, I had promised to learn to drive, as I had faithfully promised to learn to drive earlier cars, a promise which, each time it was made, I sincerely believed would result in driving lessons, a passed test and a more equal division of automotive labour, yet which somehow I perpetually failed to keep, though I resisted the suggestion that I had in any way broken my promise, because one fine day I still intended to make good on it. Still, I knew better than to ask too often for a ride into town.

'Of course not,' I said.

'Will I need to be Mrs Pevsner this time?' asked Tina warily.[2]

2 This is not a euphemism for some bedroom indelicacy. When Tina and I moved in together in the early 1990s, we rented the attic flat above the headquarters of the Victorian Society in Bedford Park, the garden suburb area of Chiswick in West London. The Victorian Society is a charity dedicated to the study and preservation of Victorian and Edwardian architecture and other arts. Amongst its guiding lights were John Betjeman, Hugh Casson and the German architectural historian Nikolaus Pevsner, founding editor of the classic *Buildings of England* series. As detailed by Susie Harries in *Nikolaus Pevsner: The Life*, Pevsner did not compile these books alone. At his side was his wife Lola. When undertaking research for one of his guides, Pevsner insisted Lola ferry him around in their Morris Traveller, wait in the car while he jotted down his observations of a church or guildhall, drive him on to the guest house she had booked, eat the sandwiches she had made for them both before setting out, and stay awake until he had finished typing out his notes. The following day, the same routine, for year after year, until her husband had filled the pages of more than thirty volumes and been justifiably

'Unlikely,' I said.

'Thank heavens for that,' she said. 'How long will it take?'

'Eighteen months . . .?' I replied hesitantly; it couldn't take much longer than that, surely.

'All right then,' said my wife, getting into the car. 'So what is my birthday present?'

'*War and Peace*,' I said. 'Will you read it with me? I've got two copies at home. I haven't wrapped yours up yet though.'

Tina looked at me with her pale blue eyes, the same eyes with which she has looked levelly at me for nearly twenty years now, a slight fleck of hazel in the right eye, eyes which are adept at communicating a range of emotions, from amusement to irritation to deep disgruntlement with the occupant of the passenger seat, who will be qualified to offer his opinion on parallel parking techniques when, and only when, he learns to drive, the eyes which have been miraculously reproduced in the physiognomy of our beautiful son, the eyes of the young woman with whom I fell in love behind the counter of a bookshop, a long time ago in a galaxy far, far away, when we were only humble service droids, she the long-suffering R2 unit to my irksome Threepio.

'All right then,' she said.

'Thank you,' I replied.

Tina studied her windblown face in the rear-view mirror. 'Look at that,' she said. 'Farmer f\*\*king Giles.'

'Farmer who?' asked Alex, who had just woken up.

'Farmer funky Giles,' Tina replied. 'He's like a farmer,

acclaimed as one of the pioneering figures of post-war British cultural life. In fact, Nikolaus Pevsner knew how to drive all along but preferred not to; and Lola Pevsner predeceased her husband by twenty years. It is this arrangement to which Tina is referring here.

251

but he's a funky farmer. On his farm, he's got a disco. After tea, all the animals go to the barn and play party games and have a disco.'

'Really?' asked Alex.

'Absolutely,' I said. 'He's really funky!'

At moments such as these, service droids stick together.

As we turned out of the car park and into the lane that leads back to the main road, I glanced over at the square-topped towers of the monastery, silhouetted against the bay and the lowering sky. '*From the water they are a moving sight on the brink of the bleak promontory,*' remarks the Pevsner guide to North East and East Kent. '*It is a disgrace that the inland road approaches through the vulgarest caravan site in the county.*' It is this kind of interjection that gives the *Buildings of England* series its inimitable character. The guide will be calmly listing the architectural properties of a building, its apsidal chancel or pilaster buttresses, and then, all of a sudden, explode with rage or incredulity at whatever monstrosity has just offended the compiler's eye: a particularly hideous office block or leisure centre, a caravan site which is not merely vulgar but *the vulgarest in the county*.

Many of my favourite books mimic the Pevsner guides in this respect, as though the narrator and their subject have become locked in an increasingly ill-tempered tussle for control of the text: *Pale Fire* by Nabokov, *Revolution in the Head* by Ian MacDonald, *Flaubert's Parrot* by Julian Barnes, most of B.S. Johnson's novels, even Roger Lewis's cantankerous *The Life and Death of Peter Sellers*. I suppose *The Life and Opinions of Tristram Shandy, Gentleman* is the prototype in fiction; and, although it was not my intention at the outset, it seems to be how *The Year of Reading Dangerously* has turned out. At every turn, the author's attempts to dictate their terms are frustrated and contradicted by the book they find themselves writing or the circumstances in which they are trying to write it; hence the term *contradictatorial*, which I have just come up with despite the hellish drilling and banging of the workmen doing up the property next door.[3]

Like many women, I suspect, Tina does not have much time for the Contradictatorial School. It does seem to be a style of writing that is practised and enjoyed almost exclusively by men, a fact which disappoints me. For a previous birthday, I had bought her Ian MacDonald's scintillating *Revolution in the Head* which, as a huge Beatles fan, I thought she would love; one of the talents that first attracted me was her ability to recite The Beatles' Christmas

---

3 They have been renovating that place for months now, the inconsiderate bastards. Their intrusion into the text would be the perfect illustration of what I am describing here, if only it weren't so bloody loud. *'Knocking, hammering, and tumbling things about has made the whole of my life a daily torment . . . I do not see why one fellow who is removing a load of sand or manure should obtain the privilege of killing in the bud the thoughts that are springing up in the heads of about ten thousand people successively.'* Schopenhauer, 'On Noise'.

Other contradictatorial books, or books with a strong contradictatorial streak: *A Heartbreaking Work of Staggering Genius* by Dave Eggers, *The Rings of Saturn* by W.G. Sebald, *U & I: A True Story* by Nicholson Baker, *How Proust Can Change Your Life* by Alain de Botton, *Leadville* by Edward Platt, as well as works by Cervantes, Samuel Beckett, Herman Melville, Julian Cope, Michel Houellebecq, Lemony Snicket and even Jane Austen (*'Reader, I married him'*) discussed elsewhere in this book. To this list, one might add the films of Jean-Luc Godard, or those of Patrick Keiller, or the stand-up comedy of Stewart Lee. Books about books, films about films, jokes about jokes. Again, this may be the influence of Douglas Adams, whose *Hitchhiker's* novels are constantly punctuated or interrupted by extracts from the fictional *Hitchhiker's Guide to the Galaxy* (the one with **DON'T PANIC** inscribed in large, friendly letters on the cover), either commenting on or disagreeing with whatever the reader has just been told. For this reason, the acid test of a book's *contradictatoriality* is whether one can imagine it being read aloud by the late Peter Jones, the voice of the Book in the original *Hitchhiker's* radio series.

1964 fan-club flexidisc in its entirety. But she could not get along with it. Maybe there is something intrinsically blokeish about a book which takes The Beatles' recorded legacy, lays it out in precise chronological order, weighs and measures it, and then complains vehemently about the parts it doesn't like. And it is this in-built, ineluctable blokeishness I find disconcerting. I have spent most of my adult life trying not to act like a typically male man, so to discover one's predilection for a book, or particular style of book, may well be governed not by taste or choice but by an arbitrary allocation of chromosomes and gametes, feels like an own goal, as though one had been compelled to conclude a thematically important paragraph with a cliché drawn from a sphere of activity one professed to despise; balls to that.

Most straight men are an embarrassment; that much is clear. They enjoy porn, Sky Sports, racing cars, barbecues and gadgets; they stink of Lynx deodorant. Though they mostly prefer the company of other men, they are scared stiff of being mistaken for women or homosexuals. In general, as we have seen, they perceive reading as a feminised activity and, although they do read books, these tend to be about either Joe Strummer or the Mafia, or have some rigid practical application, e.g. *How to Cook Great Barbecue Food without Looking Too Gay*. According to a survey from the National Literacy Trust, four out of five fathers have *never read a bedtime story to their children*, either because they see it as the mother's job or because *We're Going on a Bear Hunt* doesn't have enough lesbians in it. Four out of five! I have to share toilet facilities with these losers. In the words of Eeyore the Donkey, which four out of five men may never know the joy of sharing: '*"Pathetic," he said. "That's what it is. Pathetic."*'

*Fig. 15:* 'Down Hole', *David Shrigley, 2007.*

Tina has always said she could never have married a man who did not love books. Was she aware how reckless she had been? At a stroke, she was reducing the field of potential life-partners by up to 80 per cent. Take into account the 10 per cent of men who are gay and that leaves a shallow breeding pool consisting mostly of the myopic, weak-chested or lame. Really, as I never tire of reminding her, she was lucky to have found me. So what if I had never learned to drive? I had all my own teeth and would rather the cost of a Sky Sports subscription be spent on fresh flowers and tickets to West End musicals – and books, of course.

I strive not to behave like a manly man. Likewise Tina, though unquestionably a womanly woman, is by no stretch of the imagination a girly girl. She does not totter round the place on high heels, spend weekends being pampered with her girlfriends at a luxury spa hotel, or even possess a red lipstick ('tarty', apparently). She did confess to a little crush on David Tennant when he was Doctor Who but then so did I. In fact, when we discuss our relationship, we often conclude it is more like a double act than the traditional union of husband and wife: R2-D2 and C-3PO, Bob Ferris and Terry Collier from *Whatever Happened to the Likely Lads?*, Blanche and Baby Jane Hudson, even Steve Coogan and Rob Brydon in *The Trip*, driving around the English countryside, bickering and trying to make one another laugh. Who's afraid of Virginia Woolf? Not us.

Throughout the year of Betterment, Tina had supported and helped me. During the week, I could get most of the reading done on the way to or from the office. But on a Saturday or Sunday, with food to gather in and – yuck – 'play-dates' to organise, she had only occasionally grudged me the space I needed to accomplish that day's fifty pages. I would disappear to the town library or the shelter on the seafront, maybe bringing back a pint of milk and some Jaffa Cakes when I had finished, while Alex and one of his small-but-devastatingly-effective chums laid waste to the house.[4] I knew I was behaving like the crap dads and cowardly blokes I disliked so much – those garden-shed poltroons – but Tina seemed to realise that this was not an attempt to escape my responsibilities but to come to terms with them; and when I told her I wanted to leave a steady job and, worse than that, put the whole family through the wringer of writing another book, her response was sanguine.

'It'll be fine,' she said later that evening. 'Besides, I don't want Alex growing up with a dad who is angry the whole time.'

I kissed her.

---

4 As a parent, it has been instructive to discover that the deep, instinctive love I feel for my own child is counterbalanced by the antipathy I feel towards other people's children. *Pace* Tolstoy, it is for this reason that great nations go to war.

'Wait right there,' I said. 'I still haven't wrapped up your present.'

I had been reading alone for much of that year; my excursions into the real world – the book group, the blog – had been distractions. However, as *War and Peace* grew closer, I thought how good it might be to finish this journey in the company of someone I liked and whose opinions I respected even when I did not agree with them. At no point did I give serious consideration to how long *War and Peace* is, how drawn-out and complex, how dauntingly vast; nor did I contemplate how time-consuming such a book might be for two working people with a young child. I was thinking only of the haunting radiance of *Anna Karenina*, its colour and light, and also the relish with which Tina had demolished Antony Beevor's *Stalingrad* – as I have said, not a girly girl. I was confident she would find *War and Peace* irresistible, so confident that I had bought two copies and thrown away the receipt.

And so it proved. Together, we completed *War and Peace* in about five weeks. Tina adored it. I suppose I could tell you that we had to support one another in this endeavour, that we assisted one another through the tough patches, that one or both of us had a crisis of confidence and needed to draw on the other's strength in order to put one foot in front of the other until we both arrived at the same summit and beheld the wide plain where our persistent selves had been. But I can't tell you that because that's not how it happened. This is going to sound smug but here it is: *War and Peace* was *easy*.

*Middlemarch* is a difficult novel. *Moby-Dick*, *The Unnamable*, *Under the Volcano*: all hard work. *The Dice Man* is a fiendishly difficult read, in so far as one's eyes are constantly rebelling against the preposterous badness of what they are being asked to look at. *War and Peace*, in contrast, is merely very, very, very long. Fortunately, it is also every bit as good.

Here is Tina's five-point plan for anyone thinking of taking on, in her words, 'the only book you will ever need':

- Read fifty pages a day.
- Utilise the list of principal characters at the front.
- Pay attention! Soon you'll discover that Tolstoy is doing the heavy lifting for you.
- Don't fret if you are not enjoying the Peace, there will be a bit of War along shortly.
- When you get to the end, read it again.

Hang on a moment, Tina, you may be thinking. I haven't got time to read effing *War and Peace*, I need to pick the kids up from swimming and then take this top to the dry cleaners. Besides, I haven't even read *We Need to Talk about Kevin* yet, and Gok Wan says it's amazing. Furthermore, I am actually a man, which may come as a surprise, so just the idea of reading serious fiction makes me nervous; I don't want other lads to laugh at me and call me a puff. I tell you what, I'll wait for the app. Ok?

We all lead busy lives, replies Tina. Make room for *War and Peace*; you will be grateful you did. Fifty pages a day – that's like two episodes of *Flog It!* or one of *How to Look Good Naked*, which you can always watch on catch-up later; if *We Need to Talk about Kevin* is as important as everyone says, people will still be reading it a hundred and fifty years from now. Ignore those other boys, they are idiots. And that top just needs a dab of Vanish.

But Tina, you snivel, *why* should I read *War and Peace*? It is such a long book and my time is so precious. Why should I ever do anything difficult ever?

Because you don't have to be a lightweight your whole life, she says. Before Andy and I became parents, we were booklovers. *War and Peace* showed us we could be both. That's all. I no longer wish to discuss the matter.

Tolstoy's estate at Yasnaya Polyana lies a hundred miles or so south of Moscow. Pilgrims to the Tolstoy house have been known to remark on its unlikely similarity to Graceland. Everything has been preserved largely as it was when the sitting tenant died; and the rooms of the mansion are surprisingly poky. How could this little realm have enclosed a king?

Tolstoy's library at Yasnaya Polyana contains more than 22,000 books and periodicals, covering all manner of disciplines. There is literature from around the globe, signed and dedicated to Tolstoy by the great writers of the day: Gorky, Galsworthy, Stead, Bernard Shaw and many others. There are also numerous volumes of philosophy, religion, the history of art, science, geography and education. *'There is something almost bohemian about all these books in this cosy house with its creaking wooden floors,'* observed one visitor in 2010, the centenary of Tolstoy's death. There are even books about jujitsu and the clandestine influence of extraterrestrials in human development, so Elvis would have felt at home here.

It is said that Tolstoy had a prodigious memory for what he read. Did he work his way through all 22,000 books on his shelves from cover to cover? Of course not; Tolstoy preferred to skim each volume, establishing if it was worthy of his full attention, perhaps marking the passages that might prove useful to him later on. Did he acquire more books than he could ever hope to read? Certainly; Tolstoy spoke fifteen languages, including English, French, German,

Italian, Hebrew and Ancient Greek, but his library holds entries in a further twenty-five: Swahili, Sanskrit, Esperanto. After Tolstoy's death, a secretary called Bulgakov – not the same one, sadly – began the process of cataloguing this huge and historically significant collection; so enormous was the task that, a century later, his successors are still at it, editing 'Periodicals in Foreign Languages' and 'Music and Manuscripts', volumes four and five, respectively, of the massive *Biblioteka L. N. Tolstogo v Yasnoi Polyana*; books about books about books.

It is from his library that Tolstoy drew the learning and strength, over six gruelling years, to compose *War and Peace*. Often he felt uninspired and unsettled, but his passion for reading drove him on, as did his wife Sofya. '*He is full of ideas but when will he ever write them all down?*' she noted testily in her diary – shades of Casaubon and Dorothea.[5] Tolstoy ransacked his shelves for the social and historical background of the book, drawing on memoirs, histories and biographies, as well as his own letters and diaries, particularly those which recorded his experiences in the Crimean War, during which he had served as second lieutenant in an artillery regiment. But the one book which most affected the final shape of *War and Peace* was Schopenhauer's *The World as Will and Representation*; the German philosopher's

5 Have you ever wondered how writers backed up their work in an age before computers, Mimeographs and even typewriters? They got their spouses to do it for them. Tolstoy made the Countess Tolstoy copy out the three-thousand-page manuscript of *War and Peace* in longhand, not once but seven times; small wonder she was testy. In the same period, she also ran the estate at Yasnaya Polyana, oversaw her husband's business affairs, managed his literary career and bore him four children. All of which puts me asking for a lift to the shops into perspective, surely. Of course, a lot has changed since Tolstoy's day. Tina was asked to write out the manuscript of this book only twice, a duty she discharged with a tremendous sense of post-Feminist empowerment, like I told her to.

most renowned work. *'Do you know what this summer has meant for me? Constant raptures over Schopenhauer and a whole series of spiritual delights which I've never experienced before,'* wrote Tolstoy to a friend while he drafted the closing sections of his book; he openly acknowledged that the philosophical conclusions of *War and Peace*, especially the long passages concerning history and the will of the individual – the actions of so-called 'great men' and those of the multitude of people – derived from Schopenhauer. The general gives the order to attack but the outcome of the battle is determined by forces over which the general has little control: this is how to understand history. In our day and age, entrepreneurs such as Steve Jobs or Bill Gates seek to impose their will upon the world for reasons of personal ambition, financial gain, 'the vision thing' and so forth; but the changes in society brought about by the widespread adoption of their technologies are the result of the actions of millions of people, not one or two. Tolstoy made history when he wrote *War and Peace*; history is rewritten, just a little, every time one of us reads it.

Though we enjoyed *War and Peace* together, we found different things to admire in it. Tina, who had never read Tolstoy before, was bowled over by his broad apprehension of human nature and the astonishing verisimilitude with which he depicted all the stages of life, just as I had been at Christmas when I read *Anna Karenina*. *'It is extremely comforting to know that these are universal human struggles and universal human resolutions,'* she declared in an email at the time, an assertion she refused to retract when I suggested, by return, that this was precisely the sort of thing people said about *How to Look Good Naked*. She considers the epic scenes at the battle of Austerlitz, during which Andrew Bolkónsky is badly injured (see the extract at the head of this chapter), to be amongst the most stirring and profound she has ever read. *You go, girlfriend!*

For my part, I became fascinated with the tension in *War and Peace* between the stories Tolstoy had committed himself to telling – the saga of the fictitious Rostóv, Bolkónsky and Bezúkhov families; an accurate account of Napoleon's disastrous Russian campaign of 1805–1812; a history of all classes of the Russian people during this same period – and his growing impatience with the form in which he was attempting to tell them, i.e. a novel. For, as he wrote *War and Peace*, Tolstoy became increasingly disenchanted with fiction itself. By the time he completed the book, he was sick of fiction; all he wanted to talk about were philosophical ideas inspired by Schopenhauer. His disruptions to the narrative grew more frequent until finally, in a fit of authorial intemperance, he brought the interweaving stories to a conclusion – magnificently – and rewarded himself, if not the reader, with a protracted epilogue in which he pedantically rehearsed his philosophies of history and free will. All of which, in my eyes, made *War and Peace* a contradictatorial masterpiece.

The question of whether, technically speaking, *War and Peace* is a novel at all is one which has vexed scholars ever since the book first appeared in print; it certainly vexed Tolstoy, who found it easier to define what it was not; *'not a novel, even less is it a poem, and still less a historical chronicle'*, he stated unhelpfully. A few years later, he returned to *War and Peace* and dramatically revised it, taking out the second epilogue and all the later philosophical passages, with the intention of publishing them as a standalone volume. Shortly after completing *Anna Karenina* in 1877 – 'my first novel', as he liked to call it – Tolstoy underwent the conversion to ascetic Christianity which led him to establish his own religious sect, declare himself its head – Farmer funky Leo, the Oligarch-drude – and renounce all fiction except that which contained a strong moral purpose. In 1886, Sofya, who by now was acting as her husband's editor, literary executor and representative on Planet Earth, restored *War and Peace* to its original form because, significantly, it was this less streamlined, more didactic version of the book that the public wanted to read. The general had issued his orders to no avail; the multitude defied him.

There is plenty of fiction in *War and Peace* but there is also history, folklore, philosophy, poetry, politics: the contents of the extraordinary library at Yasnaya Polyana. This may be why it is often said of *War and Peace* that it is the book that contains all other books and the reason its devotees, who count Tina amongst their number, come back to it again and again; to them, it is indeed 'the only book you will ever need'. The List of Betterment had changed my life, gradually, slowly, through the turning of a year; book by book, the process itself had shown me another route to follow, a way forward. But here is the last-minute twist. A single book changed my wife's life decisively and forever. Almost overnight, *War and Peace* cured her of books. She has scarcely bought a new one from that day to this.

I must add immediately that I am talking about buying books rather than reading them; after *War and Peace*, Tina has probably read more, and across more genres and subjects, than she did before. She continues to give and receive books as gifts; she brings them home for Alex; she borrows them from friends and from the local library, where she takes Alex on Saturday mornings, as my parents used to take me. But the urge to acquire more books for the sake of it, to own and stockpile them, seems to have left her. I feel much the same. It is as though, having found a book with all other books within it, we looked around and asked ourselves: what do we need with all these other books?

'I think you might have to send these magazines to the dump,' said Tina a few weeks after we finished *War and Peace*. We were standing in our garage, looking at the crates of old *NME*s and piles of paper that had accompanied us from London when we moved house two years earlier.

'What about the books?' I asked. There were at least a dozen boxes of books in there that we still hadn't unpacked. Up in the house, our bookshelves were already crammed; columns of paperbacks gathered dust on the bedroom floor and stood heaped along the newly plastered sitting-room wall.

'Can you remember what's in any of those boxes?' Tina asked.

Suddenly it came to me. 'My copy of *Krautrocksampler*,' I replied. 'Other than that, no.'

'You have your answer,' she said.

So we emptied the boxes in the garage, and the attic, and the kitchen. We emptied the storage unit we were renting and paid it off. Little by little, we decided which books we wanted to keep and which would be going to the charity shops. A few we sold. The rest we offered to the members of our respective book groups, who, true to form, were irritatingly picky. A man came with a van and took most, though not all, of the magazines to the dump. Either a great weight lifted from my shoulders or a chasm opened up inside me that will never be filled. At this stage, it's hard to say.[6]

6 Julian Cope recently announced that he was planning to sell off his record collection. '*It's 2012, brothers'n'sisters,*' he wrote, '*and I have every intention of disposing of as much of our archives as I can – even personal effects*

In this way, we renewed our vow to reading.

Please don't misunderstand: we still possess an awful lot of books. Not counting ebooks, we own three different translations of *War and Peace* alone.[7] Extra shelves have been constructed in the bedroom and the sitting room and they are already flush. There are still unopened boxes in the garage and unread cookbooks in the kitchen. But, between us, we are curating a library which we mean to put to good use, which Alex can refer to and be proud of, full of books that either mean something to us or which, one day, we shall have time to read. We think twice before adding to it; we know how fortunate we are to have all these books within our grasp. It is not Yasnaya Polyana but it is ours – if you borrow something, try not to break the spine.

After *War and Peace*, there was a week left before the one-year deadline was up. The plan had always been to conclude with *Howards End* by E.M. Forster, for no reason other than the fact it had 'end' in its title. But it also included the character of Leonard Bast, the uncouth suburban clerk who attempts to improve himself with culture, for which impertinence he is symbolically crushed beneath a collapsing bookcase; 'Leonard Bast' was the pseudonym under which I had published my failed blog. And at a wedding the previous summer, a man I'd never

***

and instruments – so that my family and I can travel more extensively and live unencumbered in these coming years. Forty years of vinyl? I gotta divest myself of some of these classics . . . Love on y'all, JULIAN (Lord Yatesbury).' This is what I like about Cope; he can make something as mundane as having a bit of a clear-out sound like the affirmative action of a Forward-thinking MoFo. Encroaching clutter crisis? Er . . . Look out!

7 Tina's order of translational preference: Louise and Aylmer Maude, then Richard Pevear and Larissa Volokhonsky, then Rosemary Edmonds. She has the Constance Garnett on her Sony Reader but finds it to be 'prissy'.

met insisted to me at inappropriate length, i.e. before, after and even during the speeches, that *Howards End* is, and I quote, 'a *Bildungsroman* about the limits, no, the *limitations* of art'. But now we had almost reached the limits of the List of Betterment, I decided I would rather place my trust in a higher power.

'You choose the final book,' I suggested to Tina.

She thought for a moment. 'Have you ever read any Wodehouse?' she asked.

So this is the way the List of Betterment ends, not with a bang but with a Wooster.

I knew we had a copy of *Code of the Woosters* somewhere in the house. Propitiously, it was in the first place I looked: on a shelf next to our bed. We read it over the next few days and both thought it was great. Was it a *Bildungsroman* about the limits, no, the *limitations* of art? Not as such. It was more a funny book about a stolen cow creamer. This, I suggested to Tina, meant it was a work of *countercontra- dictatoriality*; she pointed out that even a frightful chump like Bertie had passed his driving test. We finished the book and returned it to the shelf. A few days later I handed in my notice. And that, after fifty great books and a year of dangerous reading, was that. It was time to start again.

Like me, Tina had done much of her reading of *War and Peace* on the train to and from London. One morning in late October, a couple of weeks in, she had arrived at the office with the great book still in her hand. A colleague, a woman a few years senior, caught sight of it and asked how Tina was getting on. She replied, truthfully, that we had spent much of the previous evening arguing about whether Bolkónsky's vision of a 'lofty infinite sky' represented a proof or a denial of the existence of God, a theological dispute which had grown rather heated, concluding with me sleeping downstairs on the sofa.

'That's so lovely,' said her colleague. 'I can't imagine having a discussion like that with my husband.'[8]

Late in *War and Peace*, as Andrew Bolkónsky lies mortally wounded, he experiences an epiphany: '*Love is life. All, everything that I understand, I understand only because I love.*' What graceful words these are and what a laudable sentiment. We could take them at face value and stop the book right here – in Bolkónsky's final utterance, '*How good it would be!*' However, that is not where Tolstoy leaves it. '*These thoughts seemed to him comforting,*' he observes a few sentences later. '*But they were only thoughts.*' This, to me, is the mark of Tolstoy's genius; he was too committed to telling the truth, as he perceived it, to let even a dying man off the hook. And we are all dying men.

So instead, let me suggest an alternative coda from elsewhere in the book:

'In the midst of nature's savagery, human beings sometimes (rarely) succeed in creating small oases warmed by love. Small, exclusive, enclosed spaces governed only by love and shared subjectivity.'

This is where the List of Betterment had led me, back to a small oasis governed by love and shared subjectivity; I was glad to be home.

---

8 One reader of an early draft of this chapter raised an objection to this story. It's so blissfully connubial, he told me, it just makes me want to puke. I wouldn't have minded but he was Best Man at our wedding. Anyway, the conversation about *War and Peace* did actually happen in exactly the way I have laid it out here. If it makes you feel queasy, consider this an annotative indigestion tablet.

A few days later I did read *Howards End*. Is it truly an enquiry into the limits, no, the *limitations* of art? Actually it is. Did I like it? Sorry, that's none of your business. The Countess agrees. Don't you know he's got a book to write, she says. Now clear off.

But our business here is not quite concluded. A moment ago, I wrote of Tolstoy's commitment to telling the truth in his work. I feel I must do the same.

First, that quote from *War and Peace* about small oases 'governed by love and shared subjectivity'? I'm afraid it may not actually be from *War and Peace*. It may not even be Tolstoy. When I said 'elsewhere in the book', I actually meant this book, the one you are currently reading. What happened was, at some stage during the List of Betterment, I scribbled that quote on a piece of paper but failed to make a note of which of the books it was from; and now I can't remember. I have searched several times but I haven't been able to find it again. Sorry about that.

Of course, it ought not to make any difference where those lines come from or who wrote them; I stand by every word. They may well have been penned by Tolstoy – given I read two of his books, the odds are immediately halved. And they do have a certain Tolstoyian ring to them. But the longer I gaze upon them, the less certain I am. Perhaps they come from *Middlemarch* or *Everyman* or *I Capture the Castle*; all feasible sources. How about *The Communist Manifesto* or Pevsner? Or maybe they're from *The Diary of a Nobody*; that would be neat. I doubt they are from *Moby-Dick* or *Gilgamesh* and the sentiment seems a bit chirpy for Houellebecq; but then again, 'nature's savagery'. . . Place speech marks around it and that quotation could be ascribed to almost anyone: Morrison, Bukowski, Kerouac, Brontë.

It sounds like the sort of pompous statement Ignatius J. Reilly might spit between mouthfuls of weenie, pushing his hot dog cart up the sidewalk. Or Behemoth, the infernal jabbering cat from *The Master and Margarita*; or the Devil himself for that matter. Or Sir Jamie Teabag or whatever his name is from *The Da Vinci Code*, silhouetted in a cloister in the Vatican or something, shortly after giving his albino killer monk the order to assassinate Tom Hanks . . .

Hmm. Maybe it does make a difference.

Houellebecq is fond of quoting Schopenhauer, and I have grown fond of quoting them both, so it seems right to turn the matter over to them:

Schopenhauer: 'We remember our lives a little less well than a novel we once read.'

Houellebecq: 'The fact is, in the end, we forget even our own books. And I don't know why, but this morning, I find that really comforting.'

Second and finally, you may well be asking, what about the other book? I get that *The Da Vinci Code* was the first not-so-great book but the subtitle mentions *Fifty Great Books (and Two Not-So-Great Ones)*; where the heck is the second one? Ok, I'll confess: I was going to buy another novel by Dan Brown, skim it *à la* Tolstoy and then come up with a constructive, feel-good reading to bookend the narrative. But when the moment came, I just couldn't face it. Sorry, everyone. If it really bothers you, you have my permission to get a pen, scratch out the word *Two* on the title page and replace it, neatly, with *One*. Not that you need my permission; it's your book.

I realise this may appear like the insolent gesture of defiance I promised earlier I was not about to make; yet with the finish line in sight, here I stand, hands on hips, looking you straight in the eye. Don't you see, though? The race is over and we have just breasted the tape together. I might have pretended that, after fifty great books and a year of Betterment, I ended up a nicer guy and a more forgiving reader, gentler, less scornful; but that would be a fairytale and a lie.

I am myself again. But I no longer tell lies about books.

'And now I take leave of that young man sitting alone upstairs in the lugubrious parlor reading the Classics. What a dismal picture! What could he have done with the Classics, had he succeeded in swallowing them? The Classics. Slowly, slowly, I am coming to them – not by reading them, but by making them.'

Henry Miller, *The Books in My Life*

'Arthur had jammed himself against the door to the cubicle, trying to hold it closed, but it was ill-fitting. Tiny furry little hands were squeezing themselves through the cracks, their fingers were inkstained; tiny voices chattered insanely . . . "Ford," he said, "there's an infinite number of monkeys outside who want to talk to us about this script for *Hamlet* they've worked out."'

Douglas Adams, *The Hitchhiker's Guide to the Galaxy*

'What use were his talons and fangs to the dying tiger? In the clutches, say, to make matters worse, of a boa-constrictor? But apparently this improbable tiger had no intention of dying just yet. On the contrary, he intended taking a little walk, taking the boa-constrictor with him, even to pretend, for a while, it wasn't there.'

Malcolm Lowry, *Under the Volcano*

# Epilogue

This morning before starting work, after bringing my wife her cup of tea in bed, making my son his breakfast and washing down the customary vitamin pills with the customary Svepa of orange juice, I logged on to the Internet and illegally downloaded a torrent containing 4001 ebooks. The folder occupies a little less than two gigabytes of memory, approximately the size of a family photo album or a couple of movies. At a steady rate of two titles a week, and allowing for fluctuations in technologies and eyesight, it should take me about forty years to read everything inside that folder – enough reading matter, in all likelihood, to see me out. This does not take into account any new or attention-grabbing books that might be published between now and my demise, of course. But if I live that long, I shall be eighty-five and am unlikely to be concerned with whatever passes for 'an important new voice in fiction' in the year 2054. Surely I will have read enough.

Here amongst the 4001 ebooks are *Against Nature* and *One Hundred Years of Solitude* and the complete works of Charles Dickens, George Eliot and the Brontë sisters. Here is *The Master and Margarita*; here is Dan Brown. But which titles from the List of Betterment are missing? I asked myself. Rather than doing any proper work, I set myself the challenge of hunting

275

them down on the web and, to make it more interesting, threw in every book I really loved as a child as well. By lunchtime, I had succeeded; there were dozens of new books on my laptop, either as Kindle-ready AZW files or in the easily-converted EPUB or MOBI formats. The good news is that I only had to pay for one of them; but as that was *Absolute Beginners*, I didn't really mind. And then, because what I had done was illegal and infringed the copyright holders' exclusive rights, I deleted the morning's spoils from my hard drive except those books that came from Project Gutenberg, and *Absolute Beginners*. So don't be sending me any cease-and-desist letters.

While I was writing this book, the world changed. The digital revolution had been under way for some time, of course, but the aggressive marketing of hand-held electronic readers had not begun in earnest. Consumers in the West who had been groomed to form emotional attachments with their phones and cameras responded eagerly to the idea of a device that could galvanise the outmoded pastime of reading. In the future, no one will read *Pride and Prejudice* from cover to cover, said the head of the UK's oldest paperback publisher recently; they will just tap the screen of their phone or tablet computer and find out more about the bits that interest them, the costumes or the recipes.[1] In the same period, so-called 'dead-tree' books continued their retreat from society, like Napoleon's defeated army of stragglers hobbling away from Moscow to perish in wintry and hostile terrain. Library closures continued apace. Booksellers went to the wall in ever greater numbers, chain stores and

1 The CEO concerned really said this. On the bright side, perhaps in the future I shall be able to sell the extracts from Chapter IV concerning Charles Arrowby's disgusting menus to whoever produces an app for *The Sea, The Sea*. It's all content, isn't it?

cosy independents alike; soon the only place to find printed books on the high street may well be charity shops. Where they are available to buy, books have never been cheaper or worth less. The most popular titles can be purchased at large discounts online and in supermarkets; on World Book Night, millions of them are given away for free. And of course, if you know where to look, you need never pay for a book again – though once again, I must remind you that this practice is morally reprehensible and a crime against humanity, like smoking in a crèche, or letting your dog foul the public footpath, then bagging the result and suspending it from the branch of a nearby tree.

Yet at the same time, the public's appetite for book-blah seems insatiable. Book clubs thrive in living rooms and online; literary festivals draw ever more appreciative audiences; television and radio teem with celebrity booklovers; social networks buzz with instant comment and opinion. People love talking about books or listening to other people talk about them. And for those who want to try their hand at writing one, it has never been easier to get your magnum opus out into the world; with the aid of the web and tools like Calibre or Mobipocket, anyone can be a self-published Marx or Melville. Bestsellers have been created which previously would have been overlooked by mainstream publishing, such as Amanda Hocking's *Trylle Trilogy* or *Fifty Shades of Grey* by E.L. James.[2] Glad tidings for freelancers: decent editors are suddenly much in demand.

2 I don't know why anyone was surprised by the phenomenal sales of *Fifty Shades of Grey*. When presented with some new technological breakthrough, it is only ever a matter of time before the human animal figures out how best to pornify it. The same thing occurred with previous innovations such as the gramophone record, the Internet and the Space Hopper.

In short, we have the chance to decide for ourselves how and what we read – and whether to pay for it. We need no longer rely on traditional brokers of culture and taste: agents, publishing houses, critics, booksellers, librarians. We can roam through space and history, choosing only what we know we like and ignoring all the chatter that seems irrelevant to us. If nothing takes our fancy, we can make our own books and launch them into the void. We can sell our work for peanuts or even give it away; having cut the ties to overheads such as production and distribution, we become our own typesetter, agent and publicity machine.

And what of printed books themselves? If we are bold and far-sighted enough, we can free ourselves from the burden of them – nasty, dusty things. According to some experts, they, like us, will be extinct in a generation. Hoarding boxes of books will seem like the symptom of a deeper malaise in a far-off historical epoch, quaint at best, like clots on the lungs of a Victorian consumptive. To own printed books, to value or prize them, this too may pass; it is happening already. We shall glide unencumbered through a future of clean, white lines and empty spaces, electronic, interconnected . . .

*' "I know," said Marvin, "you keep going on about it. It sounds awful." '*

It may not surprise the reader to learn that I held back from buying an ereader. I was already in a lifelong, if somewhat abusive, relationship with books; I did not need to dally with a gadget. When ebook enthusiasts said there was none of the effort or inconvenience one associated with the bulk or weight of a printed book, I dismissed them. What were they talking about? Never in my entire life, not once, had I felt myself inconvenienced by having to use either hand, or both simultaneously, to hold a book; on the contrary, holding on to books would count as one of the top five uses to which my hands have been put over the years, maybe top three.[3] Each time someone breathlessly informed me they would never have read, say, *A Confederacy of Dunces* if it weren't for their new Kindle or Nook, all they were telling me was that they were a fully paid-up confederate dunce. Was this kind? Was it fair? No, and nor is life; for if it were, our towns and cities would still boast well-stocked libraries and bookshops, and the trees would be festooned with leaves and not bags of dog-shit. But I bow to the will of the people.

Therefore, with the motivational Cope–Jung axioms from page 219 still ringing in my ears, I decided I must face up to the future and acquire a Kindle;[4] I did not want to be the man who shrinks back from the new and strange.[5] Within a few weeks, the conclusion I reached was this: if you *like* reading, this is the object, unbeknownst to you, you have been waiting for; but if you *love* reading as I do, you may struggle to comprehend what all the fuss is about. Did it make reading better? Of course not. It's a useful addition

3 The Top Five in full. 1) Drinking, eating. 2) Holding on to books, regardless of size. 3) Making models out of Play-Doh™ and sniffing fingers afterwards. 4) Giving Paul McCartney the double thumbs-up in the street and having him reciprocate with same. 5) Self-abuse.

FWIW, I believe Harold Bloom and I are in accord about at least two of the above, if not more.

4 Despite Amazon's best efforts, other brands of ereader are available for purchase and my customer comments are applicable to any and all of them.

5 'The rejection of technology is only sound when it's done through understanding. Rejection through ignorance or belief in the natural superiority of the old ways seems to me to be as bad as drably accepting all modernism.' Julian Cope, *Repossessed*.

to our library, not a replacement for it. I take the Kindle with me wherever I go. But I also take a good book.

And so we return to *Under the Volcano*, Malcolm Lowry's tale of mescal and damnation set beneath Mexican skies. I chose this novel to commence my e-reading life because it was the book from the List of Betterment I most wanted to revisit. I had blogged about it during that summer. What I did not mention then was, although the dissipated, tempestuous atmosphere of *Under the Volcano* had made a strong impression on me, I was not sure I had grasped much of the book's deeper meaning. The substance of it slipped through my fingers. This is why I wrote only briefly about it at the time; neither the book nor the blog lent themselves to adequate first impressions and I did not want to commit myself until I knew what I was talking about. However, after the List of Betterment came to an end, the mood, the ghost of *Under the Volcano* remained until, six months later, I felt compelled to return to it. On a second reading, I felt I understood it better; the narrative came into focus and chains of images started to form around it: the riderless horse, the overgrown garden, the mescal hallucinations, *Las Manos de Orlac*, the poor dead dog. I realised, as I neared the final chapter for a second time, that I was going to have to read the novel at least once more and, moreover, that I wanted to.[6] I had not recognised it at first but when all was said and done, *Under the Volcano* was one of the great Great Books.

*Under the Volcano* is a purposefully obscure novel. In his letter to publisher Jonathan Cape, to which I referred in the introduction of this book, Lowry describes it as '*my*

6 'This is perhaps the best rough test of what is literature and what is not. If one cannot enjoy reading a book over and over again, there is no use reading it at all.' Oscar Wilde, *The Decay of Lying: An Observation*.

*churrigueresque Mexican cathedral'* – a baroque and broad church. Though Cape acknowledged the novel's intricate construction, long passages perplexed or repelled him; he and two of his editors suggested major amendments to the book prior to publication, changes on which they were politely insistent. Lowry responded with a defence of the work he had laboured at for almost seven years. He contended – successfully, for the novel was published as it stood – that no reader could consciously apprehend all the meanings of *Under the Volcano* on *'first or even fourth reading'* but its cumulative effect might be felt *unconsciously*. *'The book should be seen as essentially* trochal,' he wrote. *'I repeat, the form of it as a wheel so that, when you get to the end, if you have read carefully, you should want to turn back to the beginning again . . . For the book was so designed, counterdesigned and interwelded that it could be read an indefinite number of times and still not have yielded all its meanings or its drama or its poetry.'* This was how I came gradually to appreciate the architecture and revolutionary design of *Under the Volcano*. It was a cathedral and a wheel; as Lowry said, a sort of machine.

I hardly need add that *Under the Volcano* is not for everyone. It is fragmentary and hallucinogenic. The style is intensely allusive, while the plot can accurately be described as elliptical. Some readers climb aboard the train and go for a round trip and have a great time. Others judge that Lowry's machine turns in an ever-tightening gyre until, like the mythical bird, it disappears up its own arse. In the sage words of Dan Brown, they should probably just read somebody else.

Anyway, it seemed appropriate to inaugurate a new sort of machine with an old one, and so I undertook my third pass at *Under the Volcano* on the Kindle. Or at least, I tried to. The ereader could not cope with it; more precisely, I could not cope with the ereader. I missed the slow satisfaction of accumulating pages between the thumb and fingers of the left hand. After three chapters, I reverted to my dear old paperback, such was the effort needed to overcome the innate drawbacks of reading this type of a book on this type of screen. There was no air; the blocks of text were too dense and relentless. If the driver of the book is the plot, and we are gripped by it, we read *in the moment*, thinking more or less only about the action as it unfolds and the words as they scroll in front of our eyes. But *Under the Volcano* is not a page-turner like *The Da Vinci Code* or *Fifty Shades of Grey*; it is a book that needs to be thought about, put down, reflected upon, flicked through, flicked back and read again. And this, remember, was a book I had read before. Though it would be a kind of achievement, I doubt any reader who completed their first attempt at the novel in this way would ever feel like trying it again.

Inevitably, there will come a time when the technology is up to the challenges of a book like *Under the Volcano*. Tablet computers are evolving rapidly. Right now, no doubt someone is preparing an app, perhaps using the content from Chris Ackerley and David Large's invaluable web-based companion to the novel.[7] When T.S. Eliot's publisher produced a similar guide to *The Waste Land* for the iPad, it proved a hit with consumers, who could tap the screen and learn more about the costumes and the recipes, e.g. hot gammon, a pocket full of currants, a silk hat on a Bradford millionaire. But, to come full circle, reading about *Under the Volcano* is not the same as reading *Under the Volcano*,

7 *Under the Volcano: A Hypertextual Companion*, www.otago.ac.nz/english/lowry.

diverting and demystifying though it may be. It is not the thing itself.

And yet, I have kept *Under the Volcano* on my Kindle. Irrationally, I like carrying it around with me. It is sitting on the desk here, look. The rest of the List of Betterment is on it too. Really, who needs 4001 books for a lifetime? Speaking for myself, I believe I could live out my days with just these fifty and be happy. I re-read quite a few of them while writing this book and I was never bored or let down or disappointed. The Andy Miller who exists in *The Year of Reading Dangerously*, who will be sheltered inside it once the story is complete, will spend eternity reading and re-reading that list, like Christopher Robin and Pooh at the top of the Forest, the enchanted place at the end of *The House at Pooh Corner*, sixty-something trees in a circle (*'Christopher Robin knew that it was enchanted because nobody had ever been able to count whether it was sixty-three or sixty-four . . .'*). I have granted him that life and I envy him. Though they may not necessarily be the right ones, that Andy Miller has answers.

On the Kindle, I also carry around the books I have probably read more times in my life than any other: *The Hitchhiker's Guide to the Galaxy* and its four sequels. How splendid it is to have them on an electronic book '*with a screen about three inches by four*', like the Guide itself. Douglas Adams would have approved. Unlike me, he was a man who embraced new technologies. Having begun his writing career as a self-confessed 'computer dissident' – 'I made my living making fun of computers' – he transformed, seemingly overnight, into the epitome of the early adopter. He is said to have owned the first Apple Macintosh in the UK. Was this the machine on which he wrote *So Long, and Thanks for All the Fish*, the fourth and worst of the *Hitchhiker's* books? In creative terms, Adams may have been better served by a humble typewriter, or a pad of paper and a biro. Computers presented the temptation of infinite rewrites and, as we have seen, Adams needed no encouragement in that direction.

Adams was only forty-nine when he died in 2001, a little older than I am now. This was a personal tragedy for his wife Jane and young daughter Polly. His early death also robbed the planet of Adams' humour, creativity and campaigning energy on behalf of endangered species such as the Bengal Tiger and the Northern White Rhino. And, if one subscribes to either Richard Dawkins' or Oolon Colluphid's proof of the non-existence of God, it was also a fatal error for Adams, because by doing something as uncharacteristically stupid as dying, he narrowly missed the techno-uprising he had predicted when he was alive. As his friend and fellow Apple buff Stephen Fry says, what is the confluence of the iPad and the Internet if not the Hitchhiker's Guide to the Galaxy itself, a bank of knowledge compiled by all of us? Of course, such a collaborative mechanism is not without its quirks. 'The Hitchhiker's Guide to the Galaxy *is a very unevenly edited book*,' wrote Adams presciently, *'and contains many passages that simply seemed to its editors like a good idea at the time.'*

I met Douglas Adams on several occasions, most recently around the time of his virtual sixtieth birthday party. I would like to bring this book about books to a close by briefly describing each one of these meetings. After all, now that several biographies of Adams have been published and one former acquaintance is said to be working on an entire volume about what it was like to be his flatmate, I, like Charles Pooter, fail to see – because I do not happen to be a 'Somebody' – why *my* reminiscences of Douglas Adams should not be interesting. So here they are.

## Fit the First – Websters Bookshop, Croydon, 1982

On a hot Saturday afternoon, I waited in line for three hours for Adams to sign a copy of his new *Hitchhiker's* book, *Life, the Universe and Everything*. The long wait was not down to the size of the queue, which snaked round the edge of the shop and out the front door. With a certain inevitability, it was because Adams was terribly late.

Not that I minded. Thirteen was probably the peak of my *Hitchhiker's* infatuation. I adored the novels, the LPs, the original episodes I had taped off the radio and memorised. On this particular afternoon, I had my towel with me. No one had suggested I do this, it was a spontaneous and hilarious gesture I thought Adams might appreciate; in the event, many of those in the queue ahead of me seemed to have had the same brainwave. At least while we waited, we had something to sit on.

Eventually, from a door near the back of the shop, an exceptionally tall and grumpy-looking man emerged. He marched across to the signing table and, without making eye-contact with anyone, began signing books with a gusto that can only be described as furious. In my career, I have encountered many pissed-off authors but none has ever seemed quite so nakedly unhappy as Douglas Adams did that afternoon. But I was thirteen, with a towel, and therefore equipped to screen out anyone's feelings except my own. As the queue inched forwards, I asked myself what spontaneous and hilarious message I might ask my hero to write. Then I remembered how Zaphod Beeblebrox signed photos of himself in part two of the second radio series of *Hitchhiker's*.

'Hello,' I said, as I arrived in front of his table. 'Please could you write, "To Andy, with frank admiration"?'

Without saying a word or even glancing up, Adams reached over, took a copy of *Life, the Universe and Everything* from the top of the pile, grimly scribbled the requested dedication – as no doubt he was asked to do every single time he undertook a public signing – and pushed the book across the desk towards me. Nothing further was said and, without so much as a farewell glare, our first meeting was over.

I still have the book, of course. Looking at this inscription now, thirty years later, it occurs to me that 'frank admiration' was probably the precise opposite of what Adams was feeling towards us, me and all the other towel-packing dweebs who had dragged him all the way from Islington to Croydon on a hot Saturday afternoon. But I am not sorry I asked.

## Fit the Second – Institute of Contemporary Arts, The Mall, London, 29 July 1987

Five years have passed. I am now a student at the University of Sussex in Brighton, where I am studying English Literature. I have just completed my first year's studies and am back at home for the summer holidays. In *Time Out* magazine, I notice that Douglas Adams will be appearing at the ICA in The Mall to discuss his new novel *Dirk Gently's Holistic Detective Agency*. The ICA is where I once met Fat Puffin but I am older now and much, much cleverer; just a few weeks earlier, I sat at the feet of visiting lecturer Ian McEwan and asked him where he got his ideas from. I decide I will do Adams a favour and attend.

At the ICA, Adams is in conversation with his friend and occasional co-writer, TV producer John Lloyd. There must be seventy or eighty people in the audience, several

286

of whom have brought towels with them. Sad! Adams seems far happier and more relaxed than at our last meeting. As the event goes on, I am struck by the disparity between how I have always thought of his work – i.e. funny sci-fi – and how everyone else here seems to think of it – i.e. art, philosophy, science – literature, in other words. But they have all got it wrong. I know literature; I have been studying it for nearly a year. Literature is Ian McEwan. Literature is not Douglas Adams. I must tell everyone this.

When the moment comes for questions from the floor, I raise my hand. Over the course of two minutes and twenty-three seconds, I stammer out a meandering and loaded question which, though I attempt to make it sound impressively lofty and erudite, can be summarised thus: 'Are you as surprised as me that everyone here, including you, is taking you so seriously?'

In response, Adams is thoughtful and good-humoured and, wrestling with the baffling pretentiousness of his inter-locutor, takes even longer to answer the question than it had taken me to ask it, though in essence his reply can be boiled down to three words: 'Yes. And no.'

In my seat in the audience, smiling and nodding while Adams gamely tries to untangle whatever it is I have just asked him – even I'm not sure – I wish I had something to wrap around my head, like a towel. My cheeks are burning and I have started to sweat. And with good reason: it dawns on me I have, with ill-concealed rudeness, told Adams to his face that his work is not worth taking seriously when, actually, it still means more to me than most of the 'serious' literature I have studied over the previous nine months. In short, I have behaved like a total dick. At the end of the session, I queue to buy a copy of *Dirk Gently's Holistic Detective*

*Agency* and get it signed by the author. This time I am the one who can't make eye-contact.[8]

The accidental triumph of *The Hitchhiker's Guide to the Galaxy*, I have belatedly realised, is that it is not merely literature but the best kind of literature – highbrow, lowbrow and middlebrow all at once. I say accidental because Adams had no such design in mind when he wrote it and these qualities are bestowed more by the audience than the author. But if you want big ideas about science or art or philosophy, there they are. If you want the poignant tale of a dispossessed man looking for a home, you have it. And if you want jokes – genuine, bona fide funny-ha-ha jokes – making fun of computers, digital watches and ape-descended life forms, no one has ever done it with more originality or genius or craft than Adams. If that isn't literature, I don't know what it is.

### Fit the Third – London 1992

Another five years have elapsed. Equipped with an English degree and some opinions, I have managed to find work in a West London bookshop. I am currently in charge of author events. Douglas Adams is about to publish *Mostly Harmless*, 'the fifth book in the increasingly inaccurately named *Hitchhiker's Guide to the Galaxy* trilogy'. I have a proof

8 I am able to tell you with absolute certainty that the question took me two minutes and twenty-three seconds to ask – but felt much longer – because I recently discovered to my absolute horror that the whole of Adams' interview at the ICA is now available to listen to online, as is my excruciating contribution from the audience. Twenty-five years on, it is even more mortifying than I remember it. If anyone reading this has a time machine and is thinking of going back to kill Hitler at birth, would you mind stopping off in The Mall in 1987 to kill me first? Thanks. Worst of all, this unwelcome entrance to the past has been propped open courtesy of the British Library. *You people were meant to be my friends!*

copy I have already read twice. I call the publisher to see if Adams would like to come and read at our shop, maybe on a Sunday afternoon. They say yes immediately. I put down the phone and start to feel rather nervous.

Though *Mostly Harmless* is a better book than *So Long, and Thanks for All the Fish*, it isn't great. It isn't nearly as strong as *Last Chance to See*, Adams' account of his encounters with such elusive creatures as the Komodo dragon and the kakapo. However, this is not what I am nervous about; if I have learned one valuable lesson over the previous five years, it is to keep my true opinions to myself. No, I am nervous because this will be the third time I have met Douglas Adams and neither of our previous encounters has gone particularly well. I still blush when I recollect what occurred at the ICA and I guess Adams was trying to scrub Croydon from his memory even as it was happening. As the day of the reading approaches, I am not seeking closure or a moment of connection; I just don't want the event to suck.

'This is Andy,' says the woman from the Pan publicity department. 'He's in charge today.'

'Hi Andy,' says Douglas Adams who, though greying at the temples, remains exceptionally tall. He frowns and glances sharply at me. 'Wait a minute. Aren't you that little prat from the ICA?'

This is what I fear might happen but, of course, it doesn't.

'I love the new book,' I tell Adams when he actually arrives at the shop. 'Absolutely fantastic.' And I usher him upstairs to where a sold-out crowd of admirers awaits, many of whom have reserved seats at the front with towels.

The reading is a huge success and we sell a lot of books. Adams is affable and laughs often. Watching from the back, it occurs to me that he has had to learn how to do this, or at least, how to do it in front of strangers, some of whom inevitably seek to bamboozle him with their in-depth perception of his work – is it hot in here? – or enquire repeatedly if Marvin the Paranoid Android really is dead, his complete absence from *Mostly Harmless* notwithstanding. And rather than become frustrated or exasperated by this element of his working life, Adams grins and bears it all with politeness and good grace, a forbearance for which he receives my frank admiration.

After the signing is finished and the public have left, by way of thanks we usually let our visiting authors select a book to take away with them. I walk with Douglas Adams down to the basement floor of the shop, where there are heaps of new titles on display, the latest in philosophy and history and science. Flushed with the success of the afternoon, I am seized with the urge to make a grand gesture.

'Take what you want,' I tell him. 'As many as you like.'

And I accompany Adams around the basement, as he gathers a massive pile of hardbacks, for which he does not pay and which I do not have the authority to give away. He asks my advice, I offer it. Several times he asks me if I'm sure about this, it seems very generous, etc., and I wave away his objections with an air of easy and entirely assumed munificence. Effectively, I am aiding and abetting a celebrity shoplifter. But again, thinking back, I am not sorry. For half an hour, it means Douglas Adams and I talked about books.

As Adams climbs into a waiting taxi, after I have helped him in with a clutch of carrier bags containing hundreds of pounds' worth of stock, he turns and thanks me for a very enjoyable afternoon. And I shake his hand and say what I failed to five years earlier, and five before that.

'Thank you.'

## Fit the Fourth – Queen Elizabeth Hall, Southbank Centre, London, March 1998

The twentieth century is almost over. I am now a commissioning editor; I have also started work on a book of my own. The young editor with whom I share an office tells me that Douglas Adams is giving a lecture on the South Bank this evening. He has a spare ticket. Do I want to go with him?

Adams now lives in LA, where he is still trying to get a *Hitchhiker's* movie off the ground, but he is currently in London to promote his latest project, an interactive CD-Rom video game called *Starship Titanic*. Onstage, he is full of enthusiasm, not just for the game as it stands, but for its potential in the future, as processing power increases and more people get involved via the Internet, once something called 'broadband' really takes off. After the lecture, my colleague and I eschew the queue for signed copies in favour of a drink in the Festival Hall bar. I don't mind games but I still prefer books.

*The Hitchhiker's Guide to the Galaxy* is not just a multi-brow piece of work; it also pioneered the concept of multi-platform content, back when terms like 'broadband' and 'multi-platform' were just twinkles in a crossword compiler's eye. Adams created bespoke variations of *Hitchhiker's* for radio, books, TV, audiobook and the theatre; he was still at it twenty years later, producing new drafts of the film script he hoped Disney might option. *Starship Titanic* had a precursor too; there was a *Hitchhiker's* computer game as early as 1984, though back then I lacked a computer to play it on. Some of these versions are more artistically successful than others but Adams was always a confirmed believer in the unique virtues of new media.

291

Adams' last project before he died was a four-part radio series for the BBC entitled, to his slight chagrin, *The Hitchhiker's Guide to the Future*. The series was an enquiry into how science might affect our lives in the new millennium. The second programme, first broadcast in April 2001, concerned the likely prospects for books in an electronic age. Adams already sounds excited by ebooks and the implications of epublishing. At about the halfway mark, he offers a typically warm and witty appraisal of the sentimental attachment many of us have – or had – for reconstituted wood-pulp:

'When people talk about their fondness for books, I wonder if they're really talking about their fondness for reading. It's rather like confusing the plate for the food. I mean, I like a beautifully printed and bound book as much as anybody else but I don't need a houseful of them, any more than I need a houseful of beautiful dinner plates. About twelve would do fine; that, and a good recipe book.'

He was right, of course. And yet I can't help feeling some food tastes better when eaten off a plate; and that, just because science can give us a whole meal in a tablet, we don't necessarily have to swallow it. In the future, the beautifully printed and bound book may become an endangered species, like the tiger or the kakapo. Surely that's not what Douglas would have wanted.

In the Festival Hall, we finish our drinks and make for the elevators. The lift doors open, we step inside and I find myself once again in the presence of a giant, Adams being no shorter than the last time we met. He smiles, though I am certain he doesn't recognise me. Why would he? He is talking to someone; I don't recall what about – perhaps his baby daughter or some mutual acquaintance or a new piece of tech. I do remember he was laughing. We reach the ground floor. As the elevator doors open, I stand aside to let him and his friend past.

'After you,' I say.

The last time I see him alive he is walking towards Hungerford Bridge, deep in conversation and still laughing. Our paths will not cross again for thirteen years.

## Fit the Fifth – Hammersmith Apollo, London, Sunday, 11 March 2012

Douglas Adams may be neither as tall nor alive as he once was but he remains remarkably popular. At his virtual sixtieth birthday party at the Hammersmith Apollo in London, there are towels everywhere. I am in the closing stages of writing my third book. I have taken thousands of baths and eaten many, many sandwiches, as a result of which the book is late to an extent even Adams might find outrageous. This is the first day off I have taken since Christmas.

The proceeds from this virtual birthday party / fan convention / rock concert will go to Save the Rhino (www.savetherhino.org), the charity of which Adams was a founding patron. Many of his friends and family are here. On stage, a succession of comedians, writers and scientists tell personal stories about Douglas or explain what he meant to their lives and career choices. For some, *Hitchhiker's* was the trigger for a lifelong fascination with physics or astronomy. For others, *Last Chance to See* inspired them to join the cause of conservation. A couple of the original cast members perform a specially written sketch.

Terry Jones from Monty Python explains how no one read Douglas's novels for the plot or the characters but *for the ideas*. It all feels well-meaning but also listless and unfunny. And I sit there and think: I don't give a monkey's about physics or astronomy or, if I am being scrupulously honest, the rhino, though I do put ten pounds in a bucket on the way out. These Douglas Adamses seem to have meant a lot to many of the people here but none of them was my Douglas Adams. As a reader, I loved Adams' ear for humorous inflection, the rhythm and flow of his sentences, the glorious linguistic precision of his phrasing: 'mostly harmless'; 'total perspective vortex'; 'and me with this terrible pain in all the diodes down my left side'; 'a liquid that was almost, but not quite, entirely unlike tea'. I read Adams *for the words*.

In his introduction to *Sunset at Blandings*, P.G. Wodehouse's final, unfinished novel, Adams hails Wodehouse's comic style as *'pure word music . . . He is the greatest* musician *of the English language.'* He writes of Wodehouse's *'dazzling images and conceits'* and his *'pure, creative playfulness'*, comparing him to Mozart, Einstein and Louis Armstrong. This is how I feel about Adams. He may have been inspired by big ideas and scientific concepts but he played like Louis Armstrong, bending the lyrics and the melody to express the joy of playing itself. I did not bump into this Douglas Adams at his birthday party. Nor, in retrospect, did I ever meet him in person. He rarely ventured out in public, sending forth a tall man called Douglas Adams to speak on his behalf: this was the Adams I encountered over the years and who passed away in 2001. The Douglas Adams who really mattered to me lived – and lives – in those inimitable cascades of pure word music.

The following morning before starting work, after

attending to the needs of my wife and son in the customary manner, I logged on to the Internet and illegally downloaded a torrent containing sixty computer games from the 1980s and the software with which to play them. The vintage game I was searching for – *The Hitchhiker's Guide to the Galaxy* – is available to play legally and for free at douglasadams. com, the BBC website and other locations on the web. But bad habits die hard. I installed the software, loaded the game and was rather startled to discover, there in front of me, the late Douglas Adams, alive and well. There was nothing on the screen save for a few brief sentences and a flashing cursor but as I gradually navigated my way through the opening scenes, I felt the unmistakable thrill of hearing Adams' voice after a long absence – there were whole passages of original material, unfamiliar and impeccable jokes, wonderful strings of textual DNA; the stuff of life itself. It was great to hear from him again.

Interactive Literature, Adams called it, a form of authorship which played to the strengths of the medium for which it was created, allowing the reader to decide the outcome of the story. He was delighted with the new possibilities it offered him and writers like him; equally, he never underestimated the centuries-old power of words on a page, arranged in set, unchanging lines. He was a man who loved Wodehouse, Dickens and Austen. He never lost his faith in the realignment of the synapses that occurs every time we pick up a good book and start reading, find something that interests us or makes us turn to the next page, so much so that when we look up, the world has changed.

This is the abiding miracle of the book. We choose what happens next.

# Appendix One

The List of Betterment

('Asterisks denote the easiest to get into if you are starting from scratch . . . And if I missed your favourite one out, well excuse me.' Julian Cope, *Krautrocksampler*.)

1.  *The Master and Margarita* – Mikhail Bulgakov\*
2.  *Middlemarch* – George Eliot
3.  *Post Office* – Charles Bukowski
4.  *The Communist Manifesto* – Karl Marx and Friedrich Engels
5.  *The Ragged Trousered Philanthropists* – Robert Tressell
6.  *The Sea, The Sea* – Iris Murdoch
7.  *A Confederacy of Dunces* – John Kennedy Toole
8.  *The Unnamable* – Samuel Beckett
9.  *Twenty Thousand Streets Under the Sky* – Patrick Hamilton
10. *Moby-Dick* – Herman Melville
11. *Anna Karenina* – Leo Tolstoy\*
12. *Of Human Bondage* – W. Somerset Maugham
13. *Pride and Prejudice* – Jane Austen
14. *Catch-22* – Joseph Heller
15. *Lord of the Flies* – William Golding
16. *Frankenstein* – Mary Shelley
17. *The Odyssey* – Homer
18. *Crime and Punishment* – Fyodor Dostoevsky

19. *The Unfortunates* – B.S. Johnson

20. *Fear and Loathing in Las Vegas* – Hunter S. Thompson

21. *The Heart is a Lonely Hunter* – Carson McCullers

22. *Vanity Fair* – William Makepeace Thackeray

23. *Jane Eyre* – Charlotte Brontë*

24. *Everyman* – Philip Roth

25. *Absolute Beginners* – Colin MacInnes*

26. *One Hundred Years of Solitude* – Gabriel García Márquez

27. *Don Quixote* – Miguel de Cervantes

28. *Beyond Black* – Hilary Mantel

29. *The Diary of a Nobody* – George and Weedon Grossmith

30. *The Epic of Gilgamesh* – Anonymous

31. *The Mystery of Edwin Drood* – Charles Dickens

32. *The Aerodrome* – Rex Warner

33. *I Capture the Castle* – Dodie Smith*

34. *The Leopard* – Giuseppe Tomasi di Lampedusa

35. *Under the Volcano* – Malcolm Lowry

36. *Wide Sargasso Sea* – Jean Rhys

37. *On the Road* – Jack Kerouac

38. *Paradise Lost* – John Milton

39. *American Psycho* – Bret Easton Ellis

40. *The Dice Man* – Luke Rhinehart

41. *The Essential Silver Surfer, Vol. 1* – Stan Lee, John Buscema, Jack Kirby*

42. *Krautrocksampler* – Julian Cope*

43. *Beloved* – Toni Morrison*

44. *Against Nature* – Joris-Karl Huysmans*

45. *Atomised* – Michel Houellebecq*

46. *The Handmaid's Tale* – Margaret Atwood

47. *The Portrait of a Lady* – Henry James

48. *Beowulf* – translated by Seamus Heaney

49. *War and Peace* – Leo Tolstoy

50. *The Code of the Woosters* – P.G. Wodehouse

# Appendix Two

## The Hundred Books Which Influenced Me Most

Both this and *Appendix Three: Books I Still Intend to Read* were inspired by equivalent appendixes in Henry Miller's *The Books in My Life*. Asterisks denote authors whose work I have read extensively or in full.

*My Book About Me* – Dr Seuss*
*Winnie-the-Pooh* and *The House at Pooh Corner* – A.A. Milne
*The Adventures of Tintin: The Crab with the Golden Claws* –
     Hergé*
*Asterix and the Cauldron* – René Goscinny and Albert
     Uderzo*
*Moominpappa at Sea* – Tove Jansson*
*Good Grief, Charlie Brown!* – Charles M. Schulz*
*The Eighteenth Emergency* – Betsy Byars
*Black Jack* – Leon Garfield
*Doctor Who and the Brain of Morbius* – Terrance Dicks*
*Ludo and the Star Horse* – Mary Stewart
*How to be Topp* – Geoffrey Willans and Ronald Searle*
*The People's Almanac*, 1st edition – David Wallechinsky
     and Irving Wallace
*Alfred Hitchcock and the Three Investigators in the Mystery of
     the Stuttering Parrot* – Robert Arthur*

*The Brand New Monty Python Papperbok* – Monty Python*
*The Hobbit* – J.R.R. Tolkien
*The Hitchhiker's Guide to the Galaxy* – Douglas Adams*
*The Death of Reginald Perrin* – David Nobbs*
*The Return of Sherlock Holmes* – Arthur Conan Doyle*
*The Lord of the Rings* – J.R.R. Tolkien
*Coming Up for Air* – George Orwell*
*The Beatles: the Authorised Biography* – Hunter Davies
*From Fringe to Flying Circus* – Roger Wilmut
*The Bible* ('Good News' edition) – various authors
*Hamlet* – William Shakespeare*
*To Kill a Mockingbird* – Harper Lee
*Cult Movies: the Classics, the Sleepers, the Weird, and the Wonderful* – Danny Peary
*On Broadway* – Damon Runyan
*Brighton Rock* – Graham Greene*
*The Great Gatsby* – F. Scott Fitzgerald*
*Absolute Beginners* – Colin MacInnes*
*The Annotated Alice* – Lewis Carroll, ed. Martin Gardner
*Uptight: The Velvet Underground Story* – Victor Bockris and Gerard Malanga
*The Complete Plays* – Joe Orton
*Stanley Spencer R.A.* – ed. Richard Carline, Andrew Causey, Keith Bell
*The End of the Affair* – Graham Greene*
*The Life and Opinions of Tristram Shandy, Gentleman* – Laurence Sterne
*Dialectic of Enlightenment* – Theodor W. Adorno and Max Horkheimer
*To the Lighthouse* – Virginia Woolf*
*New Grub Street* – George Gissing
*V for Vendetta* – Alan Moore* and David Lloyd
*The Life of the Automobile* – Ilya Ehrenburg

*Flaubert's Parrot* – Julian Barnes*

*Lyrics 1962–1985* – Bob Dylan

*Collected Poems 1909–62* – T.S. Eliot*

*Collected Poems* – Philip Larkin*

*Bleak House* – Charles Dickens*

*The Child in Time* – Ian McEwan*

*Pale Fire* – Vladimir Nabokov*

*The Diaries of Franz Kafka* – Franz Kafka*

*Ulysses* – James Joyce*

*In Search of Lost Time Vol 1: Swann's Way* – Marcel Proust

*The Divine Comedy* – Dante Alighieri

*London Fields* – Martin Amis*

*Jude the Obscure* – Thomas Hardy

*The Lost Continent* – Bill Bryson*

*Work is Hell* – Matt Groening*

*A Scanner Darkly* – Philip K. Dick*

*Lucky Jim* – Kingsley Amis

*Rabbit, Run* – John Updike*

*U & I: A True Story* – Nicholson Baker*

*Psychotic Reactions and Carburetor Dung* – Lester Bangs

*Madame Bovary* – Gustave Flaubert

*London A–Z Street Atlas* – Geographers A–Z Map Company
    Ltd

*Alma Cogan* – Gordon Burn

*Uncle Vanya* – Anton Chekhov*

*The Secret History* – Donna Tartt

*Wuthering Heights* – Emily Brontë

*Mon propre rôle* – Serge Gainsbourg

*The Intellectuals and the Masses: Pride and Prejudice Among the
    Literary Intelligentsia, 1880–1939* – John Carey

*Fever Pitch* – Nick Hornby*

*Trainspotting* – Irvine Welsh*

*The Life and Death of Peter Sellers* – Roger Lewis

*A Biographical Dictionary of Film*, 3rd edition – David Thomson

*Writing Home* – Alan Bennett*

*How Proust Can Change Your Life* – Alain de Botton

*Revolution in the Head: The Beatles' Records and the Sixties* – Ian MacDonald*

*Sword of Honour* – Evelyn Waugh*

*Why We Got the Sack from the Museum* – David Shrigley*

*Anthropology* – Dan Rhodes*

*Boring Postcards* – ed. Martin Parr*

*The Buildings of England: Surrey* (2nd edition) – Nikolaus Pevsner, Ian Nairn, Bridget Cherry*

*The Rings of Saturn* – W.G. Sebald*

*The Kingdom by the Sea* – Paul Theroux

*Harry Potter and the Philosopher's Stone* – J.K. Rowling*

*The Bad Beginning* – Lemony Snicket*

*The Human Stain* – Philip Roth*

*The Future of Nostalgia* – Svetlana Boym

*Lady with Lapdog and Other Stories* – Anton Chekhov*

*The Complete Peanuts: 1950–1952* – Charles M. Schulz*

*Shakey: Neil Young's Biography* – Jimmy McDonough

*Like a Fiery Elephant: The Story of B.S. Johnson* – Jonathan Coe*

*The People's Act of Love* – James Meek

*All the Devils are Here* – David Seabrook

*The Call of Cthulhu and Other Weird Stories* – H.P. Lovecraft

*Bad Vibes: Britpop and My Part in its Downfall* – Luke Haines

*Howards End* – E.M. Forster*

*The Sense of an Ending* – Julian Barnes*

*Then We Came to the End* – Joshua Ferris

*We Are in a Book!* – Mo Willems*

In addition, though they were published after the period covered by this book, I must mention Stephen Sondheim's *Finishing the Hat: Collected Lyrics (1954–1981) with Attendant Comments, Principles, Heresies, Grudges, Whines and Anecdotes* and *Look, I Made a Hat: Collected Lyrics (1981–2011) with Attendant Comments, Amplifications, Dogmas, Harangues, Digressions, Anecdotes and Miscellany* – Betterment aside, the two books to have given me the most pleasure in the century so far.

# Appendix Three

Books I Still Intend to Read

I intend to read these books and also write about them. Please visit mill-i-am.com for updates.

The remainder of *Remembrance of Things Past* – Marcel Proust
*One Flew Over the Cuckoo's Nest* – Ken Kesey
*Infinite Jest* – David Foster Wallace
*The Golden Notebook* – Doris Lessing
*The Amazing Adventures of Kavalier & Clay* – Michael Chabon
*Love in a Cold Climate* – Nancy Mitford
*A House for Mr Biswas* – V.S. Naipaul
*Naked Lunch* – William Burroughs
*The Diary of a Young Girl* – Anne Frank
*White Teeth* – Zadie Smith
*A Heartbreaking Work of Staggering Genius* – Dave Eggers
*The Summer Book* – Tove Jansson
*Masquerade* – Kit Williams
*Gulliver's Travels* – Jonathan Swift
*The Little Stranger* – Sarah Waters
*Journey to the End of the Night* – Louis-Ferdinand Céline
*Tarantula* – Bob Dylan

*Middlesex* – Jeffrey Eugenides

*The Unbearable Lightness of Being* – Milan Kundera

*The Woman in White* – Wilkie Collins

*Stoner* – John Williams

*A Brief History of Time* – Stephen Hawking

*Gravity's Rainbow* – Thomas Pynchon

The second half of *Daniel Deronda* – George Eliot

*The Man Without Qualities* – Robert Musil

*The Boy in the Striped Pyjamas* – John Boyne

*As I Lay Dying* – William Faulkner

*Wolf Hall* – Hilary Mantel

*Bring Up the Bodies* – Hilary Mantel

*Stalingrad* – Antony Beevor

*Life and Fate* – Vasily Grossman

*The World as Will and Representation* – Arthur
  Schopenhauer

*Autobiography* – Morrissey

*Inferno* – Dan Brown

# Bibliography

Every effort has been made to contact copyright holders, where appropriate. Any errors or omissions will be corrected in future editions.

The book's epigraphs are taken from *The Odyssey* by Homer, translated by E.V. Rieu, Penguin Classics 1946; and from 'Scenes from the Class Struggle in Springfield', an episode of *The Simpsons* written by Jennifer Crittenden, first broadcast on 4 February 1996.

The Introduction ('A Word of Explanation') contains an excerpt from Malcolm Lowry's letter to Jonathan Cape, 2 January 1946, reproduced in the introduction to *Under the Volcano*, Penguin Modern Classics 1985, copyright © Margerie Bonner Lowry 1965.

The epigraphs to Part I are taken from *Whatever* by Michel Houellebecq, Serpent's Tail, 1999, copyright Maurice Nadeau 1994, translation copyright Paul Hammond 1999; and from Vladimir Nabokov, *Lectures on Russian Literature*, Picador 1983, copyright Estate of Vladimir Nabokov, 1981.

'Book One' contains extracts from 'I Start Counting' (Basil Kirchin/Jack Nathan/James Coleman/Patrick Ryan), copyright © United Artists Music Ltd 1969; from *Mr Small* by Roger Hargreaves, World International Ltd. 1998, copyright © Mrs Roger Hargreaves 1972; and from *The Master and Margarita* by Mikhail Bulgakov, translated by Michael Glenny, Vintage

310

Julian Cope 1999; from 'I Have Always Been Here Before' by Julian Cope, from the album *Where The Pyramid Meets The Eye: A Tribute to Roky Erickson*, copyright © Julian Cope 1990; and from 'The Stages of Life' by Carl Jung, from *Modern Man in Search of a Soul*, Routledge Classics 2001. Unless noted, other quotes from Julian Cope are taken from his website at headheritage.co.uk; from an interview with Jon Savage ('Stone Me!', *Observer*, 10 August 2008); and from *The Modern Antiquarian*, a documentary first broadcast on BBC2 on 24 June 2000.

'Book 45' contains extracts from *Public Enemies* by Michel Houellebecq and Bernard-Henri Lévy, translated by Frank Wynne, Atlantic Books 2011, copyright © Flammarion/Grasset & Fasquelle, Paris 2008, translation Frank Wynne © 2011; from *Atomised* by Michel Houellebecq, translated by Frank Wynne, William Heinemann 2000, copyright © Flammarion 1999, translation copyright © Frank Wynne 2000; from 'Neil Young' by Michel Houellebecq and Michka Assayas, from *Dictionnaire du Rock*, Bouquins/Robert Laffont 2000, translated by the author, copyright © Michel Houellebecq and Michka Assayas 2000; from *Against Nature* by Joris-Karl Huysmans, translated by Robert Baldick, Penguin Classics 2003, translation copyright © Robert Baldick 1956; from *The Restaurant at the End of the Universe* by Douglas Adams, Pan Books 1980, copyright © Macmillan Publishers for the UK, Random House Ltd for the USA; and from Vladimir Nabokov's introduction to 'The Vane Sisters', *The Stories of Vladimir Nabokov*, Weidenfeld & Nicolson 1996, copyright © Estate of Vladimir Nabokov. The quote from Mark E. Smith is taken from *John Peel's Record Box*, a documentary first broadcast on Channel 4 on 14 November 2005.

'Books 49 and 50' contains extracts from *The Code of the Woosters* by P.G. Wodehouse, Penguin Classics 2001, copyright © P.G. Wodehouse 1937; from *The Buildings of England: North East and East Kent (Third Edition)* by John Newman, founding editor Nikolaus Pevsner, Penguin Books 1983, copyright © John Newman, 1969, 1976, 1983; from 'On

# List of Illustrations

Fig. 1: courtesy BodyParts3D, made by DBCLS; fig. 2: courtesy Gary Houston; fig. 3, 5, 11, 12, 14 and birthday card from Julian Cope: photographs by the author; fig. 4: photograph by Alex Miller; fig. 6: courtesy Gabriel Barathieu (whale); © PoodlesRock/Corbis (grail); Dan Brown: © Featureflash/Shutterstock; Herman Melville: © Bettmann/Corbis; fig. 7: copyright © 2014 National Gallery of Art, Washington, DC; fig. 8: courtesy National Gallery; fig. 9: courtesy Art Institute of Chicago; fig. 10: © Judith Kerr; fig. 13: © SueC/Shutterstock; fig. 15: © David Shrigley

# Acknowledgements

This book could not have been written without the considerable help of the following people.

At Fourth Estate, my editor Nicholas Pearson has been a friend, collaborator and shrink. He has also had to be very, very patient. I promised him I would complete this book without recourse to the phrase 'demise of the Net Book Agreement' and I have kept that promise until just now: sorry for that, Nick, and also for the major delay in delivery. I would also like to thank Victoria Barnsley for her belief in me, first as an editor and subsequently as an author. Thanks too to Rebecca McEwan, Michelle Kane, Olly Rowse, Minna Fry, Paul Erdpresser, Kate Tolley, Essie Cousins, Laura Roberts, Julian Humphries, Clare Reihill, Louise Haines and especially Jo Walker, who not only designed the cover but also filled it with precisely the right number of books without having to be asked.

At Harper Perennial, John Williams acquired the book and was a vital early source of enthusiasm and encouragement; he subsequently commissioned me to write two long essays for his online journal *The Second Pass*, in which I was able to rehearse the approach I planned to take with this book; thanks, John. Back at Perennial, the book passed through the hands of Jeanette Perez, then Michael Signorelli before ending up on the desk of my editor, the wonderful Hannah Wood. She and publisher Cal Morgan have embraced the book as one of their own and I am deeply grateful to them both for their energy, care and commitment, and to everyone at Perennial.

At Curtis Brown, my agent Jonny Geller has been an invaluable source of good humour and good advice whenever I have needed either; thanks also Doug Kean and, latterly, Kirsten Foster.

All my friends from Canongate, especially Jamie Byng – the only person I know who says he never lies about books and I believe him – and 'Digital' Dan Franklin, who was still analogue when I met him.

All my friends at Faber & Faber, especially Stephen Page, Hannah Griffiths, Bridget Latimer-Jones, Julian Loose and, all the way from Forest Hill, John Grindrod. #CroydonTillWeDie

At different times and in different ways, the following people inspired or assisted me: Mitzi Angel; David Barker; Richard Bedser; Alex Clark; Jenny Colgan; Peter and Polly Collingridge; Dick Copperwaite; Jackie Copperwaite; Steve Delaney; Peter Doggett; the late Patric Duffy; Travis Elborough; Victoria Falconer; Tim Grover; Rupert Heath; Sorrel Hershberg, Edie and Reuben; Tom Hodgkinson; Kate Holden; Leo Hollis; Tony Lacey; Stewart Lee; Sam Leith; the Lyons family; Dominic Maxwell, Emma Perry, Polly and Flora; Jeremy Millar; assorted Andrew Millers; David Miller; David Mounfield; Paul Putner; Dan Rhodes; Pru Rowlandson; William Rowlandson; Andrew Sandoval; the Sargent-McSweeney family; all my sparring partners in Sparta B.C.; Matt *Are You Passionate?* Thorne; Rob Weiss and Mary Claire Smith; and Neil Young.

Special thanks to the brilliant Jenna Russell, Dot in the Menier Chocolate Factory production of *Sunday in the Park with George*, for sharing her thoughts on performing the work of Stephen Sondheim.

Many of the books on the List of Betterment were purchased from Harbour Books in Whitstable. Thank you Keith & Emma Dickson, Vicky Hageman, Matthew Crockatt, Elizabeth Waller and Kirsten Boysen for allowing me to wander in, check the correct spelling of, say, Knut Hamsun, and wander out again. Honourable mentions to Oxford Street Books in Whitstable, Waterstones in Canterbury, managed by the doughty Martin Latham, and both branches of the Albion Bookshop in Broadstairs, now sadly defunct. Whitstable Library and the British Library at St Pancras filled in the gaps.

The book itself was mostly written in two places: a substantial part of the first draft was completed at Dot Cottage, near Winchelsea Beach in Sussex, where I learned to chop logs with an axe and operate a wood-burner, much to the amusement and concern of Michael Crosby-Jones and Margot Prew, who were wonderful hosts to a struggling writer – discreet yet touchingly reluctant to let their guest die of hypothermia; the remainder was written, and then rewritten, in a quiet house round the corner from where I live. Unlike my house, there was no telephone, no broadband and no TV to divert me. It is little exaggeration to say this book would never have been finished without the generosity and forbearance of Anthony and Julie Robinson.

I would like to award £10 book tokens to each of the following in recognition of their outstanding contribution.

For almost a century of friendship, Matthew Freedman, Michael Keane and Paul Wright.

For tough love above and beyond that which was strictly necessary, Ben Thompson and Nicola Barker.

For singing and playing guitar with me, my partner in the Gene Clark Five, Tim Donkin; and for letting the GC5 make an unlovely noise in her lovely home, week in, week out, the divine Elise Burns.

'Finished your book yet?' For commencing all telephone calls with this enquiry, week in, week out, Clinton Heylin.

For laughing and making me laugh, Neil, Sue and Nicol Perryman.

Thanks, Mum and Dad, for giving me this love of books and for letting me follow it wherever it has led.

God save the Kinks.

Finally, my wife Tina and son Alex are the not-so-secret heroes of this book and the saga on which it is based, my life. They have to go through it with me, the whole lot, in real time, without any of the funny bits. Without their humour, patience, company and love, neither book nor life would be worth persevering with. Thank you.

AM

# Notes for Reading Groups

- How many titles from the List of Betterment have you read? Which were your favourites?

- 'Everyone is entitled to an opinion.' True or false?

- Do you need to have finished reading a book before posting a review online or discussing it with your book group?

- Would you describe your book group as middlebrow?

- Throughout *The Year of Reading Dangerously*, Andy Miller has employed recurring motifs of the tiger and the monkey. What do the tiger and monkey symbolise? Anything?

- On page 148 a former colleague of Andy Miller's describes him as 'one of the angriest men I have ever met'. What do you think Andy Miller is so angry about?

- Andy Miller has painstakingly threaded images of duality through the text of *The Year of Reading Dangerously*. In your opinion, was it worth it?

- Did you understand what Andy Miller was trying to achieve in *The Year of Reading Dangerously*? If not, whose fault is that? Yours or his?

- Like Malcolm Lowry, Andy Miller has stated that he hopes people will read *The Year of Reading Dangerously* at least twice in order to engage with the text, delve into the book's many allusions and resonances, and fully appreciate its architecture and design. Can you be bothered?

- After reading an early draft of *The Year of Reading Dangerously*, a former member of the author's book group (see Chapter IX) commented: 'Andy [Miller] exhibits symptoms of clinical depression, repressed homosexuality and undiagnosed Asperger syndrome.' Do you agree?

- Andy Miller obviously has a unique mind and a fierce intelligence. But would you want to go down the pub with him?

- Which of the following Andy Millers is your favourite? The author of *The Year of Reading Dangerously*; Andrew Miller, the award-winning serious novelist; Andy Miller, guitarist with the group Dodgy; or the Andy Miller who likes women to bring him sandwiches?

- It doesn't matter anyway, because it's all a load of shit. Do you agree?

- Are these discussion notes meant to be taken seriously? Discuss.

Reading group notes © Andy Miller 2014